# STEP BY STEP ORGANIC
# FLOWER GARDENING

*Also by Shepherd Ogden*

**STEP BY STEP ORGANIC
VEGETABLE GARDENING**

# STEP BY STEP ORGANIC FLOWER GARDENING

SHEPHERD OGDEN

HarperCollins*Publishers*

HarperCollins books may be purchased for educational, business, or sales promotional use. For information please write: Special Markets Department, HarperCollins Publishers, Inc., 10 East 53rd Street, New York, NY 10022.

FIRST EDITION

Designed by Barbara DuPree Knowles

Photographs by Stephen R. Swinburne

Illustrations by Karl W. Steucklin

---

LIBRARY OF CONGRESS CATALOGING-IN-PUBLICATION DATA

Ogden, Shepherd.
    Step by step organic flower gardening / Shepherd Ogden.—1st ed.
        p.   cm.
    Includes bibliographical references and index.
    ISBN 0-06-016996-6
    1.  Flower gardening.   2.  Organic gardening.   I.  Title.
SB405.O48   1995
635.9′87—dc20                                                    94-34270

---

95  96  97  98  99  D/RRD  10  9  8  7  6  5  4  3  2  1

# CONTENTS

# 5 A Festival of Flowers   *96*

## 6 Gardens for Flowers    *248*

## Appendices    *269*

# PREFACE

Perhaps the oddest thing about this book is that I wrote it at all. I will state for the record that I am not now, nor have I ever been, associated with the American Flower party. Until recently, never did I ever harbor in my Yankee heart the slightest sympathy for something so sensuous and frivolous as a flower. I began gardening as a vegetable man—an organic vegetable man, no less—devoted to plants that people can eat, that feed the world, and that people would give me money for at our farm stand down in the village of Londonderry. I didn't take up gardening for fun; I did it for the money.

I was tricked into growing flowers. One spring about ten years ago, my wife, Ellen, who ran the farm stand while I stayed here at the farm and took care of the plants, persuaded me to pot a few extra tomato seedlings, buy in a couple of six packs of petunias, and see if they would sell. Well, they did. The next season, along with the tomato seedlings and petunia plants, I grew some marigolds, some impatiens, a few geraniums, even a few delphiniums that came from seed I'd taken off my grandmother's plants the previous summer. They sold, too . . . immediately.

Now, Yankee practicality becomes Yankee ingenuity only when freed from Yankee stubbornness, so I like to think it was not inconsistent to have erected eight greenhouses over the following five or six years and gradually filled each in turn with vegetable and flower seedlings for sale. Nor did I have to think of myself as weak, wanton, or effete when I began to arrange those flower seedlings in pots and baskets for the summer trade and placed my first wholesale order for the perennials that began to steal space from the vegetables in our fields. We began to sell cut flowers, dried flowers, perennials. No, I did it for the money, to support my family, to fulfill my God-given obligations as a provider, a family man.

THEN I GOT HOOKED. Coaxing that warm, moist greenhouse full of plants into uniform bloom while a wintry gale blew just outside became a challenge; taking a handful of seeds, so insignificant in March, and by May turning it into thousands upon thousands of bright and various flowers became a pleasure, if an exhausting one (at our peak we grew about five hundred hanging baskets and two thousand trays of seedlings).

Even more, the incredible diversity and amazing hardiness of the perennials, and the way that one, over the course of a season, became many, caught my inborn love of creating something out of nothing. As much as I had loved the idea of growing my own food (I still do), the creative outlet provided by learning about all the perennials adapted to our Northern climate, how to use them to build a landscape, and how to help them increase—these became, for a while, consuming passions. I couldn't visit a friend's garden without trying to remember and name all the plants, and I couldn't look at any space without mentally filling it with perennials that were ideally adapted to its conditions and that would provide the maximum pleasure to its owners.

Eventually, Ellen and I left the garden-center business. Our exploration of vegetables ideally suited for the new, more adventurous cuisine led to the genesis of both a seed catalog, *The Cook's Garden*, and a book of the same name. As the catalog business grew, not enough time was left for the garden center, and, forced to choose, we took the catalog. Why? It was more fun, because it gave us the opportunity to play more in the garden, to concentrate on quality and diversity rather than quantity and uniformity, to search out new and different plants from around the world. We miss the garden center, and we wish that we could still be there, offering local gardeners alternatives to the widespread and now conventional logic that demands a high-tech, usually chemical solution to everyday garden problems. But we decided that our catalog would only help with this, and it could help on a broader, national scale, to provide alternatives.

Around that time, I wrote a second book, actually an update of a book written many years ago by my grandfather, *Step by Step Organic Vegetable Gardening*. In that book I tried to offer American gardeners a reasonable, commonsense approach to growing their own vegetables without chemical fertilizers or pesticides. The relationship between that book and the current volume bears some discussion. In the vegetable book there is a complete discussion of such matters as tools and equipment, soil preparation, composting, and general garden care. That material has not been repeated here, but summarized. In this volume the same space has been given over to a more thorough discussion of the structure and physiology of plants—in layperson's terms—and practical discussions of how to propagate them. In addition, the much wider variety of plants grown in flower gardens has caused the A–Z section (Chapter 5 in this volume) to expand considerably. Finally, there is a chapter on the different considerations for specific kinds of flower gardens.

What I hope comes across in both volumes is the simple, level-headed, hands-on reasonableness of the methods presented. The reasons why one would want to grow vegetables organically are abundantly clear: Nobody in their right mind would want to spray their own food with chemicals developed fifty years ago to kill enemy soldiers. And only someone with a product to sell or a career to defend could claim that those chemicals represent a proven method of gardening and that our chemical-free method does not, when our methods have been successful worldwide for 10,000 years—and here in Vermont, on our family's land, for more than fifty. The fact that when we garden organically the environment is not only spared the insult of those chemicals, but actually improved by our more attentive method of gardening, is just the gravy on the mashed potatoes, the fragrance on the lily.

This book is an attempt to extend that basic understanding to flower gardening. Forty million American households have flower gardens, fully a third more than have vegetable gardens. Yet the logic and, again, the common sense of the organic method seems to be less immediately compelling to flower gardeners than to vegetable gardeners, 70 percent of whom consider themselves organic gardeners. It is my hope that through this book we will be able to help American gardeners take back their gardens from the chemical and machinery companies and regain some of the simple pleasure we used to take in our plants and their habitat.

# ACKNOWLEDGMENTS

First I have to thank my wife, Ellen, who introduced me to growing flowers, and the customers of our garden center, who forced me to learn more about flowers than I otherwise would have in order to serve their needs. Thanks also to Sally Ogden and Anne Woodhull for early encouragement; Nancy Rice and David Talbot for Latin rigor and the collector's enthusiasm; and Alice and Angie Higuera, both for their companionship in the business of growing flowers and their help in checking the manuscript over for errors and possible improvements. The gardens are what they are due to the influence of these people.

Thanks again, too, to the people who helped make the book: Susan and Larry on the editorial side, Stephen Swinburne for the photos, and Karl Steucklen for the illustrations. Thanks also to readers Jill, Sam, and Warren.

STEP BY STEP ORGANIC
FLOWER GARDENING

*We all feel in the garden something of the humility that comes from knowing we belong to the Earth's web of life, larger than ourselves, and not just to the web of mechanical gadgets and systems, as though we were caught in corporate influences too remote and too big to understand or combat. Everything is alive in a garden. The soil itself is teeming with microscopic life. The delight of observing and learning about all the wonderful happenings of nature is reason enough, some gardeners say, for keeping right with it—no matter how many other purposes it serves.*

# Good Reasons for a Flower Garden

There are many pleasures to the flower garden. While I am a vegetable gardener and feel that food is a pleasure—that both the garden where it is grown and the uses of it should be aesthetic and sensual—the appeal to the senses with flower gardening is clearer.

There are more kinds of flower gardens than there are food gardens. While a food garden may hold vegetables for a particular cuisine, say Latin American or Oriental or Italian, the design and care of each kind will be essentially the same, with only the plants grown being different. With flower gardens this is not the case. A garden of cut flowers not only looks different than a garden of bedding plants, it is likely to be in a different place, a totally different size and shape, and tended differently all the way from seed to senescence. The same is true of a garden grown for fragrance, or for making dried-flower arrangements, or to attract butterflies. A sunny perennial border is markedly different than a wildflower meadow or a bog or woodland garden, and will require a whole different approach.

As mentioned in the Preface, this diversity requires a different approach. Over the next five chapters we will try to provide the basics: the facts about a wide range of flowers, how they are grown, and how they can be used. We'll look at the tips and tricks that have

—Catherine Osgood Foster,
*Organic Flower Gardening*

1

been accumulated by hundreds of generations of gardeners, stretching back to the first discoveries of how plants can be cultivated, and forward to a sustainable future of joyful and humane interaction with the natural world. But first just a bit of background.

GARDENING HAS LONG BEEN split between food gardeners and flower gardeners, and even where the same gardener pursued both, the gardens themselves became Balkanized, separated by a green line of well-trimmed lawn. Food gardeners are often overtly practical people, and yet—if my own first interest in gardening is any guide—prone to feeling a bit holier-than-thou. After all, we are pursuing an art and an act that asserts the continued place of the individual within an increasingly mass-market society. Unimpressed by the cheap food of the markets because we know ours is better, we draw great satisfaction from our self-reliance and individuality. The majority of us—about 70 percent—claim to use organic methods, variously defined of course. Why? Because the connection between chemicals put on a garden and the food eaten from that garden is so clear, so plain. Only the most foolishly pretentious would spray plants they are about to eat just to make them look as picture perfect as the supermarket produce they disdain.

Flower gardeners, on the other hand, have generally been a bit more urbane, if you'll permit the term. As social anthropologist Jack Goody points out in his massive historical study of the place flowers hold in secular and religious life, *The Culture of Flowers,* the rise of ornamental horticulture seems inextricably bound to the rise of advanced agricultural systems and the social stratification that virtually always accompanied it.

While those of us who pursue both kinds of gardening are perhaps the best testimony to the validity of Goody's theory, those gardeners who grow only flowers often mistakenly think *they* are. Flower gardeners who eschew vegetable gardening for the cheap and easy convenience of the supermarket reason that growing food is something one does only if one *must.* With their "food" needs met, they use the extra space to grow "the finer things." They can, in their own estimation, raise gardening from mere craft to an art.

Please excuse me for painting some of my fellow flower gardeners with such a broad stroke, but I want to explore two important aspects of this often unconscious perspective. First is the implied faith in the success of a modern, technological agriculture, which is seen to have given flower gardeners the "freedom" to pursue aesthetics. Second is the way which the apparent severance of the connection between the way we care for our gardens and our own health seems to weaken the rationale for organic methods; after all, we don't eat the flowers.

To begin with, the faith in modern technological methods of growing food is hardly justified. Out of nearly ten thousand years of tilling the soil, the current conventional chemical methods have been in widespread use for only about fifty years, yet they have caused a number of significant problems already, from overt pesticide poisonings (first among farm workers, but also now among homeowners) to groundwater pollution, which has a much more insidious and long-term effect. As reported in the *Washington Post*, a paper in the *Journal of the American Medical Association* this past February revealed two unsettling discoveries by a team of epidemiologists. First, an American male nonsmoker like myself, born in 1949, is three times more likely to develop cancer than my grandfather, who was born in the 1890s. My wife's risk is "only" 1.7 times as great as her grandmother's. Why? According to the study, "cancer-causing hazards in addition to smoking have been introduced into the population in the past several decades." Second, cancer rates among farmers—who are otherwise healthier than the general population—match these increases but precede them in time, which "suggests that more detailed studies of agricultural exposures might yield important clues about preventable common causes," in the cautious language of the medical establishment. To me it means that farmers —who embraced the use of agricultural chemicals decades before homeowners—are reaching the end of the latency period that makes it so hard to prove a particular cancer has a particular cause. What is the majority of the U.S. population that lives in metropolitan areas going to do once they realize that the earth and water beneath them have been polluted for no other purpose than to maintain a kind of static, landscaped perfection?

All of this pollution will have to be cleaned up someday, paid for with somebody's tax dollars, and somebody will have to pay for the treatment of those whose illnesses are caused by their involvement in this "modern miracle." Yes, food is cheap and available now, but the money that we have "saved" on our food bills is just paid out elsewhere, in the Superfund hazardous-waste cleanup bill and the cost of health care. There is no free lunch. We are borrowing from the future, from our children and grandchildren; our "freedom" will be their burden.

Some critics of the traditional, organic approach have pointed out that preindustrial agriculture was also responsible for destruction of environments—the desertification of the Middle East, for example—

but that point only strengthens the argument that we should examine all the new methods we use for potentially harmful effects *before* they become widespread. A common objection to my line of reasoning is that many of the newer pesticides break down quickly and thus are not dangerous. While it may be true that some break down quickly, the chemicals resulting from the breakdown of a given pesticide may be more dangerous than the pesticide itself, as is the case with the systemic fungicide Benomyl (Benlate) and the insecticide Acephate (Orthene). Both of these chemicals, widely recommended for use on ornamental plants, are suspected cancer-causing agents. They are also highly toxic to the birds and bees, not to mention earthworms, all of whom contribute in important ways to the stability and sustainability of organically grown gardens.

The companies that market chemicals like these complain when asked to submit conclusive evidence that their products aren't harmful. While testing may be expensive it is nonetheless necessary, so the important question, honestly stated, is this: Whose burden should it be? The answer is clear: Any company should be willing to prove that their products (and by-products) are not harmful; otherwise, we taxpayers may well be left to pick up the tab for the next disaster, as we have in the past. This is, after all, not just a case of someone building a new machine, or some other limited-distribution, limited-use product. When a new horticultural chemical like Benomyl is introduced, it is mass-produced (Benomyl use is about 3,000,000 pounds per year in the Unites States alone). That is the only way the economics work—with or without the costs of testing.

But why should all this matter to flower gardeners? The pesticide itself, or its breakdown product, may not be eaten as it would if sprayed on a vegetable or fruit, but it is still a part of the overall environmental burden, as an ecologist would call it, to which each of us contributes and to which each of us is exposed by every action we take and every product we use. And the average pesticide use by suburban gardeners—per acre, six times that of agricultural land—does create a very real, aggregate effect on the water beneath our towns and cities.

Finally, the dangers we face from synthetic chemical pesticides are not just from the residues that might end up on something we eat or in the water we drink, but from the use itself. Dusts and sprays have a nasty habit of not staying where we try to put them, and I have known very few gardeners who actually follow the complete, detailed directions on pesticide labels—even with organic pesticides. To do so you would have to spend your days in a rubber suit or double-washing clothes, and telling the children to stay off the lawn or away from the flower garden for a while. I'd rather spend my time in the garden hand-picking insects, as archaic as that might seem.

The simple fact is that the earth is a closed system, and all pollution is a fouling of our communal nest that will eventually come back to haunt each of us. There is no way that we can live in this world without creating some sort of impact, so it only makes good, old-fashioned common sense that we choose which kinds of impacts, that we prioritize. Personally, the kinds of ephemeral benefits that chemical pesticides provide to a flower garden are not very high on my list of survival needs.

But, some will ask, can it be done? And aren't the benefits real and important? Consider roses, beloved by many gardeners but reputed hard to grow without chemical sprays. It would seem to be a clear case. But if you ask the rosarian Steve Scaniello at the Brooklyn Botanic Garden, as I did, whether he uses any chemical sprays to take care of one of the world's most important rose collections, he will tell you that he uses none whatsoever. "Why not?" asked one of the other garden writers on the tour. "I love roses," Steve replied. "I want to still be here enjoying them in twenty years."

So the two implicit assumptions, that the current conventional chemical gardening is a success, and that plants we don't eat can be sprayed without repercussions, are false. Lest it seem that we have been robbed of our bliss, I'd like to say quite the opposite: This knowledge saves us, stops the swindle, the con whereby efficient, manual, and humane methods were replaced with expensive high-tech mechanical and chemical methods. It frees us to go back out into the sun and the wind, to listen to the birds and enjoy a quiet moment observing the daily drama of the insects, luxuriate in the Elysian fragrances of the garden rather than accommodate ourselves and our time to the clamor and stench of industrialism. Organic gardening was here long before the merchants and their machines, and we organic gardeners will still be here long after the oil is gone and the world has quieted down again.

# CHAPTER 2

*Gardeners, particularly new gardeners, are usually ready to accept—indeed clamor to be told—the wisdom of the ancients on precisely how, and particularly when, to plant and sow and prune. The drawback to any such information, couched in exact terms, is that it can only ever be an average estimate over scores of soils and millions of microclimates. Reading and re-reading the textbooks is no substitute for a clear understanding of the principles, and a minute observation of the particulars. If you examine a plant closely, and use your common sense, the plant's health or debility, like condition of the soil, is written all over it.*

# The Basics of Good Gardening

## A PLACE FOR THE FLOWER GARDEN

The first question many gardeners face is "Where?" For some it is a simple question of finding out where the soil is best, or which spot on their property has the most sun, but for others the question of where to put the garden needs to be more thoroughly considered. There are three main considerations. First is the physical, mentioned above: Where will the plants thrive? After all, not every desirable garden flower wants full sun and a deep, rich soil.

Second is the utilitarian consideration: What do you want from your garden? Do you simply want a place of beauty, or a source of flowers for the table (or perhaps some other pleasure), or will the garden have to serve multiple needs? The third main consideration is how the garden will fit into your daily activities and the overall design of your property. The best solution is to try to answer all three questions at once; pull back a bit and study the situation.

—Hugh Thompson,
*The Principles of Gardening*

Here's how: Draw a rough scale map of your property that includes buildings, trees, and other permanent landscape components, including not only those that you like, but those you don't like. It doesn't need to be fancy. On this homemade site plan you should indicate such things as slope of the land, prevailing breezes in summer and winter, shady areas, and any spots that are especially soggy. Make a few copies of this overall plan and play around with different possibilities. Keep the original so you can make more copies if necessary.

Working on one of the copies, locate areas (indoors or out) where you spend time and map the view from those places. At our house we spend a lot of time in the kitchen during the winter; in summer we practically live outdoors, especially on the porch. I also spend a lot of time in my study, so the view from its window matters a lot to me. From each of these important spots on your own site plan, draw what I like to call a "visual fan," a pair of divergent lines that indicate the limits of your view from that spot. Using this annotated chart you will not only be able to place your garden (or gardens) where the soil and aspect are right, but also where you will get the most enjoyment from them. You can block views you don't like, provide a fragrant path on the way to the back gate, or put a bouquet garden just outside the kitchen door.

Once the location has been determined and the garden designed, basic preparation can begin. For new gardens, one of the first steps should be to have a soil test done. Each state's Cooperative Extension Service (part of the United States Department of Agriculture) runs a soil-testing lab that will analyze a sample of your soil and make recommendations on how to improve its fertility. Directions for taking the sample are included with the soil-test kit they supply.

## PREPARING THE FLOWER GARDEN

Healthy soil grows healthy plants. Whatever soil you begin with—whether it is a light sand that dries, drains, and starves quickly, or a soggy but nutrient rich, clay-based, acid upland like ours—good care will improve it and guarantee you the best possible results for all your efforts.

Soil improvement comes down to one basic rule: Always put in more than you take out. The number one addition to most soils is organic matter, or roughage, such as the unharvested remains of garden plants or mulch. The soil microbes—as many as a billion per handful of healthy soil—break this plant roughage down into humus, which is the granular, crumblike guts of a good soil. During this

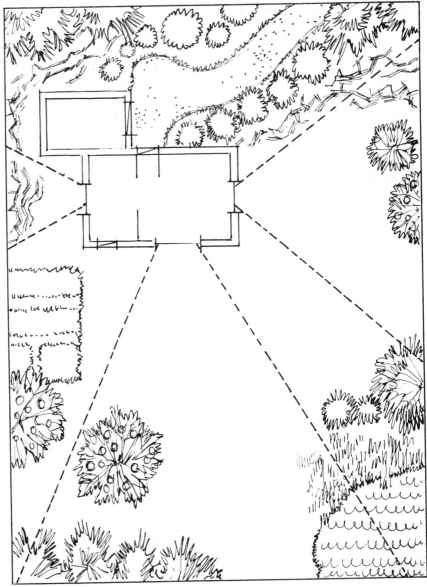

Basic design requires a site plan with all permanent features drawn in. On copies of this plan you can sketch in the view from different areas where you spend time and thus know from which aspect to plan your flower beds.

process, the microbes secrete chemical substances that break down and release mineral elements present in the soil, converting them into forms that growing plants can use. The physical and chemical structure of humus then holds these nutrients at the ready.

Perhaps the simplest way to build the organic-matter content of the soil in your flower garden is to mulch—spread a top-dressing of some bulky organic matter that suppresses weeds and conserves soil moisture—and turn under the mulch when you next prepare the beds. Mulching has many benefits, which will be discussed later in this chapter. For annual plantings, apply the mulch once the flowers are well established, and then turn it under with their remains during the normal end-of-season garden cleanup. For permanent plantings, simply allow the mulch to decompose in place and continue to add new mulch on top. This mimics the process by which nature builds soil: Year upon year of plants grow, then die and add the green matter produced by their growth to the ground on which they grew.

**Compost**

Compost provides the same soil-building benefits as mulch (which isn't surprising since it is a result of the same process), and the use of these two organic materials is often all a flower garden needs to thrive. The major difference is that with compost the materials are removed from the garden and stacked in a convenient location to decompose, then brought back to the places where the nutrients and organic matter are needed. There are many variations on this basic process that will allow you to create composts of particular types, or to speed up the process of making the compost if you need a lot right away (these are discussed in *Step by Step Organic Vegetable Gardening* and will not be covered in detail here); but the process itself need not be complicated at all.

Essential for a compost pile are a well-drained location and a supply of plant and kitchen waste to be composted. Ideally you want a pile of about one-fifth green, moist material, and four-fifths dry, brushy material, mixed together in the process of building the pile. If you have access to animal manure, so much the better; add up to two-fifths to the pile as you build. The best size for a compost pile is three to four feet on a side and about as tall. Once built, keep the pile moist but not wet, as the bacteria that live in it and accomplish its work need both moisture and air to thrive.

The pile, if properly built, will heat up—noticeably. Once it begins to cool down, turning it with a garden fork will remix the materials and get more air inside; that will cause it to reheat. Turning isn't necessary; it just gets you to the end result faster. Mature, finished compost is a dark, crumbly, soil-like material, rich and earthy smelling, like forest soil, with only vaguely recognizable bits of the original material in it.

Under the best of conditions, with close attention to the materials and prompt turning, a compost pile can be ready in as little as a month or two. Made by the "lazy man's method" my grandfather and I use—we just pile the materials and let them rot as they will—it can take a season or two, but because we start one or two piles every year, we've had plenty ever since the first pile matured.

There are many kinds of bins you can build or buy to house your composting operation if a simple pile doesn't fit in with your overall garden plan. A ring of wire fencing three feet high and three to four feet in diameter, held upright by several fence posts works well; when the pile is finished just take the fence down and the pile is accessible. Recycled wooden warehouse pallets held on edge by long stakes also work well as an enclosure, or if you have hay, you can build an enclosure from spoiled bales. Use your imagination.

Whether you enclose your pile or not, remember that compost is the gardener's black gold, and it pays to protect a finished pile from drenching rains that can wash away much of the nitrogen that has accumulated. Something presentable for a roof—or simply a piece of black polyethylene—will keep rain off the mature pile.

Well-made compost rivals the best fertilizers you can buy for a flower garden. Apply it at the rate of three–four bushels per hundred square feet in the spring, or when planting a new garden; place a spadeful in the holes dug for new transplants or where spring flowering bulbs are set each fall. Every spot that receives some compost will be better for it and, over time, as the whole garden receives its share, so will the whole garden be improved.

**Manure**   In the beginning, before you have had a chance to build a compost pile, one of your best sources of organic matter is animal manure. Manure is usually available in all but the most built-up suburbs and inner cities if you are willing to look around a bit. In rural areas, cattle or sheep farmers will often sell manure, but in small towns and suburbs the best source is usually horse owners. Horse manure, when fresh, is too strong for direct application to the garden, but it is usually mixed with some form of bedding, such as sawdust or straw, and with enough additional brushy, dry plant material added, it will compost nicely. Even if most of the nitrogen burns off (as often happens with horse manure that isn't mixed with enough roughage), it is still a valuable source of organic matter.

The best time to apply animal manure to flower gardens is at the beginning of their dormant period. In temperate regions, this is in the fall, at the time the garden is being put to bed for the winter. The manure will be aged by the time plants begin to grow again in the spring. With new gardens, it's best to turn under the manure as soon as it is spread so that as much of the nutrient content is captured as possible. In existing gardens, cover the new manure with mulch right after spreading to protect it from sun, wind, and rain while soil microbes break it down, "fixing" the nutrients in their bodies for later release when they die.

Fresh manure should not be spread on the garden if the plants are not dormant. In warm climates where some plants are actively growing all year, or if manure becomes available during the active growing season, it should be composted first, then applied. This will also serve to stabilize the nutrient content so that it isn't lost before the plants have a chance to use it.

## Soil Preparation

Now that you've built a healthy, friable soil, you'll want to keep it that way. An important part of this maintenance involves working the soil only when it is neither too wet nor too dry. Soils with a significant amount of clay are the most vulnerable. Worked when they are too wet, clay soils form into clods that later dry as hard as bricks, and only natural weathering over the passage of time— sometimes as much as two or three seasons—will bring them back into good condition. When too dry, clay soils shatter to dust, then pack so finely they can't hold enough air for good root growth and are in danger of blowing away in the first strong wind.

While clay soils are most susceptible to damage, the same principle applies to all types of soil: Wait until the time is right to prepare and plant your garden. How can you tell? Take a handful of soil in one hand and squeeze it into a ball; if water is visible between your fingers, the soil is too wet to work. Open your hand. If the compressed soil is shiny, with the small lines of your hand imprinted in it, flick it with a finger from the other hand. If the clod doesn't break apart, the soil is still too wet to work. Ideally, the soil ball should crumble when you nudge it. If the soil doesn't even stay in a clod when compressed with your hand, then it is too dry and you should irrigate or wait for rain. Extremely sandy soils may never hold together, and if yours is of this type, you will need to water frequently, especially after seeding.

The basic process of soil preparation is as follows: First, apply any soil amendments necessary, based on a soil test or your own observations; second, turn the soil; third, break up the clods; and fourth, level the surface of the bed. This can be done to the whole garden plot at once for annuals and bedding plants. For established perennial beds, though, work on the areas that you are replanting, and try to avoid disturbing areas that will remain intact. Ongoing maintenance of an established bed is a simple matter of early spring cultivation (as soon as the plants begin to break dormancy and you can see where their margins are), followed by an application of an inch-deep layer of compost and a fresh layer of mulch.

Let's take each of the steps above in some detail. First, we add whatever soil amendments that may be necessary. This way, they are turned under during the next stage and more fully mixed into the surface of the soil. Here in the northeastern United States, lime is necessary on most soils, and in our garden we add it first, at the rate of five pounds per hundred square feet. The soil test will tell you how much lime, if any, is appropriate for your plot. Other nutrient needs will also be listed. The biggest problem with these tests is that their reports are rarely in organic terms and will thus need to be converted into terms of compost and manure. Generally speaking, a half-pound of 5-10-10 synthetic fertilizer is equivalent to a bushel of compost or aged manure. Fresh manure varies in its nutrient content.

The best fertilizer and soil conditioner you can use for your garden—any garden, whether flowers or vegetables—is compost. If you don't have compost, you should start making it, following the method provided earlier. Three or four bushels per hundred square feet will provide all the nutrients that a flower garden needs, and at the same time will improve the soil structure. If you have no choice but to use bagged fertilizers, 3–4 pounds of an organic 2-3-3 mix per one hundred square feet will be plenty. When buying bagged fertilizers, remember that the three numbers printed on every bag of fertilizer stand for nitrogen, phosphorus, and potassium (abbreviated as N-P-K). Flowers have a much greater need for phosphorus and potassium than for nitrogen, so whatever fertilizer you buy, check the numbers carefully. Too much nitrogen in relation to the other elements will make your plants grow too large and flower too little, as well as make them more vulnerable to infection.

After spreading amendments, turn the bed to incorporate them, as well as to aerate and loosen the soil. Though you can use a rototiller for this purpose, I prefer to use a garden fork. Here's how to do it: Stand at one corner of the bed; turn and face outward, just in from the edge. Push the fork into the soil as you would with a shovel, then pivot the handle back toward yourself to loosen a forkful of soil. Lift fork and soil a foot or so, then quickly drop the fork halfway back down. As the soil falls back toward the tines, give them just a bit of a twist and swat upward with the fork. This will shatter the falling soil and simultaneously mix in the amendments added in the previous step. Take a step back into the bed, lift another forkful, and repeat the process.

Work your way across the bed until you reach the other side, and then either return to the beginning and start another row, or simply turn around and work back, turning and mixing another thin cross-section of the bed. By this method you can prepare about a hundred square feet of garden per hour.

Soil prep is simple. Start at one edge and work across the bed, one fork width at a time. Raise each forkful of soil about a foot above the ground, then drop and twist the fork to shatter the clod of soil you removed. Repeat this process until the whole bed is done.

Standing on a board will help you avoid compacting the soil.

To make raised beds lay out the paths with stakes and string,
then pull soil from the paths into the planting area.
Work from the opposite side of the bed, if possible.

Once the entire plot has been turned, the surface needs to be prepared for planting. In the case of an open garden that will be formed
into raised beds for planting, lay out the paths with string and stakes;
then, using the rake, pull soil from the path areas into the planting
areas. This is most easily done from the opposite side of the bed,
pulling the soil toward you with the rake.

If your garden is in permanent beds, final preparation is simply a
matter of leveling the surface and raking it smooth. In either case,
any clods can be broken up during the process of preparation by
striking at them on the diagonal so that the tines rake over them in
succession and grind the clods down. Another quick pass will distrib-
ute the newly broken clods and incorporate them into the surface of
the bed. Once the bed has been leveled and put into a fine state it is
ready to plant (a matter which will be covered in Chapter 4).

## CARE OF THE FLOWER GARDEN

**Mulching**

Once the garden is planted, the beds will need to be cultivated on a regular basis to keep weeds down. After seedlings or transplants are well established, however, mulching can reduce the amount of cultivation necessary. A mulch is simply any material laid on the soil that prevents the growth of weeds. Commercial gardeners make extensive use of plastic mulches, but in the home garden, those made from organic material (that is, plant parts) are more appropriate because they feed the soil as they break down over the course of the season.

Some important considerations when deciding what kind of mulch to use are: speed of breakdown, nutrient content, resistance to wind and erosion, presence of weed seeds, and the appearance of the mulch. Each kind of mulch that you can use has its pluses and minuses; see the chart below for a comparison.

## MULCH MATERIALS AND THEIR CHARACTERISTICS

| Material | Comments |
| --- | --- |
| Bark | Excellent for paths; should be finely ground for flower beds. |
| Buckwheat hulls | Attractive, but blows away easily. |
| Cinders | Paths only, and only if beds are separated with a hard edge. |
| Cocoa hulls | Attractive, but blows away easily. |
| Grass clippings | Supplies nitrogen, but should be dried first to avoid rotting. |
| Gravel | Paths only, except in special situations. Holds heat. |
| Hay | Informal-looking, but supplies organic matter. May contain weed seeds. |
| Pine needles | Looks great, and slow to break down. Very acidic in quantity. |
| Salt marsh hay | Informal-looking, slow to break down, no weed seeds likely. |
| Sawdust | Blows away easily, very acidic, robs nitrogen unless rotted first. |
| Seaweed | Informal-looking, but long-lasting. Wash first. Will supply nutrients. |
| Shredded brush | Informal-looking, but available on-site. Long-lasting. |
| Shredded leaves | Looks good, supplies nutrients and organic matter. Shred well. |
| Straw | Informal-looking, but long-lasting and free of weed seeds. |

Hay, for example, is nutrient-rich and breaks down quickly, enriching the soil. But it often contains weed seeds, and many gardeners consider it too visible for use in perennial borders. For that use many prefer buckwheat or cocoa hulls, which are dark in color and don't break down as fast. Both of these, however, are easily wind-blown and contribute little fertility to the soil when they do break down. Grass clippings are readily available, but if applied too thickly will rot into a hot, slimy mass; they should be used only as a thin covering, or mixed with other material. Leaves are an excellent mulch, nutrient-rich and weed-free, but if they are not allowed to sit a season and partially decompose, or not shredded before use, they mat down and smother the soil. Pine needles are nice looking and break down slowly, but are quite acidic and prone to blowing in the wind. In every case there are trade-offs; consider both what is available in your area and what you want from the mulch.

The nature of mulch is to slow down changes in soil moisture and temperature so don't spread it on cold and soggy or hot, bone-dry soil, as it will prolong these conditions. Wait until the soil is in good condition, then apply at least an inch of mulch over the entire surface of the growing bed, leaving a small area of open soil right around the base of the young plants so they can breathe. Paths, if not covered by a permanent, long standing mulch like stone, sawdust or wood chips, should be mulched more deeply—three inches or more.

Renew the mulch as necessary, and pull up any weeds that poke through. Annual beds and temporary paths can be turned over, mulch and all, at the end of the growing season. Perennial beds and permanent paths will simply need a new layer of mulch added yearly to keep the mulch thick enough to stop weed penetration.

**Cultivation**    As hinted above, areas that are not mulched will need regular cultivation. Many gardeners seem to find cultivation a real chore, but it needn't be, if done promptly and regularly. In my opinion, two of the most important garden habits you can develop are timeliness and consistency. If you weed your garden before it seems to need it— that is, while the weeds are still small and struggling to establish themselves—the process can be a joy, not a chore. Instead of a bent-knee, sore-arm, bug-sweaty, weed-yanking exercise in discomfort and frustration, timely cultivation can be a chance to enjoy a quiet few minutes in the garden, whisking barely sprouted weedlings from between the vigorous young flower plants. At the same time, the view from close quarters will give you a chance to observe any deficiency or infestation in the plants—before it becomes a problem—and to remedy it.

Timing in planting is as important as timeliness in cultivation. Plants that are started or set out too soon or too late have a harder time establishing themselves in the garden and are more likely to suffer from disease or insect attack. As a gardener you need a sense of the season, and a sense of the weather as it cycles through your own piece of the world. This natural worldliness is not difficult to develop, if you allow yourself to do so. It doesn't require any particular study or intelligence—at least in the normal sense. Study and intelligence too often attempt to reach across a gulf humans mistakenly feel separates them from the rest of nature. This attempt to reach out, to conceive of nature and its workings, actually prevents us from perceiving what we seek because we substitute our ideas of nature for the reality of it. Natural worldliness requires a sort of receptive attention, a willingness to immerse oneself in the fluid passing of the season, eyes and ears open, but not looking or listening too hard.

Time and the seasons flow like cool air down a hillside on a September morning, and the worldly gardener gains a sense of the nature of the place through a relaxed, yet complete attention to the entire milieu in which he or she gardens: soil, plants, weather, climate, season. One comes to know the microclimate of one's garden, the seasons of one's garden, the particular problems and advantages of one's garden as intimately as a spider knows the air of the particular glade in which it has built its web, or as a trout knows the stream in which it lives. And a gardener with this level of awareness senses when to plant and when to mulch and when to propagate with the same surety that the goose shows heading north after a long winter, that the apple tree shows when opening its bloom to the bees, and the iris displays when sending its first green shoots from the resting rhizome just as the ground warms to its suiting. This nonliterate understanding is difficult to communicate, but it is the acknowledged heart of the truly great gardener's art. And with it comes the timing that makes a garden work and seem, at its best, inevitable in its own time and place.

Consistency, on the other hand, is mere technique, or skill. Its payoff is an ease of care that gives us the freedom to relax and enjoy our garden. Just as a gymnast need not think about how a somersault is done once it has been practiced and learned, we should practice and learn the basic skills of gardening—the seeding, the transplanting, the dividing, the weeding, and watering—until they are second nature. Plants thrive on consistent care, and the larger the garden, the more each plant will be able to have only a moment of our attention on any given day. We need to make that moment count.

For example, setting all the plants of a given type the same distance apart when transplanting makes cultivation easier, and in the case of bedding plants is critical to the overall effect as the pattern will be upset if each plant is not precisely placed. The same is true for plants that are direct-sown and thinned to their final distances.

**Irrigation**    Irrigation is another area where timing and consistency are important. I am a firm believer in the premise that plants should be pampered when young and left alone as they mature. Thus, regular watering to keep the soil at optimum moisture levels while the plants are establishing themselves is critical.

The general rule of thumb is to make sure the garden gets an inch of water a week. An inexpensive rain gauge will help determine the amount of rainfall. When left under the sprinkler while watering, it will also measure irrigation. A quicker method is to take a handful of soil from two inches below the surface and apply the squeeze test mentioned earlier. Soil that won't stay in a ball is too dry.

The best time to water depends on your climate. In hot, dry climates, water in the evening or in the very early morning so that the moisture has a chance to seep into the soil before evaporating. In warm, humid climates, the best time is morning so the foliage has a chance to dry off before evening. Persistent humidity combined with irrigation, can keep the plants wet for long periods and lead to disease outbreaks. The key is to make sure that the foliage has a chance to dry off completely at least once every eighteen hours, to keep fungi or bacteria from getting established.

In cold climates, mid-morning is best for watering. Cold irrigation water can slow the growth of plants, so watering just before the maximum heating period of the day gives the sun a chance to warm the soil and the plants back up to optimum levels. Just as in hot, humid climates, frequent heavy dew and ill-timed irrigation can combine to foster diseases.

Consistency is important here, too, because irregular outdoor irrigation leads to irregular growth, which is unsightly. Groups of seedlings that are watered erratically will suffer even more, a topic we will touch on in Chapter 4.

**Plant Supports**    We live on a southwest hillside, and the prevailing wind in this neck of the woods is northwest-to-southeast. Since we are in a part of the world that has cool summers and frequent cloudy periods, we have kept our main gardens open—free of trees—to let in the sun. This means we have a windy site, and tall plants that aren't deep-rooted need protection or support. We plant sunflowers and other tall, well-rooted plants on the windward side of the garden—two rows deep, minimum—and they cut the wind somewhat, but we generally need to stake plants that grow taller than a couple feet if they are going to be out in the open.

Even gardeners in less exposed sites will want to support their plants, as rain, too, can bring them down. Aside from the preventive aspect there are many aesthetic reasons to support flowers. A nasturtium at the crest of a wall may grow three or four feet and still be safe within the warm clasp of the stone; morning glories may run and thrive within the thorny jungle of a rose hedge, but many others will depend on us for support if they are to look their best; certainly, if we want to use the flowers our garden presents, we need to keep them upright.

There are as many kinds of plant supports as there are climates and gardens, ranging from the simplicity of brushy branches stuck butt-end in the ground among growing annuals to elaborate trellises and arbors (beyond the scope of this book) on which perennial vines are grown to give basic structure to the layout of a garden. Even at these extremes, however, the benefits and functions of plant supports remain the same: to get delicate plants up off the ground and into the air so they get not only more sun, but less exposure to the countless bacteria in the soil and the more persistent humidity close to the ground. Many of the best flowers we grow for cutting also benefit from having support simply because it provides strength and direction to the stems, which makes them more attractive in the vase.

Let's look at the basic ways one can support flowers and the uses of each. As mentioned above, brush is an effective and natural support for flowers, and is, in fact, the traditional method used at such famous gardens as Kew, outside London. For relatively wide spreading plants up to two feet tall, fan-shaped branches of freshly cut brush firmly stuck upright in the soil provide a framework around which the plants can grow, and in the resulting tangle the brush and plants all lend support to each other while the brush disappears among the foliage and flowers of the growing plants. Taller plants, if they twine or climb like sweet peas, can use a brush teepee in much the same way.

Taller, clumping plants like veronica or some of the taller campanulas will do better with a ring of thin stakes securely set close around the clump and then ringed with several tiers of soft, untreated twine. The first tier should be about a foot off the ground, and the second a foot below the expected final height of the plants, but definitely below the lowest flower. Bamboo is especially good for the stakes as it is a renewable material, natural-looking, and has ribs that keep the twine from sliding down over the course of the season. All that is necessary is to tie the twine to one stake, then loop it once

Four methods of supporting plants *(clockwise from upper left)*: fresh-cut brush stuck upright in the ground; perimeter stakes and twine; wire quonsets; and single stakes for solitary blooms.

completely around each stake in turn, keeping tension as you go, until you return to the first stake. If you'd like to have a less casual look, there are a number of coated metal plant support systems available, and they are described in the Tools and Equipment section of this chapter.

Some flowers require a different approach. A large lily or delphinium spike loaded down with rain weighs far more than its stem can support in a wind, and given the amount of room allowed by a stake and twine ring it would simply throw itself against the twine and crumple. Therefore, plants with large, single-flowering stems will do better with a single stake per stem and a loose tie of twine every foot or so along its length so that it can't rack in the wind. The ties should not be tight or they may choke the plant, but they must be secure to hold the plant against the wind. To accommodate both of these seemingly contradictory aims, set the stake on the windward side—again, bamboo is just about the best material around—and tie the twine in a figure eight, with a complete loop around both stake and stem; this way each is held firm, but the extra twine between them allows the stem to expand, while the crossover of the twine in the middle creates friction that dampens the movement between the plant and its support.

Cutting gardens, where appearances are secondary to efficiencies and plants are grown en masse, can be supported a whole bed at a time. There are a couple of good ways to do this. One is to create a twine cage, as described above, for the entire bed, and then crisscross it with additional lines so that the plants grow up through a grid of twine which keeps them from moving more than a foot or so in any direction without restraint. For even more control, put $2'' \times 2''$ stakes every six feet around the perimeter of the bed and then hang a piece of concrete reinforcing wire (available from building supply stores) between them. This is a stiff, usually rusty, wire grid with welded joints every six inches in both directions; it comes in rolls six feet across and can be cut to a length that matches the width of your bed so that it just reaches across. For shorter plants the wire can be set up quonset style without the stakes. This kind of support is widely used by professional growers, and does not have to be ugly; the weathered surface of the wire blends in well if set up early and unobtrusively.

Probably the most important thing in a good staking job, aside from making sure the supports are set deep enough to resist the wind, is to set them early, before the plants have grown. Your flowers should grow up with the support in place so they adapt to it, cover it, and hide it. Trying to stake mature plants rarely helps the plant or pleases the gardener; all it does is take what had become the plant's natural habit and wrench it around to fit some new conception that you hadn't had the foresight to anticipate.

## DISEASES AND PESTS
## OF THE FLOWER GARDEN

You will have some pest and disease problems in your flower garden. Why? Because at some point during a given season they are virtually bound to show up. Healthy plants grown in the proper conditions will be much less affected, but that doesn't mean your garden will be problem-free. After all, pests and diseases are just fellow organisms whose lifestyles happen to be inconvenient for us. I know that sounds awfully "modern," but it's true. Of the billions of microbes in every handful of soil, only a few cause problems, and even then only on occasion. And of the million or so insect species on earth, again only a handful cause problems. Seen from this perspective we should feel fortunate. Still, when the garden is attacked we feel we must fight back.

**Diseases**   For our purposes there are three major causes of disease that affect the flower garden: fungi, bacteria, and viruses. Each of these can take various forms: Fungi can cause damping off, rusts, mildew, and some stem, root, or crown rots; bacteria can cause root or stem rots, galls, leaf spots or blights, and wilts; and viruses generally stunt or deform the plant or its parts. This may sound daunting, but it is rare for any of these problems to become widespread in a well-tended garden because the wide diversity of plants grown limits the spread of diseases that are specific to one plant or group of plants.

Specific problems are covered in relevant sections of Chapters 4 and 5: Damping off is primarily a disease of seedlings, and is considered in Chapter 4; the others are discussed in Chapter 5 under the species affected. There are, however, some general rules of pest and disease control that apply to the whole garden because they are preventative in nature, and prevention is the best solution to garden problems. Second best is promptness because problems caught early can be controlled more easily.

*Preventing Disease.* First and foremost is good sanitation. We will discuss this again in Chapter 4, but it is equally important outdoors. Inspect all plant material (seeds, seedlings, cuttings, or divisions) that comes into the garden and solve any pest or disease problems before they become established. If you are unsure about the condition of a plant, keep it isolated and in a container until you are sure; not all problems are immediately apparent.

Be ruthless: Diseased or pest-ridden plant parts should be removed from the garden immediately and destroyed. It is better to sacrifice a few plants than risk the infection of more. It's best not to compost infested plants even if the pile is built properly and heats up as it should. Burning the plants is most effective, but if local ordinances prohibit burning, take the plants to the dump. When pruning to remove dead or dying tissue, always cut well beyond the obvious damage so that you are sure to remove the problem; it only takes a few individual spores or insects to reinfect a plant. If the plant has root rot, be sure to remove the soil immediately around the plant, too.

*Controlling Disease.* Your best weapon against disease is your own ability to observe and analyze. When you first become aware of a problem, try to identify it and the conditions that led to its development. Then you will be able to control it in the least intrusive way possible, by changing those conditions.

Fungal diseases are really the only ones that can be effectively treated, and then only if you act promptly. There are a number of organic sprays that can prevent or treat fungal infections on leaves, and organic dusts that can help fight fungal attacks on stems and roots. The elemental mineral sulfur, when ground to a fine powder, works for both: Mixed with water, it makes an effective preventive or curative spray against mildew and rust; as a dust it is effective at preventing fungi from attacking the cut surfaces of newly prepared cuttings and divisions. Sulfur is readily available in a number of forms both at garden centers and by mail order. Common household baking soda, mixed at the rate of one tablespoon per gallon, has also been proven not only to kill fungal spores, but to prevent their germination if a preventive spray program is used during periods when infection is likely. Other sprays, such as garlic (which contains sulfur compounds), specially formulated soaps, antitranspirant sprays—even water sprays—have been found to have some positive effect on preventing mildew, but baking soda and sulfur, being both cheap and effective, are our first choices.

Unfortunately, bacterial and viral diseases cannot be controlled as easily as those caused by fungi. As mentioned earlier, if these problems do rear their ugly heads in your garden the best solution is simple but painful: Remove and destroy the plants. The best prevention is to avoid introducing the disease in the first place. In addition, time your irrigation so that the leaves have time to dry at least once every day and a half if possible, and try to stay out of the garden when it is wet. As you brush through wet plants, disease can be swept from one plant to the next, kept alive by the moisture on your skin or clothes, and you can quickly turn a local problem into a general one if you are careless.

**Pests**   Insect pests are even more troublesome than diseases, but, as with disease problems, they fall into a few groups, and by knowing the modus operandi of each group—and a bit about the biology of its members—it is possible to formulate a defense that doesn't require the use of harmful chemical pesticides. The four major kinds of flower pests are suckers, chewers, miners, and borers; the problems they cause are well indicated by their names, and they fall into two groups according to the method of control.

Sucking and chewing pests are relatively easy to control (compared to miners and borers) because they stay on the surface of the plant where you can get at them. Within this group are aphids, leafhoppers, slugs, and caterpillars, plus various kinds of bugs and beetles. While most of these can simply be picked off the plants and destroyed, there are more efficient ways to deal with them, and these are noted in Chapter 5 under individual plants. Thrips, whiteflies, and mites are also included in this group, but because of their size and their nearly invisible feeding, they are more difficult to control.

Miners and borers live and dine within the plant itself and so are not easily controlled, even by chemical sprays. The surest control for these hidden pests is first to destroy their natural overwinter hiding places, and second, to remove any plant parts they have infested and burn them, pest and all. Again, specific cases will be considered in Chapter 5.

Of course not all pests are insects, or even mollusks or arthropods. Any animal that interferes with your garden can be defined as a pest, whether it be a mouse nibbling at your fall-planted bulbs, a cat burying scat in your newly planted annuals, or the neighbor's kid (even your own kid!) looking for a lost baseball in the perennial border. As the German plantsmen Hansen and Stahl wrote in their comprehensive reference, *Perennials and Their Garden Habitats*, "Dogs, hens and a gardener's folly are the only enemies against which no perennial can prevail." But we can do our best to make our garden one that is as naturally resistant to the depredations of pests as possible.

Also, keep in mind that not all animals are pests. Frogs, toads, moles and shrews, and even bats are not pests, but pest predators. They spend their days (and nights) in a constant search for food, and what they eat is bugs, slugs, grubs, and worms—they are helping not hurting—so take care of them, don't chase them out. Birds can be a great help—even chickens if you don't let them in the garden until after the season is done. They will happily claw for grubs and worms until the ground freezes solid and drastically reduce the pest population you'll have to face the following spring. Robins are great consumers of caterpillars, cutworms, and slugs; Chickadees love aphids, potato beetles (who love nicotiana!), and leaf miners; finches, sparrows, starlings, wrens, and warblers are all voracious eaters of insects. Swallows, like bats, practically live on mosquitoes; not only will these anti-pests patrol your garden tirelessly, they will make it a more enjoyable place to be with their antics and their songs. Even snakes are helpful in most cases; they eat the field mice that eat the bulbs.

There are also a large number of insect species that, rather than bothering your flowers, are actually protecting the plants from harm! Take the ladybug, whose other name, the aphid lion, more clearly portrays her aggressive nature. One of the biggest follies of chemical pest controls is that they indiscriminately kill both good and bad insects, thus destroying the natural controls that nature maintains and allowing any new pests that come along—and they will—a free rein until new predators, too, appear. Even bacteria and viruses, at times a plague on the garden, play a part in the natural controls on pests. Some of the major tools in the organic gardener's control kit (discussed below) are naturally occurring diseases of pest insects that, given the need, can be introduced into the garden environment.

*Preventing Pest Damage.* Fences, or the more thorny kinds of hedges, are probably the only sure way to keep out the larger pests like rabbits, dogs, and deer. But for the smaller but more numerous kinds of pests that aren't much affected by such architectural barriers, there are still things we can do to minimize their presence rather than just react after the damage has already begun. In fact, many of the same general principles that apply to disease prevention apply equally to pest prevention.

First off, again, is sanitation. Don't bring new plants into your garden without first giving them a thorough inspection for resident pests or their eggs. It is much easier to treat a single plant than to treat a whole garden. Second, keep your yard and garden free of debris where pests can overwinter. In cold climates this means you should remove mulches at the end of the season and not replace them until after the ground has frozen; this drives the pests out into the open where they are killed by the cold. If you wait until after the ground has frozen to mulch your bulb beds, the mice will have already taken up residence elsewhere rather than finding a snug home in the mulch—right next to a winter's food supply of juicy bulbs!

*Controlling Pest Damage.* The major strategies for control of pests in the organic flower garden are hand-picking, trapping, and spraying. Hand-picking is the most basic and most effective, at least for pests that are large enough and slow enough to treat this way. Japanese beetles are a good example. A scourge to virtually all gardeners east of the Rocky Mountains, once the population builds up, they can be difficult and time-consuming to control. There are long-term controls; the most common is milky spore, a bacteria that infects the overwintering beetle grubs in the sod of your lawn, but after application (which can be expensive for large areas) it takes two or three years to become fully established and effective. In the meantime the scourge remains!

The trick is to begin patrolling for Japanese beetles as soon as they emerge or arrive in your garden; that way you get them before they breed, and you can make a serious dent in the numbers that continue to plague you. I go out early in the morning with a bucket full of soapy water and walk among the roses—one of their favorite plants—and when I see the iridescent sheen of a beetle's back hunched in the leaf or bud axil of a rose bush, I hold the bucket beneath her perch and flick her into the "chemical" brew. Because Japanese beetles are lethargic in the cool morning air, they aren't able to hold on or to fly away. My boy, Sam, given the choice, prefers to crush them, and that works just as well—no bugs have yet developed a genetic resistance to this technique like they have to the chemical sprays!

Trapping is another way to cut into the population of pests in the garden. Japanese beetle traps are one of the big sellers at the garden centers around here each spring, and you can actually tell when the beetles have emerged by the rush of gardeners into the store asking after them. But, in fact, this is not a pest where a trap is necessarily the best idea. We have noticed that the traps, which use a sex lure to attract the beetles, often attract beetles to our garden rather than simply trapping them, and we end up with more beetles than when we began. The problem is not in the traps' effectiveness but in their placement. Rather than placing them *in* your garden where you already see Japanese beetles present, you should place the traps *outside* your garden, upwind, so that they will tempt the beetles to leave the garden before succumbing to the wiles of the trap. That way those who, for one reason or another, are not enticed into the trap, will not be a further problem to you.

A case where trapping is very effective is with slugs. Of course you can buy slug traps, too, but they aren't really necessary unless you think the appearance alone is worth the money. A half a tin can, sunk in the ground, filled with beer—this is an old wives' tale told by some very smart old wives—will indeed attract, trap, and drown slugs, but it is an unconscionable waste of beer. Much simpler is a flat stone a foot or more across and at least an inch or two thick: Laid on the ground in a protected area where slugs are known to be, it will, overnight, collect them beneath. They will go there as morning approaches to hide from the hot, dry sun, but you, the gardener, need only flip over the stone and crush them—or if you are squeamish, knock them into the soapy water with the beetles. If you don't have stones, use a piece of scrap lumber eight inches wide and an inch or more thick; it will work the same way.

The final step, if more direct methods fail, is to spray the pests with an organic pesticide. These pesticides come in a number of forms: From least to most harmful, they are bacterial, botanical, or chemical. Bacterial sprays, like the milky spore mentioned above, are preferable because they are specific to particular pests and thus don't harm other possibly beneficial organisms. The most commonly used and one of the most effective of the bacterial sprays (though its overuse is beginning to create a problem with insect adaptation) is *Bacillus thuringiensis* (Bt). Bt is a naturally occurring bacteria that causes disease only in soft-bodied caterpillars. As it turns out, this encompasses a wide number of destructive garden pests. While Bt will not infect many of the beneficial insects you want in your flower garden, it will infect some that you might be willing to put up with because of their beauty: Butterflies spend a part of their life as caterpillars, and if you spray with Bt, you will risk losing them.

Botanical sprays, while considered relatively harmless in the long term because they are naturally occurring and break down into harmless constituents fairly quickly, are nonetheless what professional applicators call "broad-spectrum" pesticides. Basically that means that they kill everything. When used at all, they should be applied only to the particular plants that are infested to minimize the damage to beneficials that may be nearby. I might add that these natural poisons are harmful to humans as well as garden pests, and if you do use them you should take all the same precautions you would when using a chemical pesticide. Look for pyrethrum, rotenone, neem, or sabadilla. You can buy them in virtually any garden center or hardware store, and they are regulated and labeled just like their chemical cousins. Follow the directions!

The final form of control is chemicals, but lest you think I am going to recommend them—wait—the chemicals I am talking about are soaps. Specially formulated soaps make effective insecticides when properly applied, and now they are, at last, widely available.

They, too, are broad-spectrum killers, though, and should be used only when necessary, and only on the minimum area possible. Household soap—not detergent—will work for pest control, but is not made to the same standards as insecticidal soaps, and so cannot be counted on to have consistent results; it may even harm the plants you set out to save. Soaps degrade in seven–ten days, and are not harmful to humans in the quantities used (though your kids may tell you differently!).

In sum, try to prevent disease and pest problems, both by providing the best conditions for the plants and by giving them good care. Block diseases and pests from entering your garden by inspecting and/or quarantining new plants, and with any barriers you can. Keep a close eye on your garden, and when diseases or pests do appear deal with the problem at once before the problem becomes entrenched. Deal with the problem in the most immediate and physical way possible, and use more complicated and technological methods only if basic methods fail. Finally, note when and where the problem occurred and how it was solved, so that in future seasons you will be prepared.

## TOOLS AND EQUIPMENT

There are so many garden tools available that too often they become an end in themselves, and their actual contribution to making the work of the garden more pleasant and efficient is lost. *In Step by Step Organic Vegetable Gardening,* we examined this techno-cornucopia and discussed in detail the pluses and minuses of each tool, so we will not do so again here. Suffice it to say that the number of necessary tools to tend a garden is few. If you plan to do any propagation (which I heartily recommend) there are some other pieces of equipment that will make your time more productive and enjoyable, and your success at running a home nursery more certain. These items will be covered separately.

**Tools for Tending the Garden**

Basically, all the tools necessary to care for a garden up to about 1,000 square feet in size are: a garden spade, a garden fork, a cultivator, a planting trowel, and a rake. A good pair of flower shears is helpful, and also, if you will be cutting flowers for the table, some sort of bucket in which to hold them during harvest. Permanent plant tags will help keep the identity of your perennials straight, and if you want to keep their stems straight as well, consider having something with which to support them on hand. If you live in a dry

Five tools essential to the flower garden *(from left):* iron rake, garden spade, garden fork, stirrup hoe, and *(at bottom)* trowel (in this case a right-angle Korean trowel).

area, some form of irrigation will be necessary, whether a watering can, hose and sprinkler, or a more permanent and elaborate setup. I also think that a wheelbarrow is worth having—even for a small garden—though it is not strictly necessary.

*Tools for Planting and Cultivation.* First the spade: It should be solid forged, and as near to flat and vertical as possible so that it cuts straight. The offset, concave blades on American long-handled shovels are made to cut a tapered, round hole, which is good for transplanting shrubs; however, most of our transplanting will be done with our hands or a small trowel. We need the spade for cutting sod, edging, and trenching. The spade chosen may have any number of handle types, but I prefer the "D-handle" for general use. The handle's construction should be solid; the best are formed from a single piece of wood that spreads, properly called a "Y-D," or from solid metal, with no wood at all. Avoid those with a stamped metal handle that is merely riveted to a wood crosspiece—they will not last. Spades made entirely of steel (or a modern composite and steel), are virtually indestructible, but very expensive.

The same handle type will do for the garden fork as well, but once again there are some important differences among blades. If you will be growing vegetables as well as flowers, flat tines may be preferable, as they are superior for harvesting root crops; but absent that need, a garden fork with square section tines is more resistant to bending and easier to get into hard ground. In most cases a good quality fork of either kind will be fine, and many suppliers sell a spade and fork as a pair.

Cultivators range from the standard broad hoe to small, toothed affairs (and every imaginable form in-between). My favorite is a stirrup hoe, which has a thin steel blade that skims along just below the soil surface and cuts off weed seedlings rather than trying to uproot them. This also turns the top half-inch or so of soil without bringing more deeply buried weed seeds to the surface where they will have a chance to sprout. Unlike a normal chopping type hoe, it works both directions, in a push-pull fashion. I am also quite partial to my "hand harrow." This is about the size of a hoe, but the head holds a short axle on which are mounted three free-spinning, interlocking spiked wheels shaped very much like children's jacks. As this tool rolls across the surface of the soil, the angle of the spiked wheels and the way they interlock as they roll breaks up the top half-inch or so of soil and leaves it in a finely pulverized state. This tool is especially useful for preparing beds that will be broadcast-sown.

One of my favorite soil-prep tools is the rolling tine hand harrow, here seen with two traditional hard cultivators.

The final large tool on my short list is a stiff-tined rake (as opposed to the flexible-tined leaf rake). Once the ground has been dug and broken, the rake will be used to settle and smooth the surface. Its closely spaced tines also help pulverize the top inch or so of soil so that there is a fine seedbed in which to plant. My favorite rake has a solid edge on its back that can be used as a scraper when preparing raised beds, but that isn't absolutely necessary.

Most planting trowels resemble small spades, but I prefer the type (originally thought to have come from the Orient) that has a mold-board-plow type of blade mounted at a right angle to the rest of the handle. This arrangement makes opening holes for transplants easier on the wrist, and also makes the trowel valuable for digging furrows for those flowers that are grown direct from seed.

*Gardening Shears.* There are three general types of shears for outdoor use: passby, anvil, and grabber. Before you choose one—or all three—it helps to understand the difference among them. Passby shears range from inexpensive yet husky garden scissors up to professional pruning shears that cost forty dollars and more. True garden scissors have two sharp blades that brush past one another and thus cut whatever is between them. Because most are made with relatively thin blades, they are suitable only for light-duty cutting. Actual pruning shears have one stiff, sharp blade, and a second, curved blade that "hooks" in the stem to be cut so the shearing action doesn't just force it out of reach of the blades. The best of them come

A collection of garden shears *(clockwise from upper left):* heavy-duty garden scissors with detachable blades; professional pruning shears; garden snips; needle nose pruners; light-duty scissors; and "grabber" type flower shears.

completely apart for cleaning, and all parts are replaceable. Anvil shears also have a single cutting blade, but cut by pressing the stem against a solid surface (the anvil), usually made of brass. These are generally less expensive, but more likely to damage stems if out of adjustment (which they frequently are). Grabbing shears are a type of shear with blades specially designed to hold the stem after cutting. While most grabber shears are not up to heavy-duty cutting, they are just right for collecting bouquets.

*Plant Tags.* Permanent plant tags are an important piece of equipment if you grow perennials because only then can you really keep track of the identity of the plants you have. Even though you may remember the genus and species and even the cultivar names of your plants, as you increase them over the years you will want to be able to double-check your memory. At the least, the original plant from which you produced the others should be tagged. Also, by having the locations of plants marked you avoid disturbing them during their dormant season when otherwise you might not remember they are there.

The tags needn't be either ugly or expensive. Our favorite system is the small zinc tag and stake combinations (they come in all sizes and shapes, really) that you either write on with pencil, or incise with an awl or some other scratching implement. This makes a label that doesn't fade in the sun or rain and will last many years. Their dull color makes them quite unobtrusive during the growing season. The cost is only something like twenty cents to a dollar apiece, depending on the size and the number you buy at once.

*Plant Supports.* As mentioned earlier, brush will make a good, natural-looking support for many kinds of plants. The problem, of course, is obtaining suitable brush. Spring pruning will provide some, perhaps, but not all brush is created equal. The structure of the branches affects its usefulness; the best brush comes from young trees growing in full sun, where they branch freely. Otherwise, there is not enough spread in the branches to give the growing plants something to hang onto. The traditional material in England was hazel, and my godfather here in Vermont used birch; unfortunately neither of these is readily available anymore. If you have a bit of extra land you might consider letting an edge of it grow up to a thicket from which you can cut brush (and which, I might add, will attract birds to the edges of your garden to help with pest control). Otherwise you might need to consider metal or bamboo stakes.

I didn't mention metal stakes in the discussion earlier for the simple reason that I don't consider them either very economical or very aestheticly pleasing. From my perspective bamboo is much preferable: It is a readily available, thoroughly renewable resource. In fact, it is considered a weed in many places, and cutting it is practically a public service. If you have a spot for growing brush, you probably have a spot for growing bamboo, though you should plan carefully how you will restrain it before bringing it onto the property! If you wish to buy bamboo, it is available at garden centers or by mail. The size you want for stakes depends on the size of your plants. It would be wise to have some each of three- and four-foot lengths so that after inserting a foot of a cane's length into the ground you have two to three feet above ground and available for tying. How many you will need depends entirely on the size of your garden, but I will say I would rather have too many than too few.

The more formal metal supports that I mentioned earlier come in a number of forms. There are one-piece, L-shaped, coated metal stakes with a loop at the end of the "El" that allows them to hook together in a ring to support clumping plants (or simply to restrain a single stem). There are also flat, cross-braced, coated metal rings of various diameters, and these will accomplish the same end as the concrete wire commercial growers use, but for one plant at a time (they are often listed as peony rings in catalogs as they are especially well suited for that plant). Finally, there are rectangular, hinged, gridlike affairs that can be placed zigzag along a row for climbers to use as support. All of these are relatively expensive, from five to fifteen dollars per plant depending on the size, but in formal settings you may consider them worth the money. Myself, I prefer bamboo and twine.

*Irrigation Systems.* Irrigation needs can be met with equipment as simple as a hose with a sprayer tip on it, though much better arrangements can be put together for not too much more money. Some sort of oscillating wand sprinkler of the type used for lawns is better; better still is the rotating type, set atop a five-to-six-foot-tall shaft. These rotating sprinklers rain water down on the plants from above without drenching the nearest plants in the process or splattering mud all around.

The very best system is one that trickles water right at the base of the plants (or even underground, in the root zone); this system keeps the foliage of the plants completely dry during irrigation, which is a great help in avoidance of disease. There are two different materials used for trickle irrigation systems: relatively rigid polyethylene pipe with gauged outlets every foot or so, and porous hose made from recycled automobile tires. The first of these cannot reliably be left in the garden over the winter in cold areas, because the frost will harm it; the second is more resilient, though both will become brittle over time when exposed to sunlight. If buried they will not degrade, but care must then be exercised to avoid punctures during spring soil preparation or when moving plants.

*Wheelbarrows.* Finally, as mentioned above, I find that a wheelbarrow is a great addition to the list of garden tools, even for a small garden. There is a lot of moving to be done in almost every garden—spent plants, compost, mulch, soil, fertilizers, etc.—and a sturdy wheelbarrow makes it all much easier. If you plant in beds, and are willing to make the beds just the right dimension, you might prefer one of the new two-wheel carts over a regular wheelbarrow as it will be able to straddle the rows, but I still prefer the old-fashioned kind, with one wheel in the front. Mine has a barrow made from a sturdy construction-grade plastic, though, so it won't rust.

**Propagation Equipment and Supplies**   You'll need some equipment beyond the general garden tools discussed above if you want to raise your own flowers for the garden. It need not be expensive or high-tech, but a basic propagation setup will make handling seedlings, cuttings, and divisions a lot easier and more successful.

One of the most useful pieces of equipment you can own if you want to propagate garden flowers is a heating mat. These come in a number of forms but the principle is the same in each case: Electricity is used to heat a thin mat on which pots or trays of seeds or cuttings can be placed so that they benefit from warm soil during their gestation. A good home garden–sized model (similar to the commercial model we use in our gardens) is available from a number of mail-order garden-supply catalogs. It is nine inches wide and twenty-four inches long, and made from a clear, waterproof plastic material which has the electrical conductors bonded in between two sheets of laminate so that it is totally waterproof. This is a significant advantage, since obviously the environment where it will be used is bound to be wet. The unit plugs into any wall socket via a small transformer and thermostat unit that keeps the temperature of the mat at 72–75°F, which is good for rooting and sprouting a wide range of plants. At thirty-five dollars, these mats aren't cheap, but you will save in the long run if you have been buying plants at a garden center and instead use the mat to start them yourself.

If you have a cold frame, you can create a warm surface on the ground that will have the same effect as a heating mat. Lay heating cables directly on the ground, and cover them with a tightly woven wire mesh (to prevent their being inadvertently punctured) and two inches or so of sand. You then set the trays and pots directly in the sand, which holds and distributes the heat from the cables so that you get even heat across the whole surface. A setup like this will use considerably more electricity than mats, but will also cover a much larger space than the indoor, laminated unit.

One other essential piece of equipment you'll need is a knife. Really it would be best to have two: one with a solid, hefty blade for cutting through tough plant crowns and thick roots when making divisions, and one with a small, sharp blade for making tender stem cuttings. For the first I use a standard garden utility knife of the type made for cutting cabbages; it has a broad, steel blade eight inches long and is blunt on the end so it can be carried in your pocket without a scabbard. My detail knife is an artist's graphic knife with a removable blade; when the razor-sharp, razor-thin blade begins to dull it is easy to replace.

You should also buy a notebook to keep track of just when and how you increased your flowers. Not only will a notebook provide a backup to your memory, but as the seasons pass and you get a chance to observe your successes and failures, you will be able to

Two useful kinds of knives for the flower garden: a broad-bladed minimachete for rough garden work; and an artist's razor knife with replaceable blades for preparing cuttings and other precise work.

look back at your records and learn just what worked and why. The records you keep can be simple or elaborate, but do keep them; plants can be replaced but time can't, and time can be either friend or foe. Good records harness time to build a wealth of knowledge; their lack allows it to rob us.

*Containers.* Obviously two things that one cannot do without when growing seedlings are containers and the soil mix to fill them. The pots and flats themselves can be of any type, really, though some are more pleasant to work with and others more efficient. Wooden flats, individual clay or plastic pots, sawed-off milk cartons, recycled garden-center six-packs, peat pots, plug trays: All will work, but whatever you choose remember that the key to growing healthy transplants is consistency. All the plants of a given size and type should get equal treatment, which is difficult when using a mish-mash of containers in all different sizes and shapes.

One of the most common modular systems utilizes peat pots and strips. Many organic gardeners choose this system because they want the benefits of individual containers for each plant, yet they don't want to use plastic. Unfortunately, this reasoning does not hold up to scrutiny. Peat is a natural resource that forms in bogs at a rate of only a few hundredths of an inch per season; worldwide we are using it up much faster than it is being created. Not only are peat bogs unique ecosystems, but they also represent an important source for climatologists and archaeologists to examine ancient conditions. Peat is very useful for propagation, but we need to minimize, not maximize, its use.

Also, while the manufacturers claim that peat pots provide less muss and fuss for the gardener and less transplant shock for the plants (because the pot can simply be put into the ground, plant and all), this doesn't work as well in practice as it may sound. Special care needs to be taken at planting time or the benefits will become liabilities: the pot can wick moisture away from the plant and inhibit roots from spreading. True, these effects can be countered by cutting or tearing the pot, but then where is the advantage?

While peat containers do have the benefit of consistent sizing, they are messy to work with and, unless you use the strips, their shape makes them top-heavy once the plants have reached a decent size. Once the pots begin to tip over they are difficult to keep moist as water runs off instead of sinking in. You can buy peat pots or pellets mounted in special plastic trays that hold them upright, but if you're going to use plastic at all you might as well go with a completely integrated, reusable system like plug trays. Larger sizes of "peat" containers are often made primarily of compressed fiber rather than peat and make a good home for long-term growth of container plants.

Plugs are inexpensive plastic inserts for the standard 10″ × 20″ plastic greenhouse tray. They are similar to the six-packs that store-bought transplants are grown in, but are made of a slightly heavier gauge plastic and so are easily reusable. There are two basic types of inserts, those with parallel channels in which to sow seed, and those with a grid of conical cells that hold individual plants. For the ulti-mate in space-efficient seed germination, there are inserts which have twenty one-inch-wide, one-inch-deep rows running across the tray. With one row allotted to each flower, it is possible to start a dozen or two each of twenty different varieties, all in two square feet! Once the seedlings have their first true leaves, they can then be transplanted to larger cell plugs or individual pots.

Peat and fiber containers come in a number of sizes, shapes, and configurations. Those in front are made of peat and used for starting seedlings; those in back are made from compressed fiber and used for much larger plants.

The most useful sizes for a home propagation setup would be the 20-row tray just mentioned, plus a few sets each of 98-, 50-, and 24-cell inserts. For even larger plants, individual pots 3½ inches square fit eighteen to a tray, and 5½-inch-square pots fit eight to a tray with no leftover space (which means no tipping at watering time). We germinate most of our small-seeded annuals in the 20-row insert, while those that resent too much handling are sown direct in the 98-cell size; large-seeded annuals like sweet peas and sunflowers, as well as small cuttings, can be stuck in the 50-cell insert. Large cuttings or very small divisions fit nicely in 3½-inch pots, while larger cuttings and divisions go in the 5½-inch size. Really large summer divisions that are not immediately set back in the ground go into 8-inch-diameter recycled fiber pots of the type that fall mums are sold in, filled with our own soil mix (described below).

Raised clear plastic covers that fit over these modular trays are the final part of the system. They provide the high humidity that germinating seeds and rooting cuttings or divisions need to thrive. The whole setup is available from a number of different mail-order houses, or from some garden centers. The trays and inserts are not expensive, and with proper storage in the off-season will last a number of years. The plastic used for plug setups is recyclable.

The plants produced by this plug system are easy to transplant. The conical shape of the cells directs root growth downward, and if set out at the right stage of growth the seedlings take right off once transplanted into the garden.

*Potting Soils.* A moment's thought is sufficient to realize that the potting soil used in these plug cells is vitally important. Each cell has only a small volume of soil available for each plant, so we need to make sure the potting soil will provide ideal conditions. Young plants need excellent drainage, but they also need a constant supply of water, so the mixture we use must be well drained, but also able to store ample water to get the plants through the day while we are about our other affairs.

Commercial potting mixes are well designed to meet these needs, and if you don't want to think further on it, simply buy one that is labeled "Seedling Mix" and be done with it. I should point out, however, that not all commercial mixes are created equal. Do not buy the black, heavy bags marked simply "Potting Soil"; this stuff is suitable only for ballast. What you want is light brown, speckled with gray or white, and weighs no more than ten pounds for a sack that contains 30–40 quarts of mix. These commercial mixes often have a nonorganic fertilizer mixed in with them, so be sure to check before you start putting fertilizer in with the water; most brands also offer a fertilizer-free mix, but don't assume anything—read the label.

You can stretch the mix by adding screened, well-made compost, a quarter to a third by volume. Personally, I use the straight mix for

Inexpensive modular growing trays and inserts (*from left*): clear plastic dome to maintain high humidity during germination; germination tray with 20 individual channels for sowing seed; 50-cell plug insert with individual cells for each plant, and 5½″ pots designed to fit snugly in the growing tray. Trays are partially visible beneath inserts and pots.

germination and in plugs, and the stretched mix after the plants are established and ready to go in pots. For cuttings, which require even greater drainage, replace the compost with vermiculite, an expanded mineral material that is sterile, free-draining, and yet holds significant water. It is available at most good-sized garden centers, but if you can't find it, sharp sand will make a decent substitute.

For really large plants in large pots, say 6-inch-diameter divisions that will be grown on in the 8-inch fiber pots, or as a mix for permanent container plantings, I make a "field mix" of good garden soil, sharp sand, and rough (unscreened) compost, in equal parts. All of these variations on the standard potting soil need to be well mixed; I do this in the wheelbarrow with my fork and spade. By matching the kind of mix to the task at hand, we can provide the best conditions for our plants without wasting peat.

*Supplies.* To help keep diseases in check, keep some powdered sulfur on hand. It is a natural fungicide and is available at most garden centers. Dusting with it kills the spores of fungi that land on cut plant surfaces before they have a chance to establish themselves. Also useful to have are a 1:10 mixture of household bleach and water or a bottle of rubbing alcohol; either of these solutions can be used to sterilize the knives between cuttings so that diseases aren't transmitted from one plant to another as you work.

Finally, get a small jar of rooting powder or a bottle of liquid seaweed. These supply trace quantities of essential plant growth hormones that trigger root and shoot initiation and give your new cuttings that little extra boost that gets them up and growing quickly.

# CHAPTER 3

# Plants and
# How They Grow

*When contemplating the intricacies of the human body, its various parts and what each does, it is not possible to separate form from function. For example, a heart is not simply one of many organs, but a specialized structure for pumping oxygenated and food-bearing blood to each living cell. Similarly, the parts of a plant must be understood, not simply in terms of their appearance but, more importantly, for what each is intended to do.*

Horticulture is part art, part science, part management. A truly great gardener needs the creative courage to dare redesign nature's landscape, a thorough understanding of the plants and the site to inform this new design, and a maestro's sense of timing to keep the garden working harmoniously within the changing score of the seasons. We all have the urge, the creative spark; it's called spring fever. And we now know the basics of good gardening: that the health of our gardens depends on the health of the soil community. But this is merely the foundation on which horticulture is based.

## THE STRUCTURE
## OF PLANTS

A basic understanding of how the plants themselves are put together and how they function will help us find ways to better integrate them into our overall plans. Every element of a plant's makeup is based not on whimsy, but on need; there is a reason for everything, and nothing without a reason. Once we understand what makes plants work, we are halfway to acquiring that sense of timing that really brings a garden together.

—Brian Capon,
*Botany for Gardeners*

**Cells**   Plants, like people, are made up of cells—the atoms of biology—little blobs of protoplasm only a half-thousandth of an inch across, on which all the basic processes of life depend. Though the forms they take are varied, all plant cells have a common list of components: the cell wall, which keeps the package intact; the nucleus, which functions as the command center; the vacuole, a sac that contains the water and nutrients for, as well as waste products from, the cell's metabolism; and, surrounding these, the jellylike cytoplasm in which float various kinds of small, single-purpose organelles (cellular organs) that actually accomplish most of the work of the cell.

One kind of organelle present in all green parts of a plant is the chloroplast, which contains chlorophyll, the green pigment that allows plants—and plants only—to use sunlight as an energy source to manufacture their own food supply. When we look at a plant, the green color we see is actually the combined reflection of millions of these microscopic chloroplasts.

Within a plant, the basic cellular building block takes an array of forms as specialized cells combine into tissues and tissues combine into organs like leaves, stems, or roots. All cells are, in the end, specialized because when it comes to living things, plant or animal, there is no way to separate form and function. Let's look at these organs of the plant one by one so that we can see what part each plays in the plant's garden performance.

All plant cells have some things in common: a cell wall, a nucleus, a storage sac called a vacuole, and a range of small, special purpose organelles, all of which float in a jellylike substance called cytoplasm.

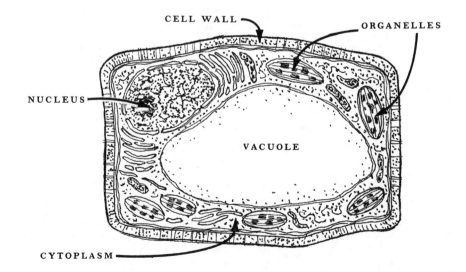

CELL WALL

ORGANELLES

NUCLEUS

VACUOLE

CYTOPLASM

Roots have three basic functions: to anchor the plant against wind   **Roots**
or removal by predators; to extract water and nutrients from the soil;
and to serve as a repository for stored nutrients.

The internal structure of roots is relatively simple. There is a thin
outer skin, called the epidermis, that is permeable to water and surrounds a thicker layer called the cortex. The cortex is loosely packed
with storage cells and acts as a kind of sump. The sugars and
starches that represent the bulk of most plants' stored energy are
here. In the center of the root are two interlocking but separate bundles of tubular tissue, the xylem and phloem (equivalent to the
human body's arteries and veins). The xylem moves water and min-
erals from the root to the rest of the plant, and the phloem distributes
plant foods to the growing points of the plant. Like arteries and veins,
they reach virtually everywhere within the body of the plant. With a
knife and a magnifying glass you can see for yourself—just cut a
thin cross section of a carrot root, a celery stalk, and a lettuce leaf,
then take a close look at their structures. You may not eat your flowers, but their structure is essentially the same.

Most of the water that enters the roots of a plant does so through
tiny root hairs that sprout from cells immediately behind the growing
tips of the root system. These root hairs greatly increase the surface
that is able to take in moisture. That is why, when transplanting,
you should be especially careful to protect the tiny feeder roots: They

While all roots are similar in cross section, tap roots are capable of storing
more nutrients than fibrous roots as they enclose a larger proportion of
cortex.

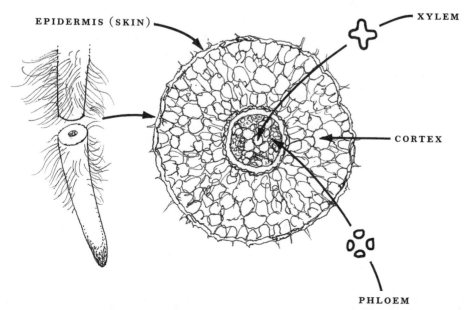

EPIDERMIS (SKIN)

XYLEM

CORTEX

PHLOEM

are essential to the plant's ability to withstand transplant shock without wilting and to restart growth as quickly as possible.

Of the kinds of plants under consideration in this book, virtually all have one of two kinds of root systems: a long, relatively unbranched taproot, or a fibrous, matlike mass of widely branching thin roots originating directly from the base of the plant. Numerous perennial species grow a wide-ranging network of more or less fleshy, underground runners, called rhizomes, which are not properly roots, but stems.

Fibrous roots are adapted to shallow or poorly drained soils, and are quite efficient at catching water and then extracting it as it percolates down through the soil. They are also able to provide ample room for the soil oxygen which is necessary for plant respiration. Tap-rooted plants are ideally suited to withstand uprooting in loose soils and windy sites; their ability to reach deep into the soil for water and nutrients also helps them to survive in locations where other plants would quickly perish.

In general, tap-roots are capable of storing more surplus nutrients than fibrous roots as the proportion of cortex to root is larger. Though roots are the most common storage mechanism for biennial and perennial flowers, other kinds of plants use swollen leaves (bulbs) or stems (corms, rhizomes, and tubers) to store energy for regrowth after a dormant period.

**Stems**  The functions of a stem are, first, to transport nutrients and water between the roots and the rest of the plant, and second, to provide a support structure for the plant's leaves—a matter of obvious importance. If you've ever closely examined young seedlings, you've probably noticed that some, like sunflowers, have two seedling leaves, while others, like alliums, have only one. This distinction between dicotyledons (two seed-leafed plants, usually called dicots) and monocotyledons (single seed-leafed plants called monocots) is important because these two basic botanical groups have different stem structures and growth habits, which affects their garden performance.

Stems, like roots, have an outer skin, or epidermis, and a cortex. They have multiple vascular bundles of xylem and phloem to conduct nutrients and water. Stems differ from roots, however, in the addition of an inner cortex called pith and in the arrangement of their parts. The epidermis of a stem is still the outer layer; inside this skin is a relatively thin layer of cortex, and then (in dicots) a ring of vascular bundles arranged around a central core of pith. In monocots, the vascular bundles are distributed throughout the cortex.

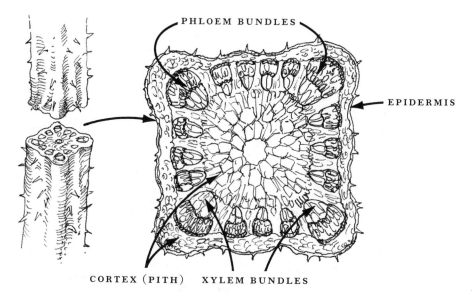

PHLOEM BUNDLES

EPIDERMIS

CORTEX (PITH)    XYLEM BUNDLES

Stems are composed of the same basic components as roots, but are arranged differently to provide the necessary strength to support their load of leaves and flowers.

Multiple vascular bundles in the stem, whether in the core of the stem or scattered about, makes it possible for the xylem and phloem to branch easily when the stem branches; they also provide alternate routes for nutrients and water should the vulnerable aboveground parts of the plant be damaged. The importance of this will become clear in the next chapter when we look at the methods of propagating garden flowers.

Unlike the roots, which are surrounded by soil, stems must be able to support themselves and the leaves and flowers they thrust into the sun and the sight of insects. Yet stems must also remain flexible so they aren't snapped off by the wind. The design of stem tissue accomplishes this aim nicely, as the hollow vascular bundles serve as reinforcement to the epidermis-enclosed pith without adding significant weight. In addition, many plants, like those of the mint family, have raised longitudinal ridges on the outside of the stem that confer additional strength. Monocot stems, with their diffuse vascular structure, are generally more flexible than those of dicots, but this makes them less suitable for propagation by stem cuttings.

## Leaves

Photosynthesis is the major function of leaves, and their entire structure is focused around bringing together all the ingredients necessary, then distributing the resulting plant nutrients to other cells in

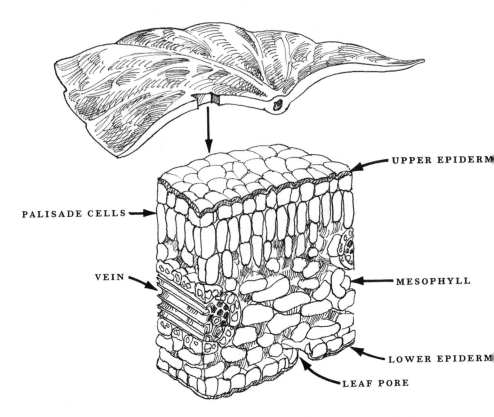

UPPER EPIDERM

PALISADE CELLS

VEIN

MESOPHYLL

LOWER EPIDERM

LEAF PORE

Leaves are food factories packed with palisade cells to convert sunlight, water vapor, and carbon dioxide into basic plant sugars, which are sent to other parts of the plant.

the plant for use in making everything from phloem to florigen, the mysterious (and as yet undiscovered) hormone plant physiologists feel is responsible for telling a flower it's time to bloom.

The structure of a leaf is much more complicated than that of a root or stem. Most leaves are flat, to expose as much surface area as possible to the available sunlight. In cross section they look like a sandwich, with a skin top and bottom, and several layers in-between. Beneath the upper skin—the side usually exposed to the sun—is a region of cells oriented perpendicular to the surface, tightly spaced, and packed with green chloroplasts, called palisade cells. Their purpose is to catch the sunlight that penetrates the leaf and perform the near magic that is photosynthesis (though other cells throughout the plant also contribute a bit to the process with their less numerous chloroplasts).

Beneath the palisade cells is an open region called the spongy mesophyll. It extends to the lower skin of the leaf and is loosely filled with irregularly shaped cells and a mixture of carbon dioxide and water vapor from the atmosphere. Leaf veins—the upper reaches of the xylem and phloem bundles—permeate this layer, supplying moisture and removing the newly made plant sugars. In monocots the veins run parallel, while in dicots they branch and split. The lower skin of the leaf is perforated with openings into this exchange area, each "guarded" by a pair of cells that open and close according to the needs of the plant.

**Flowers**

The pleasure that flowers bring—one of the main reasons we grow them—is merely incidental to their function, which is to produce seeds and thus assure the continuity of the parent plant's species. A flower is not really an organ of a plant in the same sense as the roots, stems, and leaves we have been discussing, but rather a combination of organs, including specialized leaves (the sepals, which cover the unopened blossom, and the petals themselves), plus male and/or female reproductive organs, called the stamen and the pistil, respectively. While the stamen and pistil may be together within a single flower, or on separate blooms, or even separate plants, their function remains the same, and the blossom we so desire exists solely to assist them in their mission of producing seed.

While their form varies greatly, all flowers need to have some form of perianth, composed of petals and their sheath of sepals, plus male and/or female organs. The male stamens consist of an anther atop its aptly named filament, while the female pistils have a stigma, a style, and at its base, an ovary. Not all flowers contain both sexes, however.

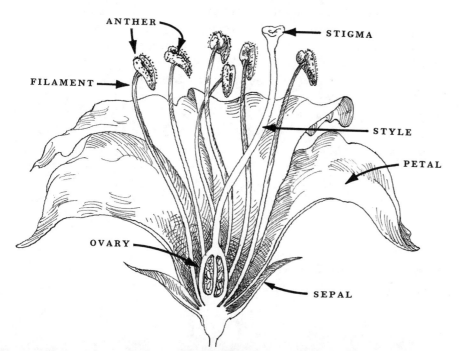

The male stamen consists of a pollen-producing anther supported atop a shaft known as a filament, while the female pistil is made up of an ovary, deep within the heart of the flower, on which grows a shaft called the style, topped by a sticky, pollen-trapping knob known as the stigma.

To produce seed, pollen from the anther must reach the stigma. In self-pollinating plants this may happen in the very process of flowering, as the growing anthers brush past the stigma and deposit their pollen. In cross-pollinating plants—which are more common— the plant is incapable of fertilizing its own ovaries, and so pollen must come from another plant. We owe the wonder and beauty of our favorite garden flowers to this need; the bright blooms and sweet fragrances have evolved over millions of years as a way to promote the passage of pollen among plants.

In wind-pollinated species like grasses, the flowers themselves are likely to be insignificant, but where transfer of pollen occurs through the visitation of insects, the flowers take an incredibly wide variety of forms. The striking patterns of an iris or sweet william blossom lead pollinating insects past the pollen-laden anthers toward a source of nectar located beyond the stigma. In the process of reaching the nectar, pollen is transferred.

Once a fertile, compatible pollen grain reaches the stigma, one of the two cells within it begins to grow down through the shaftlike style in search of the ovary, where it joins with the waiting egg, and voila! the process of fruit and seed formation begins. While this important process will provide seed to the gardener, it does spell the end of the blossom. Soon after pollination occurs, the flower will fade and fall, leaving behind the developing ovary. In some species, like nigella or poppies, the ovary itself may be of great visual interest, but in many species it is not.

The essential structure of flowers is more visible in some species than others. Foxgloves, irises, and tulips have the classical structure discussed above, but the large family of composites—including many of our favorites, like cosmos, asters, zinnias, and other daisylike formed flowers—is more complicated. Composites have two kinds of flowers in each blossom. The central part is made up of many small, tightly packed "disc flowers," and what we call the petals are actually themselves a second type of flower called "ray flowers." All together they seem to be one flower.

**Seeds**   The ultimate result of the process just described is, of course, the seed. As we'll see in the next chapter, seeds are one of the basic methods of propagating flowers and, because of the genetic mixing that takes place as an essential part of the sexual process, the dominant method of developing new and different plants. (Mutations of various kinds that appear in plants spontaneously can sometimes be propagated asexually, but their appearance is a chance affair, whereas sexual reproduction virtually assures the appearance of variation in plant type and habit.)

Seeds have three basic parts: a seed coat, to protect them from the rigors of the world during their dormant period; an embryo, with growing points at both root and shoot ends already formed, plus one cotyledon (seed leaf) if the plant is a monocot or two if it is a dicot; and food stores to nourish the seed from the time it germinates until its leaves are able to begin photosynthesis. In many plants these nutrient reserves are kept in the cotyledons themselves, but they may also be outside the embryo in what is called the endosperm. To see the difference, sprout a few bean and corn seeds in moist paper towels; the bean is a non-endospermic dicotyledon, while corn is an endospermic monocotyledon (to be fancy about it). Slice a seed of each lengthwise and you'll see the difference faster than you can say it. Flower seeds, though smaller, are similar.

Dicot and monocot seeds differ in that the dicot has two cotyledons to the monocot's one, and the cotyledons are used for the storage of the nutrients necessary during germination and early growth of the plant. The monocot seed's nutrients are stored separately from its single cotyledon in tissue called the endosperm.

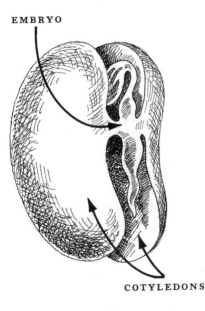

EMBRYO

COTYLEDONS

*Dicot*

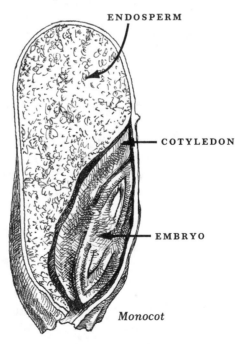

ENDOSPERM

COTYLEDON

EMBRYO

*Monocot*

The wonder of seeds is that although they contain everything needed for a plant to grow they show no signs of life. Yet they *are* alive, and their vigor is affected by the condition of the plants on which they are borne: Healthy plants produce healthy seeds. In addition, seeds must be properly cared for after harvest and protected in storage if they are to remain viable. Many flower seeds also have built-in dormancy locks that prevent them from sprouting until conditions are right for growth. This natural "insurance" must be overcome if the gardener wishes to get a head start on the growing season. In the next chapter, using our knowledge about plant form and function, we'll see just how to do this.

## HOW PLANTS GROW

Some pages ago, we began our discussion with cells. Why? Because all plant growth is, in the end, cellular growth. For our purposes cellular growth takes two forms: cell division, where one cell splits into two cells that are identical to the parent cell; and the eventual enlargement of these cells. Every cell in a plant, except the one created by the union of the sperm and egg at the time of pollination, was created by the process of cell division. The areas within a plant where active cell division is going on are called meristems; areas of active cell growth are usually nearby.

The primary growth of a plant occurs at the tips of its roots and shoots—the endmost quarter inch or so, called the apical (for apex) meristem. In dicots, secondary growth occurs from the thin cambium layer that separates the vascular tissue from the outer pith or cortex. This layer is called the lateral meristem as it grows out rather than up or down, and is responsible for the thickening of roots and shoots with age.

To see for yourself how this process occurs in a root, take the bean seed you sprouted above and mark evenly spaced lines on its root, from tip to top. Within a few days you'll notice that the distance between the lines has increased closer to the tip of the root, showing the area of fastest growth. To protect this quickly dividing area from injury by soil particles, the growing tip produces a root cap of expendable cells in front; as the walls of these front-line cells wear down from friction, their released protoplasm forms a sort of lubricant that facilitates forward movement of the following meristem.

Behind the apical meristem, the area of maximum root growth, are the root hairs that mark the primary water uptake zone (discussed earlier), which is of fixed length. Behind it, the hairs die out,

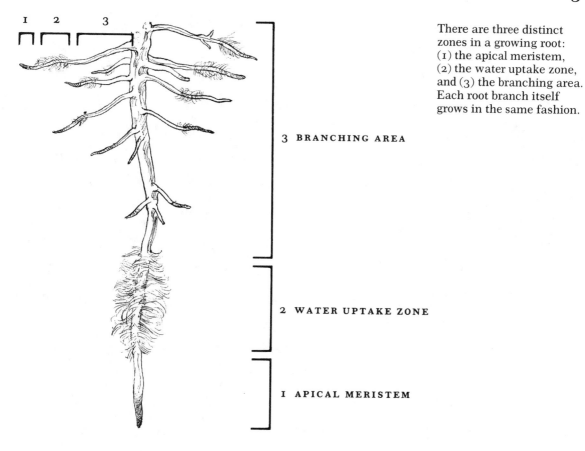

1  2  3

3 BRANCHING AREA

2 WATER UPTAKE ZONE

I APICAL MERISTEM

There are three distinct
zones in a growing root:
(1) the apical meristem,
(2) the water uptake zone,
and (3) the branching area.
Each root branch itself
grows in the same fashion.

and this is where new root branches form, sprouting perpendicular
to the existing root from inside the cortex, each a copy of the parent
root, with its own apical and lateral meristems.

Stem growth, like stem structure, is more complex, as it must
provide the entire framework necessary for growth and maintenance
of leaf, flower, fruit, and seed. As with roots, growth proceeds via
the apical and lateral meristems. The area immediately behind the
growing tip sprouts primordial leaves and branches at nodes separated by sections of clear stem. Each of these branches-to-be, called
axillary buds, has the same structure as the main stem.

Once the main shoot is formed, the cells within it begin to
lengthen, and the nodes are spread apart by the growth of the "internodes" between them. This, combined with the fact that each
node is offset around the stem from the ones above and below it,
means that when fully grown, each leaf will have maximum access
to sunlight. Whether the axillary buds begin to grow and form side
branches depends on a complex hormonal balance between them

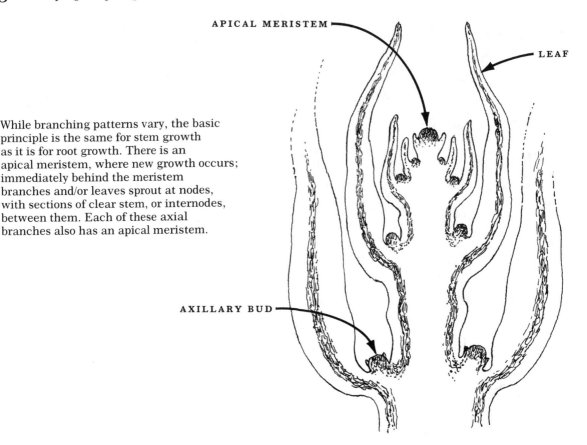

While branching patterns vary, the basic principle is the same for stem growth as it is for root growth. There is an apical meristem, where new growth occurs; immediately behind the meristem branches and/or leaves sprout at nodes, with sections of clear stem, or internodes, between them. Each of these axial branches also has an apical meristem.

and the main stem's growing point, which differs from species to species. Later in this chapter we will discuss how changing this hormonal balance can be used to modify a plant's growth to provide more or larger flowers as well as stockier, longer-blooming plants.

While the nature of stem growth is of central importance to the gardener because of the ways in which a plant can be changed by pruning and training—and new plants started—leaves are the critical organ in terms of the vigor and health of the plant. Without them there will be virtually no photosynthesis and without photosynthesis there will be no plant. As discussed earlier, the leaf provides a place wherein carbon dioxide and water vapor can be combined into the simple sugars that are the basis of the plant's metabolism. The gardener's task is to help this critical process so that the plants under his or her care may thrive; only then will there be the opportunity to utilize the other skills of horticulture.

The seasonal growth of any plant breaks into two general phases: vegetative and reproductive. During the vegetative, or juvenile phase, the plant sends up shoots, clothes them in leaves, and reaches its mature size. Then, the plant—due to the effect of the length of the day or night, the temperature, the size or age of the plants (or some combination of these)—enters the reproductive stage of life and blooms. The flowers, once fertilized, fall away, and seeds are formed. Then the plant, according to its life cycle, either goes dormant or dies.

Each of these stages of growth, from first tentative root to the setting of seed, is tied to specific internal and external cues. Knowing those cues, and the plant's likely response to each (or a combination) of them, is the basis of the gardener's art. It gives us the leverage to make the plant do as we wish, within the bounds of what is genetically and climatically possible.

## PLANT LIFE CYCLES

For practical purposes, garden flowers are generally divided into three or four categories. We will divide them for our discussion into four categories, based on how a gardener treats the plants: annuals, biennials, perennials, and then the plants that form bulbs or corms. Each group has its own needs and schedules, and though some flowers can fit into more than one category, we will ignore that complication for the present and discuss only the groups themselves. Specifics on the various plants will follow in Chapter 5.

**Annuals**

Annuals progress through their complete cycle of growth, flowering, setting seed, and dying all within a single season. Some biennial and perennial flowers can be treated as annuals because they are precocious enough to bloom the first year if started indoors in the very early spring. Tulips are also often treated as annuals, new bulbs being planted each fall for a single spring's blooming.

Within the general class of annuals, it is important to realize that different species respond best to different seasons or regions. Some are relatively insensitive to frost and can be planted as soon as the ground is ready in spring; I call these frost-hardy annuals. Because the onset of hot weather shortens their bloom period, they are often planted in early fall to bloom over winter or early the following spring in mild climates. A number of hardy annuals will even overwinter as small seedlings in cold climates if there is sufficient snow cover, and so are sometimes confused with biennials.

If a given plant can take a touch of frost, but not a lot, I consider it half-hardy. Most half-hardy plants need cool weather at bloom time and thus provide only a short display in hot climates. They may not be hardy enough to be fall-planted. They are often started indoors to give them a jump on the hot weather. In the North there is usually time to direct-seed half-hardy annuals in midspring and still get a long season of bloom.

Another group, which I call tender, cool-weather annuals, can't take any frost, yet do best in cool weather. They are ideally adapted to coastal climates, where the growing season is long, but not hot. Southern gardeners can start them indoors; as with the half-hardy annuals, planting tender annuals in light shade will help extend the bloom period. In mountain areas or the Far North they will usually also do quite well if started indoors for transplant to the garden once the weather has settled.

Finally, there are many annual flowers that can't take any frost, but can take the hot weather of midsummer, and will bloom vigorously for a long period until fall frost knocks them back. In the northern third of the country these must be purchased as plants, or started indoors to be set out after all danger of frost has passed. I class them as tender, warm-weather annuals.

## ANNUAL FLOWERS

| *Hardy* | | *Half-Hardy* | | *Tender* | |
|---|---|---|---|---|---|
| Agrostemma | Lobularia | Ammi Majus | Nicotiana | Ageratum | Impatiens |
| Alcea (Hollyhock) | Lupinus | Ammobium | Phlox | Amaranthus | Ipomoea |
| Antirrhinum | Malope | Brachycome | Rudbeckia | Begonia | Lobelia |
| Calendula | Malva | Callistephus | Salvia | Browallia | Salpiglossis |
| Catananche | Matricaria | Chrysanthemum | Scabiosa | Celosia | Tagetes |
| Centaurea | Matthiola | Dianthus | Trachymene | Cosmos | Tithonia |
| Consolida | Myosotis | Digitalis | | Dahlia | Tropaeoleum |
| Crepis | Nigella | Gaillardia | | Diascia | Venidium |
| Cynoglossum | Papaver | Gypsophila | | Gazania | Verbena |
| Eschscholzia | Petunia | Helichrysum | | Gomphrena | Zinnia |
| Lathyrus | Reseda | Lavatera | | Helianthus | |
| Linum | Viola | Limonium | | Heliotropum | |

Biennials spread their growth cycle over two seasons. The first (juvenile) year they grow to their mature size but don't flower; then they die back to the ground while the roots, with stored nutrient reserves, stay alive. The second year, they bloom, set seed, and die. Biennials are used less often than either annuals or perennials because, first, they will survive and thrive only where they can take both the cold of winter and the heat of summer, and second, most gardeners aren't willing to give them the space they need during the vegetative (nonblooming) year. Nonetheless, some of the most popular garden flowers, like Canterbury bells, foxgloves, and sweet william, are biennial.

**Biennials**

There are a number of apparent exceptions as some kinds of biennials will bloom a bit during the first season, though the better display is reserved for the second year. It is also possible to trick biennials into blooming the first year, and this will be discussed below in "Modifying the Growth of Plants." Biennials can seem to be perennial at times because self-sown seedlings will appear around the base of the dead parent plants. Close examination will show them to be entirely independent seedlings, not resprouting perennial roots or crowns.

Perennials are plants that bloom for more than one year. Some are short-lived, lasting only three or four seasons, while others will last for generations. A friend of ours has a peony plant (actually a division of it) that was given to his grandmother over seventy-five years ago! One of the most important things about perennials to a gardener is that they reproduce not only by seed but by vegetative means: that is, cuttings, division, layering, etc.

**Perennials**

Reproduction by seed is a sexual process, as we saw above, and the resulting plants are inevitably somewhat different from their parents (even if not visibly so). Vegetative reproduction, however, yields new plants that are genetically identical to the parent plant.

Like biennials, perennials die back to the ground in most climates, though the roots persist. Thus they have to be adapted to both the hottest part of the summer and the coldest part of the winter in a given area if they are to perform well in the garden. A number of our common garden annuals are actually perennials that can't take any frost and so are treated as annuals. Impatiens, nasturtiums and pelargoniums (common geraniums) are three examples.

**Bulbs and Corms**  I have classified bulbs and corms by themselves for a number of reasons. First, while they are all technically biennial or perennial, the part of the plant that lives through the dormant period (fall and winter in cool and moist climates, summer and fall in hot, dry climates) is not the roots, but the leaves or stems. The tops of the plant die back and leave a bulb or a corm underground that is not a root, but rather the compressed leaf or stem bases of the plant. Second, bulbs and corms differ from most perennials in that, with the exception of alliums and a few other, more obscure species, they are almost never propagated from seed (except by breeders). Almost all propagation of bulbs is by division.

## MODIFYING THE GROWTH OF PLANTS

Now that we know something about the structure of plants, how they work, and how they grow, let's look at how this knowledge is used by experienced gardeners to alter the growth, habits, or appearance of plants. Every plant is perfectly adapted to some particular season and climate, self-designed through a long evolution to match its growth and form with those conditions, whenever and wherever they may be. All plants want to grow, and raising them to perfection is more a matter of removing obstacles than anything else—making the conditions in your garden fit the needs of the particular plant—and then getting out of the way.

Every element of a plant's adaptation provides the astute gardener with clues about how to change that plant's garden performance in some particular way by giving it cues comparable to those it would receive from nature. Day and night temperatures and their lengths; moisture and nutrient aspects of the soil in which the plant grows; all affect the way a plant responds, and all can be manipulated by the gardener to get the plant to perform as desired.

Our knowledge of basic plant metabolism, allows us to favor some kinds of development over other kinds, to lengthen the blooming period or change it completely, even to control the size and number of blossoms (within certain genetic limits).

**Light and Temperature**  Plant metabolism is driven by the availability of light and heat. Stated simply, plants grow faster at a higher temperature and therefore require more light (as well as water and nutrients) if their growth is to remain balanced. A common problem with spring seedlings started on a windowsill is that they grow too tall and spindly. Because most people's houses are kept at a temperature that is too high for the amount of light available through the window, the plants stretch toward the light. Outdoors in the garden you see the same process if you compare a seedling set in the shade with one set in full sun: The shaded seedling will be much taller than the one that gets plenty of sun, and it will bloom later.

This relationship between light and heat can be used to tailor the habits of the plants in your garden to your needs. If you want to stretch the bloom period of a given flower in your garden, plant some in the sun and some in partial shade; you can amplify this effect by growing your seedlings under these different conditions, too.

If you want small plants, grow them in bright light and cool temperatures, with minimal water and nutrients; taller plants will be produced in conditions of moderate light, warm temperatures, and abundant water and nutrients. While you can make significant changes in the appearance of a plant by these kinds of tactics, don't go overboard. Cool temperatures, low light, and a continuously moist soil promote seedling diseases, while bright light and heat with low water and nutrients is a recipe for drought and starvation. The change in care should only be one of degree. After the plants have been out in the garden for a month or two, it will be the conditions there that will be more important; the differences seen at the seedling stage will tend to diminish.

Another way to control the height of plants without chemical sprays is by changing the relationship between day and night temperatures. This trick was discovered by researchers at Michigan State University in the 1980s, and is widely used by commercial plantsmen. What they found was this: Plants grown under warm day, cool night conditions will stretch just as plants grown in low light and high temperature. And, again, the reverse is true: If night temperatures are higher than day temperatures, then plants will be more compact. Of course, this last situation is in direct opposition to the natural cycle that occurs in spring—when the days are normally much warmer than the nights—and thus it is difficult to provide the conditions necessary to modify plant growth in greenhouses and cold frames. Fortunately, a further discovery showed that just a few hours of cool temperatures first thing in the morning is enough to trick the plant's internal thermostat into treating the day as cool, no matter how high the temperature rises later on.

For gardeners who are growing just a few plants on a windowsill, this trick is particularly important, as windowsill plants often show a lot of stretch. The key would be to move your plants to a really warm spot for the night, and then, in the morning, move them back to the coolest, brightest spot you have. If that is a windowsill, then turn down the thermostat in the morning when you leave for work, or if you work at home as we do, and the weather permits, bring the plants outdoors.

All plants are adapted to a particular regimen of light and heat for each stage of growth, depending on the region where they evolved and the season of the year during which they normally grow. In the greenhouse and in the garden we can use what knowledge we have of each plant's nature to evoke responses that we desire. One example is the way that greenhouse operators trick chrysanthemums into blooming at any time of the year by mimicking the decreasing daylengths of late summer and fall through the use of shade cloth suspended over the growing areas of the greenhouse.

It is also possible to trick biennials into blooming the first year by changing the temperature at which they grow. Most biennials have a kind of "blooming trigger" which prevents them from flowering until they have been through a minimum growth period followed by a minimum period of cold temperatures. This would normally be a summer followed by a winter in the garden. Gardeners can trick many biennials into blooming their first year by growing the seedlings in warm temperatures until they have more than five true leaves, then moving them to a spot kept below 50°F for a minimum of ten to fourteen days. While some plants will require more warmth and more chilling, this minimum can often be accomplished by starting the plants indoors during the late winter and setting them out as soon as the ground can be worked in spring. If your climate can't be counted on to provide the necessary cold treatment (without temperatures getting too cold—say below 25°F), then give the plants their cold treatment indoors, in a cool corner of the basement where they can be illuminated with a fluorescent light (total darkness will harm the plants as they will not be large enough to have sufficient reserves accumulated in the root to survive the prolonged absence of photosynthesis). Some experimentation may be necessary to learn the specific treatment required for a given plant in your particular climate, but after all, that's half the fun.

## Nutrients and Water

The primary change you can cause in a plant by altering its nutrient and water regimen is the slowing down of its maturation rate (without slowing down its growth rate). Two reasons for wanting to do this are (1) to compensate for a late spring, and (2) to harden off seedlings prior to transplanting.

Hardening transplants is discussed in the next chapter. It involves not only cutting back on the nutrients and water for the last week or so before setting the transplants out, but also adjusting the transplants to the temperature and light levels of the open garden. When hardening off your plants, don't forget that they'll also need to adjust to wind and rain and temperature changes over the course of their days and nights outdoors.

If the spring weather doesn't settle down on schedule, you can hold back seedlings either by keeping the temperature down or by increasing the amount of nitrogen the seedlings receive relative to the other major nutrients, phosphorus and potassium. (Nutrient balance in fertilizers was discussed in Chapter 2.) Most plants are greedy scavengers of nitrogen and will soak it up even when it throws their metabolism out of balance. If you have ever seen a friend's huge, beautiful nasturtium plants with no flowers, you have seen this effect in action. By keeping your seedlings well fed, well watered, and brightly lit but cool, you can keep them in a juvenile state for a week or two longer than normal. In many cases this is better than holding back the fertilizer and ending up with a small plant. Seedlings that are in their juvenile state when transplanted— that is, with no open flowers, and preferably only small flower buds— will perform better in the garden than those that are more advanced.

The problem with this high-nitrogen method is that you may need to move the seedlings up to larger containers to avoid crowding of roots and tops, and transplanting is both time- and space-consuming. If they have already started to set flower buds, some species will respond well if you pinch off the growing tips just before fertilizing, which will help somewhat with the space crunch that virtually every gardener faces when spring is late.

## Pruning and Training

Probably the most common methods of pruning and training flowers are pinching, disbudding, and deadheading. All three of these (and all other kinds of pruning, on whatever plant) affect the plant by changing its hormonal balance, although the intent and effect of each kind of pruning is different. As noted earlier in this chapter, the apical growing point of a given stem is dominant over the axillary side shoots that arise from it. When we remove either the apical or axillary growing points, the whole system shifts its growth pattern to compensate. Holding back development of the plant by forcing it to regrow some of its parts is only one of the possible effects we can cause by this kind of pruning.

Pinching out the growing tip shifts the balance of the plant from its terminal bud to its side shoots and thus promotes bushier growth and a larger number of smaller-sized flowers. To do this, pinch out the apical bud on each branch of the plant just above a set of axillary sprouts, which will force the plant to send up new growth. From a single-stemmed plant, we first create two stems, then four, then eight, then sixteen, and so on with each pinching. Chrysanthemums are probably the most common example of a plant that benefits from this kind of pruning. The schedule for pinching mums has been worked out over the years in concert with the light treatment mentioned above, to a fairly exact science that allows precise control over size and flowering date.

Not all flowers respond well to pinching (especially not monocots), but in those like snapdragons and marigolds, it pays to start pinching immediately when setting the plants in the garden. There is a double benefit to pinching at that time, as most transplants need some balancing between root and top when first set out; pinching can accomplish this at the same time it improves the conformation of the plant. Also, whenever cutting flowers for a bouquet, make your cut just above a leaf node; that way your cut will have the effect of pinching the plant at that point and will prompt it to start growing new flowering stems from the axillary sprouts at that node.

Disbudding has the opposite effect from pinching: It decreases the number of flowers produced and increases their size. You deprive the plant of all but a limited number (often all but one) of its flowers and thus prompt it to put all its reproductive energy into the remaining flowers, increasing their size. Except for show purposes, though, most gardeners I know would rather have more flowers, over a

Pruning affects the flowering habit of plants in a number of ways: *(left)* pinching out the apical meristem will lead to more, but smaller, flowers; *(center)* disbudding—pinching out the side, or axial, buds—will cause the flowers that are left to grow larger; *(right)* plants with many tiny flowers, like sweet alyssum, are often completely sheared after blooming to renew their vigor.

longer period, and so disbudding is not as common a practice as pinching, shearing, and deadheading.

Deadheading is no more than the practice of removing spent blossoms from a given plant to keep it looking good. Aside from improving the appearance of a plant, it has the effect of keeping the plant from entering senescence, during which the plant goes dormant or dies. Most flowering plants will stop or slow their production of new flowers once a given number have been pollinated and begun to form seeds. From that point on, the plant's energy is directed to maturing the seed. Once the seed crop is ready, annuals and biennials die, while perennials enter dormancy.

There are two important things to remember when deadheading flowers. First, it is not enough to cut or pinch off just some of the flowers that have been pollinated and started to go by; you need to remove all the spent blooms or the internal plant signals will remain, even if weak. Second, you have to be sure that you remove the ovary, within which the seeds are formed, as well as the petals. The ovary in some species is a swollen area behind the petals; the best idea is to remove at least an inch of the stem so that you are sure to get the ovary.

Shearing, which can be thought of as wholesale deadheading with shears—and is done primarily with small-flowered plants like alyssum—usually involves cutting the whole plant back to just above its newest, youngest growth. This will rejuvenate plants that have gotten leggy or disfigured in some way. If petunia baskets get too scraggly, for instance, you can cut them right back to the rim of the basket and, as long as there are a couple of nodes left on each plant or branch, they will quickly regrow and will bloom almost three weeks to the day after cutting.

While deadheading alone will lengthen the bloom period, shearing can totally reset the flowering schedule of the plant by requiring it to restart vegetative growth. In our garden we can radically lengthen the bloom period on our delphinium if we time the shearing just right. We take one-third of the plants and cut them back to about eight inches tall (leaving just a few of the youngest stems complete) as soon as we see the first flower buds. We cut a second third back as soon as the flower buds are fully formed and ready to open (this cutting will provide long-lasting blooms for the house). The remaining plants are allowed to flower normally, and are kept in bloom as long as possible by diligent deadheading. The early-cut third of the plants, having been set back, then come into bloom, followed by the second-cut plants. Some years this has provided us with delphinium flowers from the end of June through the end of September!

# CHAPTER 4

*Propagation is looked on by many people as a rather advanced skill, one which distinguishes the dedicated gardener from the mere dabbler, and certainly there are some plants whose propagation calls for great skill and sensitivity. On the other hand there are huge numbers of plants—the great majority of those we grow in our gardens— which are not at all difficult to propagate successfully, using very simple methods, which can easily be used by anyone willing to have a go. Plants which we have raised ourselves provide a uniquely personal sense of affinity with them and the place where they grow, which has a great deal to do with the pleasure that our gardens give us, and which the mass-produced products from a garden center can never bring with them.*

# Plant Propagation

There are only two ways you can raise your own flowers for the garden, neither of which need be difficult: from seed or by cloning plants you already have. New plants grown from seeds may closely resemble their two parents, but they are genetically unique and different from either parent. This may well be desirable in a cutting garden, or where a relaxed atmosphere is desired, but for edging or bedding, absolute uniformity is the aim. Cuttings and divisions produce plants that are identical to the parent plant in every respect—they are clones of it. A bed of plants cloned from one parent will all grow alike and bloom alike (given equal care and conditions).

As a general matter, annuals and biennials that will bloom their first year (as well as some perennials) are propagated from seed, while long-lived or highly selected cultivars of perennials are in-

—Peter Thompson,
*Creative Propagation*

62

creased by cuttings and division. At the two ends of the spectrum, common varieties of perennials as well as experimental hybrids and crosses may be initially started from seed but then increased vegetatively to maintain their identity.

## RAISING FLOWERS FROM SEED

Southern gardeners may well be able to direct seed most flowers right in the garden or in a nursery bed, while Northern gardens must start a significant number indoors. To make a nursery bed, turn over a small part of your garden, say 5 or 10 percent, to growing seedlings. This area should receive special care during spring preparation so that the soil is in fine tilth and the seedlings have the best possible conditions. Be ready to rig up shade during hot periods and some sort of cover during any unusually cold weather. If you make this nursery bed in a different section of the garden each season as part of your overall rotation, eventually you will have improved your whole garden. Even Northern gardeners, who will likely start most of their seedlings indoors, should still have a nursery bed. It makes an excellent place to stick a newly acquired plant until you decide on its final location, or to hold a group of seedlings whose eventual space is still occupied by other, still-flowering plants.

**Buying Seed**

There are a few things to keep in mind when buying flower seed. You can buy seed just about anywhere during the spring: hardware store, garden center, supermarket, discount store. Though these sources may be sufficient at first, once you get deeply involved in your garden you'll likely start wanting more unusual flowers than these retail racks carry.

Then you'll want to turn to mail order. There is an absolutely unbelievable diversity of mail-order seed catalogs in America—I know because I run one—and this is even more true for flowers than it is for vegetables. There are specialty catalogs for fragrant flowers, wildflowers, cutting flowers, rock-garden perennials, primroses; you name it and there is likely to be a catalog for it. One of my favorites lists seed for more than two dozen different species of hardy geranium, forty species of campanula, and twenty veronicas on its "Collector's List." Keep in mind, however, that these are not named cultivars, which rarely come from seed; you will need to purchase the named cultivars as live plants and then increase them by cutting or division.

Another benefit of buying seed from mail-order catalogs is that you will be able to select annual flowers by color. This makes it possible for you to coordinate color schemes in different parts of the garden, instead of settling for the shotgun effect produced by mixed packets of seed. Mixes can be very convenient where a casual look is intended, but even then it is a good idea to have some control over the mix, and you may want to buy from a catalog that offers "formula mixtures." The least expensive flower mixtures are produced by growing the seed in a field where the different colors are allowed to reproduce themselves in whatever proportions normally occur. While inexpensive, these mixtures don't allow much control over the final appearance of the plants in your garden. Formula mixtures, on the other hand, are made up by the seed company from the individual colors available, following a precise recipe that guarantees just how much of each color will be included. Not only does this assure that the colors will be in certain proportion, it allows the company to offer, as our company does, mixtures that concentrate on one theme, such as warm shades, cool shades, or, as another company does, sunset shades. All in all, the extra money for formula mixes is well spent and makes a good compromise between field mixtures and the complication of growing individual colors.

The last aspect of buying seed I want to touch on is the choice of hybrid versus nonhybrid seed. The subject of hybridization is beyond the scope of this book, but a short summary of the process is in order as much of the seed sold these days is of hybrid origin, and an understanding of its production will help the gardener decide if he or she needs or wants to buy hybrid seed. One point first, though: Any connection or conflict between the terms organic and hybrid is totally cultural; hybrid seed can just as easily be organic or not organic, and organic seed can just as easily be hybrid or nonhybrid. Anyone who tries to tell you different is talking politics, not gardening.

Hybridizing is the conscious crossing of two known (and compatible) but genetically different parent plants in the hope of producing new and valuable offspring. If the resulting generation is itself of value, the seed from this cross may be sold (and will be listed as an $F_1$ hybrid). Hybrid seed is generally much more expensive than nonhybrid (open-pollinated) seed because of the labor involved in producing it, but hybrid plants usually outperform both of their parents, as well as nonhybrids of the same type.

The seed set by these hybrids, however, will not produce uniform plants similar to themselves, but rather a wide range of types based on the characteristics of the original parent plants. Breeders may grow out those $F_1$ (first generation) plants, gather their seed, sow it, and then examine the succeeding, diverse generations for new and valuable combinations of the original parents' genes. Over four or five generations, those strains that are desirable can be "stabilized" by selection, and will then breed true, given the proper controls. For the average home gardener all this is much too time-consuming, though many a weekend hobbyist has dabbled in flower breeding with some success.

As alluded to earlier, propagation by seed is an inherently sexual process and, as such, inevitably introduces some genetic variation. The degree of variation differs widely according to both the flower involved and the actions of the gardener.

## Harvesting Your Own Seed

Some flowers, like sweet peas, are self-fertile, which is to say that the pollen from a given blossom is able to fertilize the ovary in the same blossom. The genetic similarity of sperm and egg in self-fertile species restrains variation, and while this is a convenience for gardeners who like to save their own seed (because established varieties remain stable without the necessity of isolation), it decreases the likelihood of new and interesting flower types appearing unexpectedly.

Other species, like sunflowers, not only cross-pollinate easily, but are self-sterile, that is, they require cross-pollination. While this requires isolation of a particular variety if you wish to save the seed and have it come true, it also promises greater natural variation in the garden.

As mentioned in the last chapter, the viability of seed is affected by the conditions in which the parent plant grew. Seed viability is also affected by the weather at seed harvest time and the care and storage of the seed after harvest. These factors are important if you want to collect seed from your own plants as a method of increase.

For harvesting seeds, gardeners recognize two different types of flower seeds: those that bear exposed seeds and shed them immediately upon maturity, like asters and other composites, and those that hold the seeds in pods or capsules at maturity, like nigella and poppies. Observation will tell you which type you are dealing with; different handling is required for each.

Seed pods can be harvested as soon as they begin to turn yellow or tan, ideally on a dry, sunny day. The mature flower stalks can be bunched loosely and placed upside down in a paper bag that has a few holes punched in it for ventilation, then hung in a dry, warm, airy place for a week or two to cure. The seeds can then be removed. Seeds that shed at maturity can be treated the same way, but will need to be harvested in stages, over a period of time, as the individual flowers ripen. Bag storage is even more important for these species as the bag will catch the seed as it ripens and falls during storage.

Cured seed can be separated from pods or other chaff by crumbling or lightly crushing the pods or heads, then sifting through screens of various sizes. Final cleaning can be accomplished by winnowing with your own breath: Blow across the surface of a small dish while rolling the seed back and forth so the chaff and underweight seed are blown away.

Once harvested, cured, and separated from chaff, seed should be stored in a sealed container with a small amount of desiccant. Silica gel is widely available for this use, as is calcium chloride. Sources are listed in the Appendix. For most species, the best storage conditions are cool, so keep the sealed jars in your basement, root cellar, or refrigerator just above freezing (35–40°F).

## Sowing Seed Indoors

Given viable seed, three things are necessary for germination: There must be sufficient moisture; the temperature must be right; and the seed must not be dormant.

Dormancy is a form of evolutionary insurance; it keeps seeds from sprouting except when conditions are right for growth. This can be a problem for gardeners because we often want to grow (or at least start) a plant outside of its normal season. Thus we need to understand what keeps a seed dormant, and how we can trick it into thinking the time is right to germinate.

There are really two kinds of dormancy that we need to concern ourselves with: physical dormancy, where the seed coat is so hard that water can't get to the embryo (or so tight that the embryo can't expand); and physiological dormancy, which is affected by light and temperature regimes.

Physical dormancy can be overcome by cutting, nicking, or scratching the seed coat until it is sufficiently porous for germination to proceed. This is often necessary for lupine seed, for example. Soaking seed for up to eight hours can soften the seed coat enough for germination, as it does for morning glories. Both of these processes accomplish the same thing that would happen outdoors in the soil, over the course of the plant's dormant season.

Physiological dormancy can usually be broken by subjecting the seed to conditions that mimic those of their native region. Desert plants, for instance, can be subjected to temperatures over a hundred degrees for a week, then soaked as they would be by winter rains. Plants from the Northern Temperate Zone can be wrapped in moist towels and placed in the refrigerator for a month to mimic a cold winter spent underground, then brought out and planted in warm soil.

Plants that have adapted to the competition of other plants in the same space may sprout only on bare ground, so they should be sown on the surface of the planting medium where the sunlight will trigger their reflex to sprout. Other seeds may be inhibited by light, desert plants for example, because to them light signals that they are not deep enough in the soil to survive if they were to sprout. In each case, a knowledge of the natural conditions in which the plant developed will help us understand what conditions will promote germination. This is only a quick overview of how dormancy affects the gardener who wants to grow flowers from seed.

When you are ready to sow your seeds, fill the planting trays or pots loosely with soil mix. Straight compost mixed with sand and vermiculite works well in open flats, but is too dense for plugs. In plug trays and recycled six-packs, the addition of some peat helps keep the mix from packing down; for cuttings it is a good idea to keep the peat and/or compost to a third or less of the total mix. Too much water-holding capacity will increase problems with rot. For insurance, top off the containers with a quarter inch or so of horticultural vermiculite; it drains well, yet holds some moisture, and is totally sterile, so it won't harbor damping-off bacteria and fungi.

If your compost was not properly made—that is, the pile did not heat up fully—it may contain disease spores from the plants that were composted and, in the incubatorlike conditions under which most plants are started, that can be fatal. To guard against disease, sterilize the compost by heating it to 140–160°F for at least four hours in the oven; hotter than that may harm the beneficial organisms. You can also buy commercially prepared compost. Remember, the first few days of a young plant's life make a big difference to its eventual success in the garden, and it is less resistant to problems that it might shrug off outdoors; so be sure it gets a good start.

Large seeds are easily placed, but with small seeds, you may want to mix them with a bit of sand to make handling easier. If the seeds are small and expensive, I pour them into the palm of my left hand and use a toothpick or pencil to pick them up singly. Just touch the toothpick to your tongue, and then to the seed (with a bit of practice, you will find that the moisture will hold the seed to the toothpick long enough to reach the tray); it will release as you poke the surface of the soil. I usually place two seeds in each cell of the tray so there will not be empty cells later on. If both seeds germinate, I cut off the extra with a pair of scissors: Don't pull it out or you'll disturb the one that remains.

Those seeds that need light to germinate can simply be pressed into the surface of the mix, otherwise I top off with a bit more mix, and press down on it. Then I move the flat to a 2-inch-deep tray of water and allow the moisture to soak into the mix from below while I seed the next flat or pot. When you see moisture on the surface of the previously seeded flat or pot, remove it from the watering tray to the germination area, cover it with a humidity dome or other clear vapor barrier, and put the next flat into the watering tray. Using this step-by-step method you can make quick work of even a large number of seeded flats.

The rate at which a seed germinates and grows is directly related to temperature, just as the amount of water pumped by a windmill is directly related to the force of the wind. There are three general groups of flowers, based on the temperatures at which they germinate. The largest group is adapted to late spring, and will germinate at standard temperatures between 65°F and 75°F. Early-spring-adapted species germinate at cool temperatures between 50°F and 60°F. Fall-adapted plants (which naturally sprout in the summer) will germinate best at warm temperatures between 80°F and 90°F. Those that need a particular temperature to germinate should be sown together so they can receive similar treatment.

Low-temperature flats can be set on the floor at room temperature; this will keep them cooler than they would be at eye level. High-temperature flats should go on a germination mat. Those flats that like 65°F to 75°F can be kept on a shelf unheated. If your house, like ours, is cooler than average, the flats can be put on top of the flats of heat lovers, where they will catch just enough escaping heat to provide for what they need. Bright light isn't necessary while the seeds

## SPECIAL CONDITIONS

| *Needs Light* (*Do not bury seed*) | | | *Cold Treatment* (*Seed and/or seedling*) | | *Hard Seed* (*Soak or scrape seed*) |
|---|---|---|---|---|---|
| Ageratum | Impatiens | Papaver | Aquilegia | Lathyrus | Ipomoea |
| Antirrhinum | Lobelia | Petunia | Aruncus | Matthiola | Lathyrus |
| Browallia | Lobularia | Reseda | Baptisia | Primula | Lupinus |
| Digitalis | Nicotiana | | Consolida | | |
| | | | Delphinium | | |
| | | | Eupatorium | | |

# GERMINATION TEMPERATURES

| Cool (<65°F) | Warm (65–75°F) | | | Hot (>75°F) |
|---|---|---|---|---|
| Aconitum | Achillea | Digitalis | Monarda | Ageratum |
| Agrostemma | Agastache | Echinacea | Myosotis | Amaranthus |
| Allium | Alcea | Gaillardia | Pelargonium | Celosia |
| Armeria | Antirrhinum | Gypsophila | Phlox | Dahlia |
| Aubretia | Aquilegia | Helenium | Physostegia | Gomphrena |
| Calendula | Arabis | Helianthus | Platycodon | Petunia |
| Campanula | Begonia | Helichrysum | Rudbeckia | Salpiglossis |
| Centaurea | Callistephus | Helipterum | Salvia | Tropaeolum |
| Delphinium | Catanache | Impatiens | Scabiosa | Zinnia |
| Eryngium | Centranthus | Ipomoea | Tagetes | |
| Lathyrus | Chrysanthemum | Lavatera | Trachelium | |
| Lobularia | Consolida | Liatris | Trachymene | |
| Nigella | Coreopsis | Limonium | Venidium | |
| Papaver | Cosmos | Lobelia | Verbena | |
| Primula | Dianthus | Lychnis | Veronica | |

are germinating; however, once they break ground, seedlings should be moved to the brightest area you have available.

If you don't have a good spot for growing seedlings in natural light, you can rig up a special germination area in a spare room or basement. Plans can be found in a number of books, but the essentials are the same for most setups. Build a set of shelves, at least one of which has a hookup for fluorescent lighting, and another that will hold a germination mat. The ideal setup would have lights suspended above the top shelf, and the germination mat one or two shelves below that. This arrangement produces a wide range of conditions—cool-temperature plants can be germinated on the lowest level, beneath the heat, while heat lovers can sit right on the heating mat; those with middling needs can be set on the shelf above the heat to germinate. As each flat of seeds germinates, it can be moved to the top; escaped heat will keep it relatively warm, and the lights will provide the raw material for photosynthesis. The room itself need not be heated if the whole affair is covered loosely with a clear plastic cover to hold heat and humidity. Many gardeners start all their plants this way, as it allows good control of light and temperature conditions. Seedlings raised under lights, away from breezes and strong sun, though, will need extra time to adjust to outdoor

A special germination area can be set up just about anywhere if you have a hookup for lights and a heating mat. Be sure to use lights with the balanced spectrum that plants need.

conditions before planting in the garden. If you can heat the whole room, an oscillating fan that sweeps across the grow rack is an excellent addition—it not only keeps the air in the room moving, which keeps temperatures even and helps fight disease, but it also keeps the plants sturdy stemmed by forcing them to stand upright in the face of periodic blasts of "wind."

Once the flats are seeded and watered, the seeds begin to swell with water and activate stored enzymes. As this process accelerates, oxygen is needed. This is why you soak the medium just once after planting—you don't want to drive out all the air. You will need to cover the flats with some sort of moisture barrier, though, to help keep the potting soil moist enough.

**Growing Seedlings**    After a few days, or weeks, depending on the species of plant, tiny feeder roots begin to spread through the soil. Soon the plant breaks ground and finds the last vital growth factor it needs: light. If you haven't added fertilizer to the soil mix you will soon need to start both watering and fertilizing. From this point on the growth of the seedlings is dependent on the nutrients that their roots can find in the soil, the moisture that makes the nutrients available, and the quality of light their leaves receive. The fertilizer we use, both for growing bedding plants and for later feeding outdoors, is a tablespoon each of liquid fish fertilizer and liquid seaweed per gallon of water.

The most feared enemy of a seedling is damping off, a general term for an almost always fatal disease caused by a number of different soil fungi. If it shows up, it can wipe out whole flats of seedlings virtually overnight. Damping off is favored by cool temperatures, low light, poorly drained mix, and high humidity (caused by a lack of ventilation or planting too densely). Therefore, it pays to foster the opposite conditions as much as possible. Relatively low temperatures (65–75°F as noted above) produce sturdy plants; just don't get too carried away.

Though spores are nearly everywhere, the presence of fungi can be controlled somewhat by using a sterile potting mix and disinfecting any seed you have saved from your own plants so that no spores are carried over to the new plants. A simple method of disinfecting seeds is to make a 10:1 solution of water and household bleach, then soak the seeds in it for five to ten minutes depending on the hardness of the seed coat. This same solution can be used to disinfect any containers used from year to year. To avoid cracked, dry skin and its resultant irritation, wear dishwashing gloves when handling the solution.

Since heat and light fuel plant growth, the relationship between the two is a critical factor in growing healthy, vigorous seedlings. Too little light in relation to the temperature leads to limp, leggy plants. This problem is very common with plants started early on a south-facing windowsill. The glass in house windows screens out some parts of the sunlight that plants need; in addition, the temperature inside the house is kept relatively high during the day, and the sunlight adds to this. Then at night the temperature drops, and the plants, right next to the window, get chilled, adding insult to injury. To make matters even worse, the gardener then tries to compensate for slow, uneven growth with more fertilizer, which only increases the imbalance between the factors necessary for good growth.

Plants felled by damping off collapse at the soil line, where the stem has shriveled. Remove affected plants immediately and give any survivors plenty of light and air.

The solution: Start your plants later, when conditions are better (they'll catch up soon enough), or use the warm night, cool day trick we discussed in Chapter 3 to control plant height.

It is possible for the temperature to be too high even in a greenhouse. On cloudy days it makes sense to lower the temperature in a greenhouse to compensate for the lower light levels; keeping the temperature high to get a jump on the season will, in the end, more likely put the plants out of touch with the season and cause problems later. Gardeners "ride" the season like a surfer rides a wave, and it doesn't work to be ready too soon. If you must raise the temperature, do it at night, not in the daytime, and then cool the house down for a few hours just after sunrise to set the plant's internal thermostat to "cool."

Every plant has a range of temperatures that it likes best, and within that range the cooler you keep it the better off the plant will be. Because growth is slower at lower temperatures, well-lit plants will grow strong and stout. Again, don't take things too far, though, or you'll risk damping off. If any plants start showing the symptoms (withering of the stem at the soil line and collapse of the plants) remove them from the flat and destroy them. Then get the flat out into the sun as quickly as you can; high light levels and fresh air will do wonders for the remaining seedlings.

Plants need nutrients as well as light to grow, and without enough moisture, they'll wilt and die. But too frequent watering can wash away whatever nutrients are in the growing mix. While the conventional practice states that you should feed the plants every seven to ten days, I recommend fertilizing every fourth time you water, regardless of the date. That way the feeding is based on the amount of water that the plant has taken up. The same effect is achieved by fertilizing every time you water, but at one-quarter normal strength. You then don't need to keep track of when you last fertilized, and the plants get an even, constant supply of nutrients. Again, our own mix is one tablespoon each of liquid fish fertilizer and liquid seaweed per gallon of water; for constant feed, use the same amount of fish fertilizer and liquid seaweed in four gallons of water. Read the label on whatever fertilizer you use in order to achieve the same strength.

Once again, don't go overboard or go to sleep. Watch the plants to see if the fertilizer is doing its job. Leaves that curl under are a sign of overfeeding; discoloration is usually a sign of underfeeding. If the plant is pale, it is likely nitrogen-deficient; leaves with purplish undersides indicate a shortage of phosphorus; leaves with bronze edges indicate a shortage of potassium. Since the liquid fertilizers that we use contain balanced amounts of nitrogen, phosphorus, and

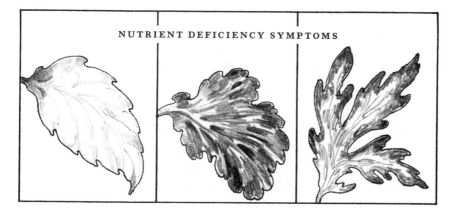

NUTRIENT DEFICIENCY SYMPTOMS

The signs of major nutrient deficiency are subtle but clear: *(left)* nitrogen deficiency shows itself through pale leaves; *(center)* a shortage of phosphorus causes leaves to be purplish on the undersides; *(right)* potassium deficiency causes the leaf edges to appear bronzy. Feed your plants regularly with ocean-derived fertilizers; they provide a wide range of both major and minor nutrients and will almost guarantee that no deficiencies develop.

potassium, the simple solution is just to increase or decrease the strength or frequency of feedings.

It's not enough to raise vigorous, healthy seedlings if they are so pampered that they can't survive the sun and wind and rain, and the seesaw effect of day and night temperature changes. This is especially important for plants grown under lights in the still air of a basement or spare room. As planting day approaches, help the seedlings adjust gradually to outdoor conditions. All of these adjustments can be made by hardening off the seedlings. Hardening off is one of the best uses of a cold frame: Put the plants in the frame and then leave the lid off for longer and longer periods each day until it is no longer needed. In hot weather the lid can be replaced with shade to protect the plants from overheating. If you don't have a cold frame, just set the plants outdoors in a protected spot. Each day they should get less protection and stay longer. Hardening off may take as long as a week, but doesn't have to; if good transplanting weather—moist and still, free from bright sun—comes along sooner, by all means set them out.

The process of setting the plants is fairly straightforward. Take the first plant and set it in one corner of the planting area. Since this first plant will border the edge and won't be completely surrounded by other plants, space it half the distance from the end and side of the planting area than it needs to be from the other plants. That is, if the

**Transplanting Seedlings**

plants need to be a foot from each other, put the first plant six inches in from the edge. If you do this with every other plant that faces an edge, the abutters will automatically be spaced correctly in relation to each other. The beauty of this method is that it works just as well for irregular, casual border designs as it does for the strictly efficient planting of a cutting garden.

Always hold seedlings by the root ball or by the leaves, never by the stem. Stored nutrients in roots can grow new leaves, and a healthy top can grow new roots, but the stem is the bridge between the two; if anything happens to the stem there is no way for the two ends of the plant to move nutrients back and forth and regenerate themselves.

If the seedlings are rootbound—if their roots have filled the container and started to circle around the bottom of it—they'll need to be "woken up," or the plants will never amount to much. Knead the root ball softly in your hands like clay or bread to break loose a portion of the tiny root hairs. This breaking of the roots will signal the plant to send growth hormones back to the roots (after having given up on them when they reached the sides of the pot). Don't be too shy; if you're too gentle it won't work.

Most dicots should be pinched back at planting time, as this makes them bushier and also balances the roots and shoots after the shock of transplanting. You can use your fingers or a pair of small shears to take off the growing point of the plant just above a node. Don't remove more than a third of the leafy growth or you'll shock the plant; all we are trying to do is shift the hormonal balance.

I don't use a trowel to make the transplant holes; the soil in our beds—and in any well-tended, highly fertile organic soil—is soft enough that my hand works just as well. For small seedlings a poke with the finger is enough. For larger plants, a quick scoop with a hand is all it takes. My grandfather often put a shovelful of compost wherever he was going to set a plant, and that is a good idea, especially for perennials. When I'm doing a bed in this manner I go along ahead of time and prepare each spot so I can be free and easy about it when I plant.

In the moist soil of spring, that's all there is to it. Later on in the season, as the soil dries out, you may want to water the seedlings in. We take a hose with a trigger grip nozzle on it out into the garden, aim the nozzle at each spot where a plant is to go, and pull the trigger for just a second. The blast of water burrows a small hole and temporarily fills it with soupy soil. It's a snap to plop the seedling quickly into the hole and draw some soft, dry soil from around the spot loosely over the area, leaving the final depth of the plant the

This transplant is well proportioned but a little too old, as evidenced by the massing of roots at the bottom of the plug.

(*Below left*) If the roots have begun to circle the bottom of the container, "wake them up" before planting by kneading the root ball to loosen the roots and get them growing again.

(*Below right*) Unfurl the roots, then transplant gently to avoid breaking off the small *feeder* roots.

same as it was in the flat. The same effect can be had with a watering can from which the sprinkler cap has been removed, though it takes more practice.

Two points to remember: First, if you are going to label the plants at all, do it now; and second, resist the feeling that the plants should be closer together—they will grow! Good labeling helps you keep track of what works in your garden, and we believe in labeling virtually everything. Proper spacing is critical for the prevention of foliage diseases later in the season, as the plants will need good air circulation to dry off the leaves after summer rain (or irrigation).

Once the first plant is set, we space another tier of plants around it, so that each plant is equidistant from its neighbor. If more plants are available and further tiers are needed, the process is repeated until the space is filled or you run out of plants. We don't use any measuring or digging tools in this process, and we don't lug anything along the row; it's just the planter and the plants. If the bachelor's buttons, say, want to be eight inches apart, well, that's the distance from the tip of my thumb to the tip of my little finger when my hand is outstretched. From the tip of my longest finger to my elbow is eighteen inches; my foot, luckily, is a foot long. Your body may be a different size, but it isn't going to change suddenly, and once you know how far across your fingers and hands are and how long your feet and arms are, you can leave the ruler back in the shed and save a lot of time and trouble.

If you mulch the bed immediately after planting it will lower the evaporation rate of water from the soil and generally temper the soil climate. Don't use field hay as mulch unless you know that it was cut before the pasturage began to set seed, or you'll just be spreading weed seed around your garden. With an organic mulch be sure not to spread it until the soil is warm, unless you are trying to keep the soil cool. I've seen more than one beautifully mulched, weed-free garden here in Vermont weeks behind nearby, unmulched gardens because the soil never had a chance to heat up. Also, don't mulch right up to the plants—there should be a ring of clear soil around each plant to lower the humidity locally and help prevent bacterial and fungal infections. Mulch is discussed in more detail in Chapter 2.

**Direct Seeding**   Perhaps you don't have room to start seed indoors. Don't worry. Some flowers are hardy enough to be sown outdoors no matter what the weather. Others resent transplanting, and so must be sown where they are to grow. Whatever the reason, there are times when you will be direct seeding your flowers.

Set transplants at the same depth they were at in the plug or pot and firm soil around the stem with hand pressure.

Plants at the edge of a bed should be half the normal planting distance from the edge so that they fill it out completely.

Within the bed, plants should be set just closer than their mature size so that the foliage meets and interweaves.

Direct seeding:
First, prepare the soil, then smooth and break up with a rake or hand harrow. Make furrows: curved rows keep the bed from looking too regimented. Sow the seed, but don't close the furrows until all the rows are done so you don't lose track of what is where.

When I close furrows, I like to draw my hands along both sides at a slight angle, drawing soil back over the seed.

Lightly firm the soil to make good contact with the seed and set the proper depth of soil over it.

Make tags now, before moving on to other tasks. On my tags, I put the name, date, and an ID number that matches an entry in my garden journal.

In early spring the soil is still cool and moist, so we should not plant as deep as later in the season when the top of the soil is hot and dry. As long as every seed is buried at a depth two to three times its width, good results can be expected; seeds requiring light to germinate should simply be sprinkled on the surface of the soil, then pressed in. These seeds that need light to germinate and very small seeds, which need to be near the surface, must still be kept moist. You'll need to give them some extra attention if the weather is hot and dry immediately after planting.

When planting in rows, keep in mind that the rows do not need to be straight, or even parallel. Cut flowers in a bouquet garden might well be grown just like bedding plants and vegetables—in strict patterns for convenience at cultivation time. But flower beds primarily meant for viewing are best kept from being so regimented. With transplants this is easy, as we saw above, but when direct seeding, planting requires a bit of imagination. At the famous Kew Gardens, outside London, annuals are sown in parallel arcs so that the viewer can't sight along any row without seeing another row as well. This gives depth to the plantings. Whatever method you use, just be sure that, after thinning, each plant has enough room to grow without crowding its neighbors.

Some flower beds may be broadcast sown. To do this the seed is sprinkled evenly across the entire surface of the planting area. Wildflowers and mixes to attract butterflies or songbirds, for instance, are good candidates for this treatment. Here's how to do it. First work over the surface of the bed with a rake or hand harrow; this fluffs up the soil and leaves the surface of the bed in a multitude of small ridges. The seed is then sprinkled on the surface of the soil. A small grass-seed spreader or a jar with holes poked in the lid can be used if the seed didn't come in a shaker can.

Once the seed is distributed, take a hand harrow or stiff-tined rake and go over the bed to settle the seed down into the fluffed-up surface created during the first pass. With all but the smallest seed you'll be able to see when you've buried it. With large seed you may need to add a thin layer of compost on top to assure that the seed will be fully covered. You will need to avoid moving the seed around after sowing, as this will lead to uneven growth across the bed where the seed has bunched up. Once the seed is covered you can tamp it by standing on a section of plywood placed on the bed or, as I do, by watering. Either way, get the seed into firm contact with the moist soil to assure prompt and complete germination.

The biggest problem with broadcasting flower seed is in knowing the difference between the seedlings you planted and any weeds that germinated at the same time. Planting in rows, even rows that wander, helps with this in that you can tell easily what you planted and what simply came up on its own. Because the rows will tend to disappear (and the bed looks more natural) as the plants mature and fill in, row planting can be just as visually appealing as broadcast planting. It just takes time and a bit of faith.

## INCREASING YOUR PLANTS

Increase means "to become greater in size or quantity." In gardening one says that "the increase from seed is five hundred fold" meaning that the seed from one plant produces five hundred more plants; or that "the increase by division is sixfold," etc. That's what I like about gardening: Not only does my collection of plants continue to grow as one plant produces half a dozen more, but each tiny nicotiana seed grows to become a five-foot-tall plant, and each lily-of-the-valley pip grows into a mature plant that, if desired, will provide even more pips to increase the following season. Aside from the fact that I was a mud puppy as a child and still have an attraction to getting dirty, the natural increase of plants is a big part of the magic that makes me garden.

While getting dirty is great fun, it has to be "clean" dirt, because sanitation is even more important when increasing plants than when growing them from seed. The possibility of carrying over disease from the parent plant is greater because of the relatively large, actively growing plant parts that are used in the process. Also, the fact that you must often break a plant's skin in the process of cutting or dividing creates a natural entrance for any bacteria or spores that might be in the air or on your tools. Thus, it is important to sterilize the knives or shears you use between producing cuttings from different groups of plants, especially after working on any plant that shows symptoms of bacterial or fungal infection. The simplest way to sterilize tools is with a dip into rubbing alcohol or the 10:1 water-bleach solution discussed earlier. Exposed ends of newly prepared cuttings or divisions can be dusted with powdered sulfur, an effective fungicide.

**Cuttings**

Cuttings are basically parts you take from one plant and persuade to grow into new plants. Stems, roots, and leaves are all suitable for cuttings on one plant or another, though most garden flowers that reproduce vegetatively respond best to stem cutting. New roots will arise from the lateral meristem; shoots will arise from the nodes of the cut stem. Rhizomes, which are horizontal underground stems, are so ready to sprout roots that gardeners often speak of *dividing* a clump of iris or *Coreopsis verticillata*, when, in actuality, they are making stem cuttings. Root cuttings are effective for a number of garden species like phlox, peonies, and Oriental poppies. Leaf cuttings are used primarily for house plants and will not be covered here.

There are three general schedules that will be most successful with garden flowers:

*Schedule 1*. In cold-winter areas, where the ground freezes solid, perennial plants can be dug in the fall, potted up, and held until early spring, then forced into growth and used to take cuttings. The simplest method is to dig the plants in the fall, pot them up, and then mulch the pots well with leaves or hay (and a waterproof cover like polyethylene). In late winter the pots can be taken into the greenhouse or sunroom, fertilized, and allowed to grow. A low-nitrogen fertilizer is best because rank growth does not root well. In very cold areas like ours this jump on the season makes a big difference. In areas where the ground doesn't freeze, you may wish to wait until the plants break dormancy naturally, but you can, nonetheless, pursue the same kind of schedule as we "arctic" types do. Just dig the plants three weeks to a month before you'll start forcing, so they have a chance to adjust to the move.

Don't mulch the pots until well after the first fall freezes—you want to wait until all the field mice have found homes for the winter—then sprinkle a few mothballs around under the mulch to repel midwinter marauders. If you have a cold frame, it is an ideal spot to keep the plants as long as it can be shaded to keep the air temperature from fluctuating too much on sunny days and clear nights.

To make the root cuttings, unpot the plant, then shake or wash the soil away from its roots. With fleshy-rooted plants like baby's breath or bleeding hearts, cut two-to-three-inch sections of roots that are about the diameter of a pencil. A well-established plant can spare up to a third of its root mass and still regrow nicely—simply repot and nurse it back to health in time for spring planting. It is a good idea to dust the cut ends with sulfur to help fight infection.

Make the cut closest to the plant straight across the root, and the lower cut at an angle; this not only eases insert of the cutting into its container, it reminds you which end was up. Root cuttings that are planted upside down will grow, but they will be slower to break ground as the shoot, once it emerges from the root, has to do a U-turn. Also, handling young plants with a crook in the stem right at the base requires much more delicacy.

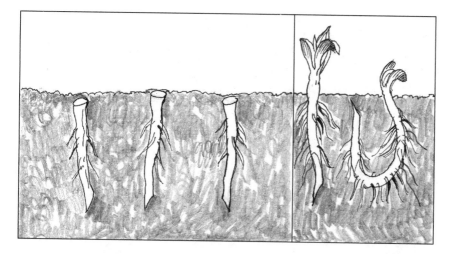

Be sure to plant fleshy root cuttings right side up; though inverted cuttings will grow, they are more easily damaged in handling. Cuttings from thin-rooted plants (*below*) can be rooted lying on their sides.

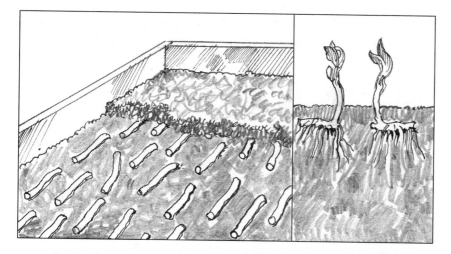

Fill the flat or pots with the cutting mix described earlier, and then insert the cuttings angle end down and deep enough so that the top cut is just below the surface of the mix. If the container isn't deep enough you can put the cuttings in at a slight angle. A minimum spacing of two inches between cuttings is best in open flats or pots; we use the 18-cell plug tray (which is equivalent to a 3½-inch pot) and put one cutting in each cell.

Thin-rooted plants like phlox or yarrow are even easier to handle. Again, you can take up to a third of the root mass, and you should cut the pieces two to three inches long. You do not need to keep track of which end is which, however, as these cuttings are planted horizontally. Take the cut root pieces and lay them on the surface of a partially filled flat an inch or two apart, and then fill the flat with another half-inch or so of mix.

Water the flat gently, and cover it loosely if you will not be able to check it often enough to keep the soil moist (but not waterlogged). If you have space on your heating mat, by all means place the cuttings on it, but if you are tight for room, just set the tray or pots in a warm area and save the mat for stem cuttings, which can put the heat to more use.

Before you can make stem cuttings, the plants will need to break dormancy and grow new stems. Raise plants for stem cuttings in the brightest spot you have, and don't pinch out the central growing point, as that will shift the hormonal balance of the plant to concentrate growth on the side shoots. While you do want the laterals to grow, the best cuttings come from stems that are high in carbohydrates and relatively low in nitrogen. When the central growing point is left, growth will concentrate there, and the side shoots, being less active (though still growing), will likely have more stored sugars and starches.

Once the side shoots are three to five inches long, cut them with a sharp knife (I like to use a graphic artist's knife that has interchangeable blades). Morning is the best time to cut, as the shoots will be most turgid (plump and full of moisture) at that time. If the cuttings are prime for rooting, the oldest part of the new growth should snap off, rather than bend, under finger pressure. With woody species like rosemary or salvia, you should cut just below the new growth, where the stem turns from green to brown. If there are any flower buds on the stem remove them, and remove all but the topmost two or three leaves. Until roots sprout from the cutting, water draw from leaves needs to be minimized or the cutting may wilt.

Succulent cuttings—ones that ooze sap, like geraniums—should be allowed to sit and dry for a day before being planted, so that the cut end has a chance to start healing over. Other cuttings will need to be kept moist until planting. If you can't set them right away, wrap the cut ends loosely in polyethylene film. Keep both kinds of cuttings out of the sun. Before planting the cuttings, they can be dipped in a rooting powder to stimulate root formation if you wish. Rooting powders come in three strengths, according to what type of plant you are trying to increase, and are available at larger garden centers (or by mail order); the weakest will do for the kinds of herbaceous cuttings we are discussing here. Rooting powders are syn-

thetic plant hormones, and if you'd rather not use them, dip the end
of the cuttings in a label-strength solution of liquid seaweed instead,
as it contains trace quantities of many growth hormones. And—it
might sound funny—handle your cuttings; it is known that human
sweat (and urine) contain some of the same growth substances. In
fact, the much vaunted green thumb that helps plants thrive under
some gardeners' care may well just be the presence of growth hormones on their hands!

For small stem cuttings we use a 50-cell plug insert; for larger
plants with more foliage, we use an 18-cell insert (which is equivalent to 3½-inch pots set side by side in a standard 10″ × 20″ nursery
tray). If you are using individual pots, multiple cuttings can be stuck
around the edges of the pot, an inch in from the rim and far enough

Take stem cuttings from side shoots, remove all but the top three to four
leaves and any flowers, and then insert in a tray or pot of moist cutting mix
and hold in bright indirect light under high humidity until rooting occurs.

apart that the leaves aren't touching. Fill the container loosely with cutting mix, poke a small hole with a chopstick or blunt pencil, and insert the cutting in the hole up to a quarter inch or so below the remaining leaves. Once the tray or pot is full, water it, then place it on the heating mat and cover it with a vapor barrier. If you are using nursery trays, the clear plastic covers used for seedlings work quite well. If you are using individual pots, a polyethylene bag is effective; just put a small stake in the pot to hold the bag up off the cuttings. Do not seal the tray or pot completely as the cuttings need air—you are only trying to increase the humidity so transpiration of water from the leaves is slow until roots form. Otherwise the cuttings wilt and then decay.

Some species, like carnations and chrysanthemums, will begin to root within a few days, though you won't likely see any activity for a week or two even with these fast-rooting flowers. Plan on leaving the cuttings on the heating mat for two to three weeks, then keeping them in the tray or pots for another two to three weeks before transplanting to larger containers or hardening off and setting out in the garden. The cover should be removed temporarily (to air out) at any sign of infection by bacteria or fungi, and permanently as soon as there are signs of renewed growth. Before setting out in the garden, loosen new cuttings from their pots and inspect them to make sure that enough roots have formed to hold the soil ball together during handling.

*Schedule* 2. While cuttings taken from greenhouse-forced plants will be ready before those taken off plants just breaking dormancy outdoors in the spring, they really are more trouble. If you wait, the whole process will be much simpler.

Most outdoor root cuttings should be taken as soon as the ground has dried sufficiently to dig without mucking things up. Take a spading fork and work underneath a healthy, young specimen of bleeding hearts, bee balm, or whatever suitable plant you've chosen. Once the edge roots are exposed, you can make the cuttings, just as you would on a potted plant. (A little sulfur dusted on both cut ends is a good idea.) Then reset the plant, firming the soil around the roots to exclude air pockets. With plants that don't mind the disturbance you can dig up the entire plant. If you take more than a third of the roots, though, be sure to cut back the top when replanting so that the root-shoot balance is maintained. With plants that resent disturbance—mostly those, like Oriental poppies, that have taproots—use a sharp spade to cut down through the soil in a circle a foot or so outside the edge of the clump and leave the plant intact. This will separate the outer part of the surface roots, yet leave them in the ground at just the right depth to sprout. Once they sprout, gently dig up these new plants and move them to their new home. In either case, water after digging if the soil is dry and rain isn't likely in the near future.

If you have taken outdoor root cuttings, you can treat them the same way as the indoor cuttings described earlier. If you have a well-drained piece of ground, though, you can simply plant the cuttings there, using the same techniques—and giving the same care. Planting inside a cold frame would be best, but you can rig a low polyethylene tunnel over the plants to keep the humidity high and protect them from sun and wind until rooted. Instead of the clear plastic normally used for tunnels, though, use white plastic—it is less likely to overheat on warm, sunny days.

Stem cuttings taken from outdoor plants in spring and summer are handled in the same fashion as those taken from forced plants. Use side shoots; take a two-to-three-inch section of the stem, cutting just above a node; remove all fruits and flowers (or their buds), and all but the top few leaves. Stick the cuttings in prepared flats on a heating mat, or in a cold frame or low protective tunnel. If the soil in the cold frame or tunnel is warm, loose, moist, and yet well drained, you can start the cuttings directly in the soil, but remember, stem cuttings are generally more demanding than root cuttings. Also, unless all the cuttings root at the same rate, planting in the ground will be less convenient than in pots that can be moved individually as their various contents are established and ready to plant out. Transplanting of rooted cuttings is the same as for seedlings.

*Schedule 3.* One of the best uses of stem cuttings is to make extra plants of a favorite annual that didn't germinate well or that you'd like to bring in the house before frost. Petunias, impatiens, and geraniums are often treated this way. Let's say you want a mass of red petunias for window boxes and don't have the space to grow them from seed, but also don't want to spend the money to buy started plants. You could buy a half dozen plants early on, pinch out the growing point, then set the plants into individual 6-inch pots. Each will grow into a large plant fairly quickly and provide a source of cuttings from which you can start many, many more plants. By the time you are ready to propagate them, the weather outdoors will likely be settled enough to stick the cuttings directly into the window boxes.

Impatiens and geraniums, as well as a multitude of other annuals, will provide mid-to-late-summer cuttings that can be established in pots and then brought indoors to continue growing over the winter.

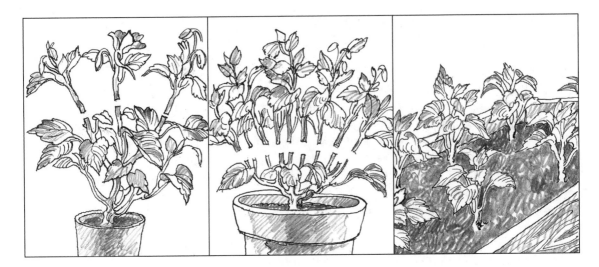

Impatiens can be increased in late summer for winter houseplants by stem cuttings. Shear the plants and you'll provide lots of material to work with.

Here in Vermont, we start thinking about fall around the first of August, and set the pots of cuttings in a protected, shady spot near the hose's faucet so they get watered regularly. By the time frost threatens around Labor Day they are well established and growing on their own roots, ready to provide us with some indoor winter cheer. Before taking them indoors, however, we check the plants closely for insects or their eggs.

**Division**     Division is probably the simplest form of plant increase, and is ideal for the beginner. If you have ever dug up a clump of daffodils that has had a few years to establish itself, you will have noticed that it is made up of a cluster of three or four plump, tannish bulbs. To divide and increase those daffodils all you have to do is gently break apart the individual bulbs and replant them. It really is that simple: the structure of the plant is obvious, and the way to proceed clear.

Other forms of division are essentially the same, though of course there are differences among various plants. Most perennial flowers actually need to be divided periodically to maintain their vigor. If not thinned in that way, they will eventually crowd themselves out.

With a few exceptions (noted in Chapter 5) most perennials can be divided in spring or fall, and some particularly tough species can be divided virtually any time if you have a gentle hand and give them good aftercare. To minimize a setback in their growth, those that bloom in early spring are best divided immediately after they have bloomed (in the case of spring bulbs, let the foliage die down first).

Fall-blooming perennials can also be divided after their bloom period if you live in a warm climate, but here in northern New England, the danger of an early winter is ever present, and if the plants don't have a chance to get their roots down, frost can heave them right out of the ground. Thus, in cold climates, fall-blooming plants should be divided in early spring before their new shoots are more than an inch or two long.

The basic technique is as follows: Gently dig up the plant, separate it into parts; then replant. I like to use a garden fork to dig the plants, as it lifts rather than cuts. The roots will need to be broken at some point, and I'd rather do that by pulling so that they come apart at a weak point, instead of cutting them at an arbitrary point with a shovel blade.

Insert the tines of the fork two to three inches away from the visible edge of the clump and press down as far as the fork will go without foot pressure; then tip it back and pry the plant loose. Clumps more than a foot across will probably require lifting all around before they come loose. Loosen the plant thoroughly before lifting so that as much soil as possible falls back into the original planting hole. Soil is the heart of the garden, painstakingly built up over seasons of composting and mulching, so try to conserve every handful.

Once the plant is out of the ground, divide it into pieces. In some cases it is possible to simply shake the clump loose of soil, and it will come right apart. In other cases it helps to pry the full clump apart into two or three sections and then work on these smaller sections. A simple way to do this is with two garden forks. Insert them back to back through the center of the clump and then pull the handles apart. Once the clump size is manageable it is easier to work a section apart. A sharp knife can be used to help this process along, cutting tangled roots and stems. Remember: Each clump must have both stem and root to grow successfully. In most cases, the older, center part of the clump is discarded, and only the vigorous new growth around the edges is replanted.

If minimal setback is your goal, each piece should be six to twelve inches across. Clumps that size, divided a few months before they normally bloom, should not have diminished bloom at all; in fact, bloom may be improved. To further increase your supply of a given plant yet still get some bloom, the divisions can be made as small as three to four inches across (a handful) as long as they contain three to four buds or sprouts. For maximum increase you can divide the plant into very small pieces—literally just a bud and a root—but you'll need to set them in a nursery bed and give them special care for the first season, setting them out for bloom the following season.

A single clump of Shasta daisies measuring two feet across, for instance, can be divided into quarters in early fall or spring with no diminution of bloom. A dozen plants could be created and most would bloom a bit, then by the second year be fully established. If desired, thirty or forty plants could be broken out of the clump, nursed for a season, then set out for a massive display the following season. This flexibility is one of the great joys of perennial gardening.

Extremely tough or overgrown plants may not let go easily from their clumps, and will need to be cut apart in situ with a sharp spade, a process I call "shovel division." Very large, overgrown clumps of upright sedum or daylilies can be divided this way: Simply chop off pieces six to twelve inches across, applying your full weight to the shovel if necessary; then replant the pieces, at the same depth, a foot or two apart in each direction. The following year they will be back in bloom and will soon fill the open space.

Try to protect new divisions from drying winds and direct sun while working. Most species are replanted immediately, but large, succulent rhizomes like those of irises should be given a dusting of sulfur on any cut ends and allowed to dry a bit before replanting. This helps fight infection. Irises are finicky about depth of planting, as are peonies. Specifics for various plants are in Chapter 5, but some general principles can be applied.

Plants that grow in rosettes (the leaves and flower stalks arise directly from the crown, where roots and tops meet) and those that grow in clumps (the leaves and flowers are borne on stems) require different planting depths. Rosette plants like primroses must be replanted at precisely the same depth or they will rot at the base of the leaves. Clumping plants like rudbeckia are generally more forgiving and can be set a bit deeper after division. If the species is one that roots readily, deeper planting may even strengthen the plant: the buried stems will send out extra roots.

You can tell when perennials need dividing because you'll notice a decrease in their "flower power." When crowded together, some species, such as garden phlox, are much more susceptible to foliage diseases like mildew. If you notice a sudden increase in problems like that, consider dividing the clumps. Bulbs may simply fail to bloom, though the leaves will be thick and healthy.

The technique for replanting divisions is not very different from that for replanting cuttings and seedlings, but larger, older divisions that you want to rebloom immediately will need some extra attention. Dig a large hole and spread the roots out so they are not doubled

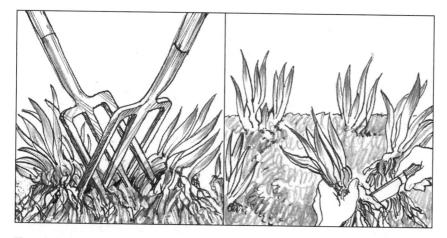

Two-fork division of daylilies is simple, if strenuous. Jam two garden forks
back-to-back through the center of the clump; then lever the handles
against each other to loosen it. Oversize pieces can then be cut apart and
replanted. Shovel division *(below)* involves simply cutting an existing
clump (in this case, sedum) apart with a sharp spade, then replanting the
pieces. For bloom the same year from a spring division, the pieces should be
at least eight inches across.

over each other. Cut out any damaged or diseased sections and, after
partially filling the planting hole, water them in thoroughly so that
there are no air gaps trapped around the roots. If the division has a
significant amount of top growth on it, sink a stake on the windward
side and tie the top to the stake with soft strips of cloth or other
nonbinding material. This keeps the wind from flexing the stem and
breaking loose the tiny root hairs—the first to regenerate—on which
the plant depends for its water supply. Do not use a slip knot—it will
strangle the plant as it grows.

**Increasing Bulbs and Corms**

While most of the plants we consider bulbs produce seed (and often lots of it), they are rarely propagated that way by home gardeners as most feel that the three-to-five-year wait for the plants to reach blooming size is too long. By far the most frequent method of increase is division. Division is done just after foliage dies down in early to midsummer. Lift the bulbs gently and pull off the bulblets attached to the mother bulb, making sure to take a bit of root with them. If you find any soft or rotten spots, either cut them out and dust with sulfur, or simply throw out the bulb.

Bulbs can also be increased—and somewhat more quickly—by making cuttings. One of the ways that bulbs and corms differ from many other kinds of plants is that their stem and leaf structure expands laterally instead of vertically; their characteristic plumpness is the result of leaf nodes that are all bunched together. What this means is that the axillary meristems (the potential side shoots) are bunched around the main growing point instead of below it.

The way to make cuttings from a bulb is to cut it into pie-shaped sections, making sure that each section has a bit of leaf and a bit of the base plate, which is the plant's crown. Again, the best time is midsummer, after the tops have died down. There is no technical limit to the number of divisions that can be made from, say, a single daffodil bulb—commercial propagators may make a hundred or more—but most gardeners stop at eight to keep the size of the pieces manageable.

To make cuttings from bulbs, cut into sections as you would an orange or an apple; then dust with sulfur and pot up in moist cutting mix. Hold in the dark at 50–60°F until leaves begin to sprout; then move into the light.

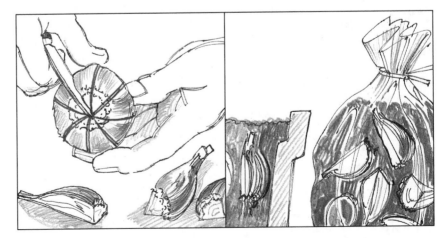

As soon as they are cut, the sections should be dusted with powdered sulfur, then potted up (if big enough) or put in a poly bag filled with moist potting mix. Either way, the cuttings should be kept in the dark at 50–60°F until new leaves begin to sprout. Once the young plants are established they can be planted out, though they might appreciate protection in a cold frame for their first winter.

With lilies all that is necessary is to gently pull off the many scales that make up the bulb. Up to a third of the scales can be removed early in spring without affecting the plant's bloom in the current season; the entire bulb can be split if your desire for more plants outweighs your desire to see them bloom that year. The scales should be stuck two-thirds of their height into the potting mix used for cuttings and nursed along for the first season—until they form small bulbs themselves—at which time they can be planted out in the garden. It will be another year or two before they bloom.

Lilies also form miniature bulbs in their leaf axils, and these too can be planted out for bloom in two or three years. The production of such bulbils is generally increased if you cut off a third to a half of the flowering stem—before it flowers. (I know, I know; you decide if it's worth it!)

## BUYING PLANTS

It might seem odd to discuss buying plants in a chapter about plant propagation, but realistically that is how many flower gardeners get started. Only later do we start trying to increase plants on our own. Because of this, I thought it a good idea to touch briefly on a few points about buying plants from a garden center or a mail-order catalog. If you do buy started plants, be sure to examine them closely. You could bring more problems home than you'd care to deal with. Forewarned is forearmed.

**Garden Centers**

Obviously, plants should be free of insects and their eggs; be sure to check the undersides of the leaves, and look closely where the leaf branches meet the stem and at the growing point of the plant—where the youngest, tenderest leaves are—as those are favorite congregating places of many feeding insects. Also check underneath the flats themselves, as night-feeding pests will crawl up between the sections of a six-pack container to spend their days safe from harsh sunlight and the prying eyes of the greenhouse proprietor. Do not put purchased plants in with your own until this inspection has been done.

Second, buy only young, vigorously growing plants. Bare pots may have dormant yet healthy plants in them, but there is no reason to buy them until the tops are well up and looking good. Let the nurseryman take the chance that something may happen to the plant before it breaks dormancy; you shouldn't have to. At the other extreme, avoid large, pot-bound plants unless you have something particular—like making your own root cuttings—in mind for them. Overgrown plants will be shocked at transplant time and will not establish as easily as younger plants. Also, you are always better off buying seedlings that haven't bloomed. It is a universal tendency— and mistake—to buy bedding plants that are already in flower; the moment you get them back to your garden for transplanting, you are just going to pinch off the flowers anyway (or at least you should!).

Third, the plants should be well proportioned and well fed. Greenhouses are expensive to operate, and the garden-center operator needs to fit as many plants as possible into the space he has available. This means that the seedlings are too often crowded; consequently their tops have developed all out of proportion to their side branches. The rule of thumb is that at planting time a seedling should be as wide as it is tall. If you are unsure that the plant has been properly fertilized, look back at the discussion of nutrient deficiency symptoms earlier in this chapter, under Growing Seedlings, so you will learn how to recognize the signs of both over- and under-fertilization.

## Specialty Nurseries and Mail-Order Catalogs

There are many plants, especially named cultivars of perennials, that you might want to grow but can't find at the local garden center. If so, you owe it to yourself to check out the wide range of specialty nurseries and mail-order catalogs. While specialty nurseries are exciting to visit, doing so can take a significant amount of time away from the garden unless you are lucky enough to live near them. Mail-order nurseries, because they are able to serve a national audience of gardeners, can stock a much wider range of varieties than all but the best specialty nurseries, and they are as near as your mailbox. Just one example is a pelargonium (common geranium) specialist who offers more than one thousand kinds of geraniums! Similar catalogs exist for other popular garden flowers like peonies, daylilies, iris, and hostas.

The cautions noted about your local garden center apply equally to specialty nurseries. Any time you bring actively growing plants home you need to check them over thoroughly. Plants ordered by mail, if seedlings, will need the same attention. Unpack and inspect them immediately upon arrival, then plant as soon as possible just as you would your own seedlings.

Older perennials that arrive in the mail will almost certainly arrive bare root. This means that the plants have been dug during their dormant period and all the soil removed from around their roots. Obviously this not only saves the soil for the grower's next crop, it saves on shipping (soil is quite heavy). Bare-root plants are likely, though not certain, to be free of pests, because most pests are found on actively growing parts of the plant, in the soil, or clinging to the underside of the pots. None of these is present in a bare-root plant, so there is less likelihood of a problem.

Bare-root plants require special attention, however. On their arrival, the shipping container should immediately be taken to a cool, dim place and opened. Strong sun and drying winds are the great enemies of bare-root plants. The plants will likely be wrapped in moist newspaper or moist wood shavings; if they are enclosed in a plastic bag, open it and examine the contents for moldy or rotten spots. If there are any, cut out the bad parts with a sterile knife and dust with sulfur. Resterilize the knife between plants. Be careful not to break off any shoots that may have begun to sprout.

Unless you can plant (either in pots or direct in the garden) immediately, store your new plants in a dark, cool, moist place. Leave the plastic bags open at the top with the plants in them and the wood shavings or paper in place. At temperatures between 30°F and 50°F they will hold in good condition for three to four days. If the intended spot for your new plants isn't yet available, either plant them in your nursery bed—see, it's a good thing you had that spot ready!—or into containers.

On the morning that you intend to plant, it is a good idea to soak the roots for an hour before planting; this will help wake them up and let them know it is time to get growing again. After soaking, treat the plants just as described above in the section on replanting divisions. If you will be putting the plants in containers, be sure the pot is big enough to hold the entire root mass without doubling over. Water all bare-root plants immediately after transplanting; new growth should be visible within a week or so. Keep records of when the plants arrived, what you did to take care of them until planting, and the planting date so that if you have a problem, you will have the information necessary to seek help or a refund from the nursery where you bought them.

# CHAPTER 5

# A Festival
# of Flowers

~~~~~~~~~~~~~~~~~~~~~~~~~~~~~~~~~~~~~~~~~~~~~~

## ACHILLEA

Within the achillea clan, also known as the yarrows, are some common weeds of waste places and some of the finest cut flowers you can grow. The species responsible is *Achillea millefolium,* which in plain English means, "with a thousand leaves," but it is generally just called common yarrow. The Latin name refers to the finely cut texture of the ferny leaves, however, rather than to their actual number. When we bought our property, white yarrow was one of the most common weeds of the dry ground (wild daisies covered the wet, open areas, with wild azaleas at the woodland edge). We also saw an occasional pink plant, a color more often seen among the cultivated types. In cultivation, yarrows can reach two feet in height, and have more or less open and flat-topped flower clusters. There are a number of cultivars available from seed, but once you find a particular plant with a color and habit you like, it is best to increase by division, as plants grown from seed are quite variable.

*Achillea filipendulina* is the true fern leaf yarrow and has somewhat broader leaves and grows considerably taller: three to four feet in good conditions—sunny and dry, but not too fertile. If the soil is too rich the plant may grow to five feet and require staking. Flower color is yellow, and different cultivars have different shades; Parker's flowers are golden yellow while those of Gold Plate are a deeper yellow. Fern leaf yarrows are more consistent from seed (though you may still want to select individual plants for increase) and can be easily started in spring by the standard method from Chapter 4, using a temperature of 70–75°F for germination. A hybrid between *A. filipendulina* and the Balkan species *A. clypeolata,* however, is superior to any of the standard kinds: Named Coronation Gold, it is somewhat shorter at just under three feet, and flat golden flower clusters numbering in the dozens can reach as much as four inches across. In addition, the foliage is a very attractive gray green and is strongly aromatic. This is one of the all-time favorite landscape and garden plants, and deservedly so; increase purchased plants by division in spring.

Another interesting hybrid is Moonshine. Much smaller than the others at only one to two feet tall, it has all the good characteristics of Coronation Gold writ small, and the flower heads are a wonderfully subtle pale yellow.

Finally, there is a different type of yarrow, *Achillea ptarmica,* unfortunately called sneezewort (*ptarmica* means "plant that makes you sneeze"), that has undivided leaves and half-inch, mostly double, white pom-pom flowers on one-to-two-foot plants. The best cultivar is The Pearl, and it should be increased by division to maintain its appearance and performance.

All the yarrows make excellent cut flowers and will dry well. Harvest when the flowers are fully open and add to arrangements or bunch and hang them in a dark, airy location to dry.

## ACONITUM

The tall, brooding spires and covered faces of monkshoods along with its preference for cool, shady places put this plant among a select number of perennials that serve, like *aruncus, ligularia, cimicifuga,* and a few tall species of *hosta,* as a backdrop for dimly lit corners of the garden. Also known as wolfbane because its tubers were reputed to cure those doomed to life as werewolves (probably by killing them), this dangerously poisonous plant has had a long relationship with humankind and is the source of the drug aconite, which was used to reduce fever and quiet irregular heartbeat.

Here in the North monkshood grows well in sun or shade, but its range is limited by an intolerance of heat to areas from Virginia north, except in cool hollows. There are two basic types, which can be distinguished by their leaves: *A. napellus,* native to the mountains of central Europe, has deeply divided leaves, while *A. carmichaelii,* named for plant collector J. R. Carmichael, who first brought it back from the mountains of central China in the 1860s, has broader leaves. By far the most common flower color is a deep violet blue, but there are other colors. Both have numerous forms that grow anywhere from three to six feet tall and are quite variable, so it is best to buy plants of named cultivars and divide them in spring or fall to increase your collection. Because of the poisonous nature of the roots, bury any leftover pieces and wash up thoroughly afterward.

Some *A. napellus* types to look for are Bressingham Spire, which has an upright habit but grows only two to three feet tall, or Newry's Blue, which is taller, at four to five feet. Spark's Variety grows to a similar height, but has a more open, arching habit; another variety, usually sold as Bicolor, is only three to four feet tall and has blooms that are blue and white. Even more unusual is Carneum, the pale pink form which grows to four feet.

Among the cut-leaf forms, the most popular is the three-to-four-foot-tall, large-flowering Arendsii, named for the famous and prolific German breeder and nurseryman Georg Arends. There is one called Kelmscott, however, that has lighter, lavender blue flowers and grows to an impressive six feet.

A lesser-known relative to these common aconitums is the woodland wildflower form *A. vulparia,* which has smaller, longer flowers that range from creamy white to yellow. It is an open, branching plant with arching stems. You may also find white forms offered by nurseries under the name Ivorine or Album, classified as either a *napellus* type or as its own species, *A. septentrionale,* which in its native Sweden actually has lilac flowers. Don't worry about what it is, just get it.

Monkshood can be started from seed, but to do so it is best to collect your own and sow it immediately. Seed that is not absolutely fresh enters a deep dormancy, and even after a cold treatment may not germinate for up to a year.

## AGERATUM

The ageratum most people think of is a tender bedding plant that grows only eight to twelve inches tall and is covered first with cushiony warm blue buds, sort of like a blue button mum, and then small monochrome daisy flowers that from a distance appear furry. It is a valuable plant simply because it is blue, a relatively rare color in flowers. Lobelia, brachycome, browallia, myosotis, and *Campanula carpatica* are just about the only other blue edging plants that come to mind.

Unlike these others, the blue of ageratum is almost always a bit pinky, though breeders are working hard to improve on existing varieties. Most of what is available these days is hybrid, as hybrids are much more uniform and compact than the standard type typified by Blue Mink. Among the hybrids, a southern favorite is the Hawaii series, available in blue, lavender blue, and white, which is especially heat-tolerant. Popular bedding hybrids in the Northeast are Blue Danube and Adriatic. If you look hard enough you may find the bicolor standard known as Bavaria, or even the pink form.

Far more useful in my mind than these bedding types, though, is the cut flower ageratum, which reaches two to three feet tall. By far the best available is Blue Horizon. It can be recommended especially for filling a bouquet primarily composed of more dramatic flowers. An open-pollinated form of equal value is the prosaically named Florist's Blue.

Ageratum is indeed a tender annual. We had to keep it away from the greenhouse vents at our garden center because just a puff of sub-freezing air was enough to turn the foliage black and set the plants back. It needs high temperatures (80–85°F) and light to germinate, so do not bury the seed when sowing and put the planted flats in the warmest spot you've got for best results. Once the seedlings break ground in a week or two's time, they can be grown at the standard 60–65°F. They should be ready for the garden in six to eight weeks, but neither the bedding nor the bouquet types can be set out until all danger of frost is past. When planting out in the garden, bedding types will need six to eight inches between plants, while the cut-flower types need a foot between them. For bouquets, harvest the flowers just as they open. They do not dry well, but will last seven to ten days in arrangements.

## ALCEA

Hollyhocks are, in many areas of the country, short-lived perennials grown, at best, as annuals. Here in the mountains of southern Vermont, however, they seem to last longer than in warmer climates. Still, we start most of our plantings from seed, which if started early will allow some strains to bloom the first year. Start indoors in a 50-cell insert or larger eight to twelve weeks before the frost-free date and transplant to the garden twelve to eighteen inches apart after the danger of hard frost is past.

To grow hollyhocks as biennials or perennials, start the seeds in the summer and let the young plants spend the winter in a holding or nursery bed. Sow in June or July and transplant to the nursery bed or their final location when the plants have from four to six true leaves.

Whether you grow hollyhocks as annuals, biennials, or perennials, allow plenty of room in the garden as most of the old-fashioned types (our favorites) grow six to nine feet tall in the fertile, sunny locations they like. Keep them deadheaded for extended bloom time, and hope they don't get rust. Rust is a fungal disease that nearly drove hollyhocks from garden use a hundred years ago; it can be battled with sulfur sprays, but the best defense is to give the plants plenty of room and keep the foliage as dry as possible.

Hollyhocks are also very attractive to Japanese beetles, which can be controlled by hand picking or trapping. Go out early in the morning with a bucket half full of soapy water and hold it beneath the leaves and buds that are infested; then tap the stem. Being lethargic from the cool temperatures, the beetles will fall into the soapy water. We also keep beetle traps outside the garden, on the upwind side, to draw these pests away, and we visit the traps each morning with our soapy water bucket. One last (excellent) line of defense is kids;

Japanese beetles are lethargic in the cool of early mornings and can be easily shaken off plant leaves into a bucket of soapy water.

Japanese beetles are an intriguing iridescent blue black color and make a fantastic (to kids) crunching noise when stepped on. Enough said.

Our favorite hollyhocks are the old-fashioned, single-flowered types from the species *Alcea rosea*. The variety we grow is Indian Summer, but Summer Carnival will also bloom the first year from seed. The color range is generally long and strong on the pink, salmon, red, and white end of the spectrum, with an occasional yellow shade. The standard double hollyhock is Chater's Double, and it is the only mix that is also available in separate colors, which include the full range from yellow through the warm pastels to purple. A dark red, almost black, strain that grows six feet or more is *A. rosea* "*nigra*," a single, or *A. r.* "*nigra plena*," with double flowers. There is also a pale, lemon yellow type that is sold under the name *A. rugosa*. If truly perennial hollyhocks are your wont, and you haven't had luck in the past, try *A. ficifolia*, the fig-leaf or Antwerp hollyhock. This related species is much more vigorous than *A. rosea*, and has interesting fig-leaf foliage. It has the usual range of colors, but with more yellow, and will usually outlive the standard types.

## ALCHEMILLA

Lady's mantle is an unassuming but useful plant with intriguing foliage and flowers that, while not colorful, fill a important function in the design of a garden: The neutral chartreuse flowers set off brighter neighbors in a way that allows the gardener to change color schemes from one section of a bed or border to another without a clashing effect. Lady's mantle also makes a good edging plant as it is both tough and uniform and looks good up close due to the way moisture beads up on the leaves.

There is only one species in general use, *Alchemilla mollis*, though more than two hundred others exist. It grows from one and a half to two feet tall depending on conditions, with an equal spread. Propagation is easy—by division spring or fall—and no special treatment is necessary. In our gardens it has proven unkillable and is never bothered by disease or pests. The leaves and flowers are also useful in bouquets as a filler.

## ALLIUM

Alliums were the first perennials I ever really took an interest in collecting. I began as a vegetable gardener who loved all the edible members of the allium family—onions, leeks, garlic, shallots, chives, and the like—and just branched out from there. While the flowers of ornamental alliums all share certain characteristics, the way in which those traits are varied to such different ends, yielding such radically different plants is a vivid example of the phenomenal diversity possible even within such a well-known species. For example, *Allium giganteum* has a broad basal rosette of succulent aloesque leaves and huge spherical flower head three to four feet in the air, while *A. narcissiflorum* (the daffodil onion) is less than a foot tall, with thin, flat leaves and clumps of nodding, half-inch, dusky rose blossoms that look like the raised center of a daffodil.

Alliums are propagated primarily by bulbs that are planted in the fall at a depth three times their diameter. They will come true from seed, but most are slow to flower, taking two or three years to grow sufficiently large to be worth the trouble. Two notable exceptions are *Allium schoenoprasum*, or common chives, which regardless of what the effetes say is a fine plant, and *A. tuberosum*, the flat-leaved, white-flowered Chinese or garlic chives, which blooms in late summer. Both of these are unkillable yet controllable, and are absolutely uniform plants that are good for edging, in my estimation. There is a giant form of common chives, sometimes sold as "giant chives" and sometimes by the name *A. s. "majus."* To keep chives of all kinds vigorous, shear them after the flowers begin to fade to force secondary growth.

Of the kinds best grown from bulbs, we find the following most interesting: *Allium giganteum* is the king of the family, and to many a bit too much, but we like it. The plant is well named, with a basal rosette of gray-green, fleshy leaves almost two feet across that wither in late May to early June, just as the seed stalk begins to rise three to four feet into the air bearing a large, three-to-four-inch diameter, spherical flower head comprised of hundreds of tiny lilac flowers. They make excellent cut flowers. After two or three years, the base-ball-sized bulb splits and can be divided and replanted. This reliable and spectacular plant is hardy all the way from the coldest parts of Zone 4 to the warm regions of Zone 8 (see Appendix 5 for hardiness zones). A smaller form is the two-to-three-foot *A. aflatunense*.

While the plants are not as large, the largest flower of the commonly cultivated alliums belongs to *A. christophii* (sometimes *A. albopilosum*), the star of Persia. Again the basal rosette is made of wide, straplike, fleshy leaves that die before the plant flowers, leaving the lonely flowering stalk on its own to rise a foot or two before exploding into a loosely constructed foot-wide sphere of small metallic blue flowers. Similar in habit but only half as tall (and with less striking color) is *A. karataviense,* the Turkistan onion. Hardiness is similar to *A. giganteum.*

All four of these alliums virtually require some kind of companion planting in all but cutting gardens because their dead and dying foliage is unattractive, and the gaps left when they go dormant can ruin the design of a border. The ideal companion plants sprout late to allow the alliums a chance to have the ground to themselves, and then form a mass of foliage by June to disguise the withering foliage and provide a visual canvas above which the flowers can be displayed.

Three species that don't need hiding are *Allium senescens, A. ostrowskianum,* and *A. narcissiflorum.* These make good container plants as well as thriving in most gardens. *A. senescens,* known as curly chives, has wonderful, flat grayish foliage that grows in an arching spiral from a basal clump, and dark, rosy pink flowers held a foot or so above the foliage. While very slow growing, the clumps divide easily, and we have never had a problem with winterkill here in our low Zone 4 garden, so it appears perfectly hardy. This is a wonderful edging plant.

*A. ostrowskianum,* named for a Russian government minister of the late nineteenth century who was a patron of botanists and plant collectors, is a foot-tall, flat-leaved clumping onion from the mountains of eastern Turkey and Afghanistan. The foliage is a vibrant green, with blunted swordlike leaves that clump lazily, rather than standing erect and last well into midsummer. The flowers are larger and more loosely clustered, less spherical than most of those we have discussed so far, but they still dry well.

The narcissus-flowered onion is a wildflower species from the Italian Alps and, unlike most of the cultivated alliums, likes a semi-shady spot with a moist soil. The foliage is grassy, and the nodding pink, half-inch flowers, which resemble the raised cup of a daffodil, are held in clusters of four or more on foot-tall, arching stems. This plant is slightly smaller, but with a bit larger flowers, than the native American nodding onion *A. cernuum,* which is widely grown as a rock garden plant.

Another open-flowered species is *A. neapolitanum,* the Naples onion from southern Europe, which grows a foot tall and blooms in early spring, bearing two-inch-wide, upward-facing clusters of fragrant white flowers. Unfortunately it is only hardy in the South, though it makes an excellent pot plant here in the North. Plant four to five bulbs an inch deep in a 6-inch pot and chill for eight to ten weeks before bringing out into a warm, bright area.

*Allium moly*, also known as the lily leek or golden garlic, is one of the oldest known ornamental onions—prized and revered by the ancient Greeks—and one of the most delicate, with a mere pair of two-inch-wide leaves that are a foot long, and a two-inch cluster of upward-facing golden yellow starlike flowers. The lily leek can be grown from seed for bloom in one year, but bulbs are widely available.

Perhaps the best of the alliums for cutflower use is *A. sphaero-cephalum*, drumstick chives, so called because the tightly packed oval flower heads are held atop three-foot-tall bare stems like drumsticks. At bud stage in early summer the heads—composed of a hundred tiny, unopened flowers—are green, but during the next few weeks they become more and more purple and once cut will last almost two weeks in the vase. The bulbs are inexpensive and should be planted six inches deep; after two or three seasons you can remove new bulblets to increase your supply.

## ALYSSUM, annual—*see* Lobularia

## ALYSSUM, perennial—*see* Aurinia

## AMARANTHUS

Amaranth is an ancient food plant in Central America and a striking specimen in the garden, though rather coarse and weedy. The plants are large: four to six feet tall and two feet or more across, and the flower spikes themselves are over a foot long. There are both upright and drooping forms. The drooping form is *A. caudatus*, which means, once translated out of the Latin, "never fading, hanging like a tail," but it is commonly called love-lies-bleeding because of the blood red color of the flowers (though there is a green form as well). A somewhat cheerier name for the same flower is kiss-me-over-the-garden-gate. *A. cruentus* is an upright form with strong spikes that resemble a cross between cattails and celosia, also of red or green. While its common name is prince's feather it is better to look under the names Cathedral or Oeschberg to be sure you are getting the right plant.

Amaranths are tender annuals that thrive in hot, sunny places though, because of their size, some protection from wind is advisable. Sow indoors four to six weeks before the last frost, and delay planting out until the weather is fully warm and frost-free. Both *A. caudatus* and *A. cruentus* plants should be set two feet apart in each direction. Amaranth can also be sown directly in the garden after all danger of frost is past. Love-lies-bleeding makes a good tub or container plant as the blooms hang down over the side of the planter.

For bouquets, harvest blooms when two-thirds to three-quarters of the tiny individual blossoms in a given flower spike have opened. Fresh-cut stems will last a week or more in the vase. Blooms to be dried should be left on the plant until fully opened and then dried with the stems standing upright in water (the flower spikes themselves can be left hanging) to preserve their natural appearance. Once dried they make a nice alternative to bows on dried wreath arrangements.

Some related species are used as foliage plants for bedding schemes, much in the same way as coleus is used. *A. tricolor*, also known as Joseph's coat, has a bright (dare I say gaudy?) combination of fiery red, sunny yellow, and lime green splashed across each leaf; while *A. bicolor* is two-tone red, but still visually striking if you like bold statements. The only one of these we have much use for is *A. salicifolla*, or willow-leaved amaranth; the smoldering, threadlike leaves of Flaming Fountain are just different enough (and just subdued enough) to make it worth growing.

## AMMI MAJUS

This simple and unassuming plant is a real star in cutting gardens and as a winsome companion in mixed borders. The flat, white flower heads of *Ammi majus* have all the beauty and simplicity of Queen Anne's lace, which it resembles, but it is easy to grow all over the United States as long as the season is matched to its need for cool growing conditions.

Seed should be sown outdoors in early spring where it is to grow and the resulting seedlings thinned to nine to twelve inches apart. Southern gardeners can also sow in the fall as the plants will withstand temperatures down into the teens. If the weather is warm at sowing time, chill the seed in the refrigerator for a week or two before planting.

Seedlings started indoors should be kept where temperatures drop below 50°F at night for the one to two weeks required for germination. A daily variation in temperature will help the seeds to sprout. Seedlings will be ready to transplant in three to four weeks.

For bouquets, cut the flower heads when three-quarters of the blossoms are open. If the apical (center) stem is cut early, the plant will send out strong side shoots. Note: Some people are quite sensitive to the sap of *Ammi majus,* so wear gloves when picking the blossoms. Cut flower heads may be dried in the same fashion as dill, by hanging in a dry, dark, airy place for two to three weeks.

## ANEMONE

Windflowers are a diverse and long-cultivated group of perennials, some rhizomatous, some tuberous, and that is probably the best way for us to get a handle on them in practical terms. Of the tuberous kinds, probably the best known is the diminutive *Anemone blanda,* or Grecian windflower. Only six to eight inches tall, but possessed of brilliant, daisylike flowers up to two inches across, this plant is a natural choice for open, deciduous woods with dappled shade. Buy the inexpensive corms in fall, soak them overnight, then plant in clusters for an early spring display. In the mid-Atlantic states they will become established within a year or two and spread. In the South they will naturalize, though more slowly; in the Far North, they may require some light mulch such as balsam boughs for winter protection and might be better spring-planted. The natural color is blue, but other colors are available; the corms can be potted up in fall for winter bloom.

*Anemone coronaria* is taller, at eight to sixteen inches, with more finely cut foliage and slightly larger, poppylike flowers—hence the name poppy anemone—that have fewer but broader petals. Though not as hardy as its relative, it is easily grown on the same schedule, and because of the low cost of the corms, makes a good annual cut flower. The Mona Lisa series is considered the premiere single-flowered type, while the St. Brigid series includes a wide range of double-flowered forms. The species is generally available only from specialists.

The most important of the nontuberous anemones, and the type most widely available from catalogs and garden centers that deal in perennials, is the hybrid or Japanese anemone, *A. X hybrida.* There are many cultivars, and most are outstanding garden perennials. Unlike the other anemones discussed above, they flower in fall and are tall plants, growing three to five feet tall and bearing large numbers of single or double flowers anywhere from two to five inches in diameter, in the full range of whites and pinks to almost purple. Propagation is by division in spring, or by root cuttings taken from dormant plants in winter (see Chapter 4). Mature plants resent disturbance, so they are a good candidate for in-place root cuttings: Dig a circle around the plant with a sharp spade and wait for new shoots to appear from the severed root tips that will grow into new plants.

Gardeners from Zone 4 to Zone 8 should do well with these fine garden hybrids; see one of the many perennial catalogs listed in the Sources appendix for descriptions of individual cultivars.

*A. sylvestris* (snowdrop anemone) is a charming, spring-blooming woodland plant a foot or so tall, with small, upward-facing, cup-shaped white flowers with yellow centers. It runs freely in moist, loose soils and the dappled shade that it prefers, so don't put it in close proximity to plants that are less competitive. You'll enjoy its fragrant show each spring. It is hardy in Zones 4–8.

Two smaller types of anemones are the European (*A. nemorosa*) and American (*A. quinquefolia*) wood anemones. Only half as tall as the snowdrop anemone and not fragrant, they are nonetheless valuable for naturalizing in moist woodlands because they bloom considerably earlier than the snowdrop anemone. Again, make sure you have room for them to run.

Finally, the meadow anemone (*A. canadensis*) is a hardy, ground-covering charmer that will quickly spread across sunny, moist meadows and provide an annual spring show of two-inch white flowers with yellow centers. Plant height is one to two feet. They can be easily propagated—in fact they will do it themselves whether you have the room or not—by division.

Seed for all anemones should be sown fresh. To tell if the seed is ripe, rub the seed heads between two fingers; if the seed drops free, it should be ready to sow. Remember that named cultivars will not come true from seed and should be increased by cuttings or division.

## ANTHEMIS

Anthemis is a relative to the daisy, with bright yellow or orange flowers and deeply cut, aromatic foliage reminiscent of yarrows. There are two common types, both of which thrive in full sun and well-drained, rather poor soils. The golden marguerite (*A. tinctoria*), grows to three feet and becomes so covered in bright two-inch blooms that it exhausts itself unless cut back in late summer so it has a chance to rejuvenate. St. John's chamomile (*A. sancti-johannis*) is a strong orange-blooming plant that is slightly smaller than the golden marguerite; its blooms have very large, raised disk flowers (the "eye" of the flower) and much smaller ray flowers (the "petals" of the flower). This markedly different proportion in sizes of large disk flowers and small ray flowers, combined with the strong coloring, often causes a strong reaction in most gardeners—you either love it or hate it. Because the two types of anthemis cross freely, purchased plants or seed are likely to be a natural hybrid of the two. There is also a less common form, *A. cupaniana,* which is less than a foot tall, with traditional daisy flowers, white with yellow eyes. All of these species increase readily from cuttings or from fresh sown seed.

## ANTIRRHINUM

The most common name for *Antirrhinum* (an-tee-*ree*-num or anty-*ry*-num; take your choice!) is snapdragon, but another common name is toad's mouth. Not a very engaging pair of names, but they do describe one of the oddities of this common hardy garden annual: The lower petals of the flower are "hinged" and a small squeeze with the fingers on the sides of the bloom will cause them to move. This ability of snapdragons to "talk" has kept our children occupied for many pleasant summer hours.

There are three major classes of snapdragons: carpet types that grow only six to twelve inches tall and are used for bedding; three-foot-tall cut-flower types that are also at home in borders; and a midsize that spans the uses from bedding to borders to limited cutting, given their eighteen-to-twenty-four-inch height.

You can do two things to help get snapdragons off to a good start. First, sprinkle the fine seed on the surface of your potting mix, press the seed in, and then allow the mix to soak through from the bottom. Then place the sown pots or plugs into a refrigerator or cold cellar for a week or two. After that, put them on a heating mat at 72°F in bright light and they will sprout within seven to ten days. To keep the soil moist without blocking light, cover the flats or pots with clear plastic and hold them out of direct sunlight. The plants should be up and growing six to eight weeks before the last frost, and the seeds need to be started two to three and a half weeks before that. As soon as hard frost is over they can be hardened off and set out.

The second trick to good snapdragons is to pinch out the terminal bud, or growing point, right after transplanting. This forces side growth (as we saw in Chapter 4) and produces bushier, more wind-resistant plants. (It is also important to keep cutting and pruning the plants over their useful season to keep them producing new blooms.)

Bedding snapdragons should be set six to eight inches apart; larger kinds need eight to twelve inches apiece. Very tall cut-flower types will also benefit from some sort of support, like the wire cages or string and stake arrangements discussed in Chapter 2. The biggest problem with snapdragons in our gardens are a leaf miner that makes tunnels in the foliage and rust. Leaf miners are best controlled by cutting off affected stems and burning them, miner and all. Rust is best prevented by not crowding the plants and avoiding overhead irrigation if possible. If rust does show up, it usually begins with small pale spots on the underside of the leaves that gradually redden. Soon problems appear on the tops of the leaves, then on the stems, which brown and die. At first sign, either remove infected plants and burn them, or spray with a wettable sulfur (see Chapter 2 for details on sprays).

Bedding snapdragons will bloom en masse, then go by; to prolong their display, shear the plants promptly after they peak. Tall varieties need frequent deadheading as well to remain attractive. For bouquets, cut when about two-thirds of the blooms on a spike have opened. Blooms last a week in water, and can be dried if you have silica gel in which to immerse them.

The most widely grown variety of "carpet" snapdragons is the appropriately named Floral Carpet, but other notables of the type include Tahiti and Floral Showers. All three grow less than ten inches tall, and are suitable for containers as well as bedding out. A few catalogs sell them by separate colors, but most are offered only as a mix. By far the most popular of the tall snapdragons is the Rocket series, which grows to three feet and is available in nine different colors (as well as a mix). If you'd like to try something a little different, though, consider the open-faced azalea-flowered series Bright Butterflies or its double-flowered counterpart, Madam Butterfly. Both are available only as a mix, but could add some extra interest with their unusual blooms.

Snapdragons germinate more readily after a cold treatment. Sow the seed; then hold at 30–40°F for one to two weeks; then raise to 72°F and provide bright light. At transplant time pinch out the terminal bud to force extra flowering stems from the axial buds.

The standard strains for medium height are the Liberty and Sonnet series. Both are available in a wide range of single colors as well as mixed, and both grow just over eighteen inches tall, yet are good for cutting as well as beds and borders. For something unusual in this height range, there is the 1987 AAS winner Princess White/ Purple Eye, which has striking bicolor blooms.

## AQUILEGIA

Columbines are native to North America's airier woodlands and have the easy grace of a longtime resident. The plants themselves have a buff, amphibian green leaf, and an open long-stemmed frame that holds the flowers out like the mouths of trumpets playing Handel's royal flourishes. In the garden columbines can take sun, at least here in the North. They are best among other plants so that their sparse nature doesn't run the risk of making them seem inconsequential in spite of the bold contrasts the blooms often present, with their starkly different colors on the sepals and petals and long rearward "spurs."

Here in the East, *A. canadensis,* or common columbine, is the native species, and its flowers are usually some form of red and yellow, borne on plants two to three feet tall. Farther west, the Rocky Mountain columbine *(A. caerulea)* is native, the coloring is blue and white, and the plants are about a foot shorter. Also from the West is the golden *A. chrysantha,* which is the only fragrant columbine I know of; it grows a little larger than the common eastern type under the right conditions. These are all essentially wildflowers and, as such, they will reseed themselves once established; you can start off with purchased seed, which it would be wise to refrigerate for a week before sowing. A germination temperature of 70°F should be fine once the cold treatment has tricked the seed into expecting the heat. Even though it comes well from seed, particularly fine plants can be maintained from year to year by division.

Most of the columbines seen in gardens today, however, are hybrids formed by crossing the species already mentioned among themselves and with a few others that have particularly desirable traits but less than ideal overall garden value. Thus our gardens have gained such first-rate performers as the McKana hybrids, a colorful, long-spurred mix that grows to about three feet; the Dragonfly series, similar but smaller at about two feet; and the Music series, smaller still at eighteen inches. The smallest you are likely to see is Biedermeier, which is usually blue with white, but sometimes in other colors as well, at a foot or less in height. These hybrids, of course, must be increased by division, not seed, if you wish to maintain their distinctive qualities.

The only double columbine I know of is Nora Barlow, which grows to two feet or more and has quilled or ruffled—or whatever you want to call it—bicolor flowers in pink to purple and white. To me it has always looked confused, but most people seem to love it, and on occasional days I find it interesting myself, as it is certainly unique and unusual. Nora Barlow is a nonhybrid form of the European *A. vulgaris* and will come true from seed, though a few off types will show up and should be removed—unless you like them, of course!

As mentioned in the introductory remarks, the best place for columbines is in a semishady, moist soil that mimics their ancestral home in open woodland. Give them this and they will thrive, establishing a semipermanent colony for your continued enjoyment. The only significant problem we have had with columbines is leaf miners, which can riddle the plants. The solution is simple: If you see any damage, which appears as small light-colored tracks ambling about within the leaves, remove these parts of the branch where the damage occurs and burn them, miners and all. The plant will quickly replace the branch. If you wish to pick the flowers for bouquets, cut them in the evening (or early morning) just as the blooms begin to open.

## ARABIS

Arabis is first of three rock garden plants in the Mustard family that we will discuss (aubretia and aurinia are the other two). Rock or wall cress is a creeping white or pink perennial that blooms in early spring, raising its half-inch single flowers in great drifts up to a foot above the low, glaucous gray-green foliage. Like most rock garden plants, arabis likes a very well drained spot and thrives in the sun here in the North; south of Virginia, it may suffer in the summer and should be planted as an overwintering annual and then removed. In northern areas, a shearing after bloom will rejuvenate individual plants and keep them better-looking through the summer. Seed germinates easily and does not need bottom heat. In the North, new growth stimulated by early summer shearing will be ideal for cuttings, which root easily. Cultivars such as Snow Cap and Rosabella, widely considered the best of the white and pink types, will need to be increased by cuttings to maintain their identity.

## ARMERIA

You can think of armeria, whose common name is thrift, or sea pink, as something in between chives and catananche. The globular pink flower heads are borne on long, brittle-looking stalks above a grassy tuft of narrow-leaved, green-to-gray-green foliage not more than a few inches tall. Over the years, breeders have produced strains with many different shades of pink in the flowers (as well as a white form), and plant height ranges from a mere six inches to over eighteen inches, making armeria useful for edging or the front border. The flowers are also useful for fresh and dried arrangements. For best results in bouquets, cut just after the flowers have opened, and stand the stems in water for several hours; for drying, hang the flowers in small bunches in a dark, airy location. Armeria germinates easily from seed at 70–75°F, and will bloom the same season it is sown; but to maintain named cultivars such as Alba (white, six inches tall), Ruby Glow (deep pink to red, ten inches tall), or Robusta (pink, twelve to sixteen inches tall), divide established plants. Thrift is also a good container plant.

## ARTEMISIA

This famous family contains not only a number of green- and gray-leaved plants whose foliage makes it widely useful in the ornamental garden, but also such relatives as the culinary herb French tarragon and wormwood, from the which the psychoactive liqueur absinthe was made until the first part of the twentieth century.

The same plant (*A. absinthium*) makes an excellent border plant, growing up to four feet tall in upward-arching branches covered with silver gray lacy foliage. Lambrook Silver, at two and a half feet, is considered the best cultivar generally available and can be increased easily by cuttings or division. It is worth cutting back in midseason just to keep the clump compact and tidy, and the fragrant branches dry well to make an excellent component for herbal wreaths. Similar in texture but much smaller is Silver Mound (*A. schmidtiana*), which grows into a neat, uniform mound eight to twelve inches tall and twelve to eighteen inches across. Silver Mound is ideal as an edging plant or used to separate areas of competing color in the front border. It, too, benefits from midseason shearing and will provide good material for dried arrangements. Division is more difficult with Silver Mound due to its smaller size, but cuttings root easily.

Two members of the species *A. ludoviciana* grow slightly larger than Lambrook Silver and have much simpler foliage, so they make a different kind of visual statement. These are the "royal" artemisias: Silver King, which has long narrow leaves with smooth margins, not at all lacy like the previous types; and Silver Queen, which has lightly serrated leaves but is otherwise similar. Both of these plants grow to about three feet in height. They share many of the same growth and flowering habits as the other artemisias, except that here in the North—and perhaps a good distance south, though none of these species relishes hot, humid conditions—the royal artemisias are rapid spreaders and need to be kept in check. Fortunately, their usefulness makes them worth having and not a chore to control.

## ARUNCUS

Goatsbeard is a large plant four to six feet tall suited to the same partly shady, moist woodland edge conditions as monkshood, hosta, and astilbe, which it faintly resembles—though its arching, feathery flower spires are more open and casual than astilbe, and goatsbeard is much larger overall. The leaves of goatsbeard are compound, in pairs or trios, and are broad and oval in shape with serrated edges. Of interest is the fact that goatsbeard is dioecious—meaning that male and female flowers are on separate plants—with the male flowers more upright and plumose, while the females arch gracefully, laden with seed. Given the right conditions, which rarely exist south of the Mason-Dixon line, goatsbeard will form large clumps, so it is best out of the main garden and in a transition area where it can establish itself and mount its dramatic display as spring turns to summer. For cut-flower use, cut morning or evening just as the flowers are beginning to open. Increase by division, but be prepared for a bit of work as the clumps can be tenacious.

## ASCLEPIAS

This close cousin of the common milkweed is not only a striking perennial that provides a wealth of excellent material for bouquets, but one of the most attractive plants to Monarch butterflies, hence its name, butterfly weed. It has a vigorous habit, which is also implied in its name, but as long as it is grown in a place where it can be allowed to spread—or where the flowers are removed promptly—it is not as invasive as its more common cousin. One of the endearing traits of asclepias is that it competes well with grass, and so can be grown on the wild edge of an open garden in relatively poor, sandy soils. The plants will not only thrive happily under such conditions, but form striking specimen plants. The stems are sturdy, green, and upright, even if a bit coarse; they are branchless, with tight-clasping leaves right up to the flower heads. The blooms are six to eight inches across and made up of domed two-inch clusters of tiny, half inch flowers, in bright and often contrasting reds, yellows, and oranges. Each plant may have half a dozen or more stems at any given time, and if cut they will be quickly replaced in a month's time, making butterfly weed one of the great cut-and-come-again bouquet flowers.

As this is a plant that self-sows freely, nature may be allowed to take her course and will provide a continuous supply of new plants. To start seed indoor, either sow as soon as the seed is harvested or, if the seed has been stored any appreciable time, moisten the seed and then refrigerate for four to six weeks before sowing. Choice plants can be increased by root cuttings or by careful division. It is necessary to be delicate, however, as asclepias does not like to be transplanted.

## ASTER

This is not the common garden aster of summer, but rather the thin-petaled, perennial aster. The annual or Chinese aster belongs to a different genus, *Callistephus,* and will be discussed under that listing. The most common kinds of true asters in this country come into their best after the first frosts knock down many of the less hardy garden plants, but there are some asters that bloom in midsummer and even spring.

The alpine aster, *A. alpinus,* is a diminutive plant only six to ten inches tall, best suited for rock gardens or well-drained raised beds in the North. The foliage is green to gray-green, and the one-to-two-inch daisy flowers are a purplish blue with yellow centers. The alpine aster is a relatively short-lived plant unless it is divided frequently. (Do the division immediately after flowering in late spring to early summer.) It also comes easily from seed.

Frikart's aster (*A. X frikartii*) is considered one of the best asters for hot, humid climates, and it serves as an example of the little-realized fact that heat hardiness in a plant is as important as cold hardiness. The two-to-three-foot-tall, mildew-resistant plants bear multitudes of two-inch light-blue-to-lavender flowers with yellow centers. Both of the preferred cultivars, Mönch and Wonder of Staffa, prefer a relatively infertile soil in full sun or they become too luxuriant and require staking. Pinch out the growing tips in early summer (before flower buds form) to further restrain the plants. Divide every few years when the center of the clump becomes open, and replant only those pieces from the vigorously growing edges, discarding the center. Both of these fine, summer-blooming asters make good cut flowers; they should be cut in the early morning just as the first few flowers of the chosen cluster have opened.

The two most common perennial asters in American gardens are native here, and have latinized names that pretty well spell out their heritage: the New England aster (*A. nova-angliae*) and the New York aster (*A. nova-belgii*—for New Belgium), which is also called the Michaelmas daisy in England where it blooms on Saint Michael's Day at the end of September. Both plants have been intensively bred, and there are hundreds of cultivars of each. Some differences: New England asters tend to have smaller, thinner, and more numerous ray flowers, and some cultivars have an annoying habit of closing their flowers at night or even on very dark days; the New York asters, however, are less resistant to mildew and wilt than the New England asters. Both tend to flop even more than Frikart's aster and should be grown lean and pinched early to keep them compact; they will require staking if you don't. Both the New England and New York asters will require division every few years to keep them attractive but, placed well and well cared for, they will provide not only a brilliant late-summer-to-fall show, but also immense numbers of stems for flower arrangements.

One last perennial aster that is not as well known as it should be is the white wood aster, *A. divaricatus*, a two-foot part-shade-loving plant with broad, serrated heart-shaped leaves and masses of tiny white flowers that cloud the plant from midsummer to fall. This aster, too, is an American native.

## ASTER, annual—*see* Callistephus

## ASTILBE

Astilbes are funny plants; they look delicate, yet are tough as nails. Given a moist, shady location with rich organic soil, they will thrive with little attention, and the soft, feathery plumes really brighten up dark corners of the garden. Most of the plants seen at nurseries these days are hybrids, a large portion of them (over seventy!) developed by the justly famous German nurseryman Georg Arends beginning just after the turn of the century and continuing into the 1950s.

The *arendsii* hybrids range from two to four feet tall and bear, given different cultivars, flowers ranging from white, pink, and salmon, to bright or glowing red blooms. Season of bloom ranges all the way from late spring to early fall, and even when not in bloom the compound, fernlike foliage is attractive in and of itself, especially on red cultivars, with its bronze tinge. While species astilbes can be raised from fresh seed, hybrid cultivars need to be increased by division. As astilbes are vigorous, hungry plants, it is a good idea to divide them every few years anyway, just to keep the colony looking good. Astilbes make excellent cut flowers and dried flowers if harvested when half the tiny flowers on the plume have opened.

A species astilbe that makes a good ground cover is *A. chinensis*, the Chinese astilbe, which grows a foot or two tall and has rosy pink flowers. A lot of variations on this plant are floating around in the nursery trade, so you should check out what you are getting. As a technical matter, the lowest kind, at eight to twelve inches is *A. chinensis Pumila*, and the really tall version, called *A. c. Taquetti*, is four feet or more tall, with huge, bright panicles of a hotter pink. In practice, though, the name and plant don't always match up. All three of the species astilbes are more tolerant of drought than the hybrids.

One last kind of astilbe is *A. simplicifolia*, the star astilbe. This dwarf type grows only about a foot and a half tall, but has gracefully arching branches of bloom that are much more open than the others. The pink form Sprite; introduced a number of years ago by the Bloom nursery in Britain, was chosen Plant of the Year for 1994 by the Perennial Plant Association in recognition of its usefulness in rock gardens, shade borders, and as a groundcover. It is hardy all the way from the Canadian border to the deep South.

## AUBRETIA

Aubretia is the second of the big three wall and rock garden plants—arabis, aubretia, and aurinia—and its common name is false rock cress (arabis being the real thing). It is similar in its needs and habitat to arabis and comparable in its appearance, though only half as tall at six inches, with smaller, quite crowded wedge-shaped leaves that have less gray than green. Aubretia has larger, lilac-to-reddish-purple flowers, whereas arabis flowers are, at most, pink (though more commonly white). Some hard-to-find cultivars of aubretia, like Aurea Variegata, have variegated foliage and it is possible to find blue-flowered cultivars—J. S. Baker and Royal Blue are two examples.

Aubretia demands a sunny, well-drained soil to succeed. It does not tolerate hot summers, so it does best in northern areas. South or North, its appearance and vitality will both be helped if the foliage is cut back by a third to a half after blooming. Aubretia comes easily from seed sown indoors in spring under the standard warm conditions, and named cultivars can be increased by division of cuttings (the late-spring shearing will provide plenty of material).

## AURINIA

This is the third of our big three rock garden plants. Until recently, this plant went under the Latin name *Alyssum*, and was thus sometimes confused with the fragrant annual edging and wall plant commonly known as sweet alyssum. Botanists broke up the family, and that annual species has now been changed to *Lobularia*, but has kept the common name alyssum. This hardy perennial, whose common name is basket of gold, has been rechristened *Aurinia*, which loosely translated means "golden plant." It is well named, as the tiny (one-eighth-inch) but brilliant flowers cover the foot-tall plants in spring. Like our other wall and rock garden plants, aurinia should be cut back after flowering by a third to a half to reinvigorate it. It is not well adapted to hot climates, but comes easily from seed with the standard warm treatment; it can be grown as a fall-planted, spring-blooming annual, the plants being discarded after blooming. Where it persists through the summer, it can also be increased by stem cuttings taken from the shearings, or by division in spring or fall.

## BAPTISIA

This hardy legume is commonly known as wild or false indigo because the flowers were once used to make a substitute for the dye indigo. It is native to the eastern United States and the most common, blue form is hardy throughout the Lower 48 and all but the coldest parts of Alaska where it may still survive due to the insulating effects of a heavy snow cover. This blue color of wild indigo—responsible for its name—makes it an especially valuable plant here in the North: it emerges from the cold spring garden more quickly than most plants and then just as quickly grows into a substantial, upright clump of attractive branches festooned with foot-long flowering stalks, ascendant with pale-to-deep-blue one-inch flowers. Following the flowers are large, pealike seed pods that will stay on the plants until fall frosts knock them down. If you wish to increase baptisia by seed, though, they should be removed as soon as the seed rattles within, and sown promptly. Otherwise, it will be necessary (as it is in spring, with purchased seed) to subject the seed to a three-to-four-week cold treatment before it will germinate satisfactorily. Once thus treated, though, it will sprout readily under the standard care. Baptisia can also be increased by division.

## BEGONIA

There are more than 1,000 species and 10,000 hybrids of begonia, a plant native to the Tropics and Subtropics worldwide. For our purposes, however, we can lessen confusion by considering them as divided into two broad groups: the smaller, bedding type, fibrous-rooted begonias, and the larger, tuberous-rooted types that are used primarily in pots, baskets, and planters. There is a third kind, the rex begonias, grown mostly for their large, variegated foliage, but we will not discuss those here.

The small kinds (six to twelve inches tall) that one sees today in broad, sunny beds in parks or edging the walk to a sunny front door are hybrids of a number of South American species, and as such are called *B. semperflorens-cultorum*, which means "everblooming cultivated," and the name is apt, for these are sturdy, long-blooming plants. The common name is wax begonia, in reference to the shiny leaves, which may be either green or a bronzy to almost chocolate color. The flowers are generally one to two inches across, with broadly splayed, rounded petals in a range of colors from white to red—salmon seems to be as close as they come to the yellow-orange range; tuberous types have no such inhibition, and also have bright yellow stamens.

Wax begonias are an excellent candidate for buying, already started, at a garden center. Why? Because, although they are easy to grow, they need to be started a full three months before the frost-free date, yet cannot be set out until that time. What this means, on a practical basis, is that begonias started at home will take up space for a really long time, yet the kinds you might start are pretty much the same you can buy. It has always been our approach to buy the common things and use what limited space we have for starting unusual and hard-to-find flowers.

Nonetheless, to grow your own seedlings, the process is straightforward. Begin twelve to fourteen weeks before the last frost and sow the seed on the surface of flats prepared with commercial potting mix or your own mix to which an extra complement of sand or vermiculite has been added for drainage. Use the pencil-and-tongue method described in Chapter 4, pressing down the surface of the mix after sowing to assure good contact between seed and soil. Then water the flats from below and cover with a humidity dome. At 70–

75°F the seed should germinate within ten to fourteen days. From that time they should receive the standard treatment for tender, warmth-loving annuals.

The most common cultivar of wax begonias seems to be the foolishly named Cocktail series, with each flower and leaf color combination named for a different drink, e.g., Whiskey, Bourbon, Vodka, and Gin. The plants, at least, are sensible; they are dwarf bloomers at six inches or so in height, used for bedding and edging in full sun (North) or part shade (South). For taller plants consider a series like Pizzazz, which is nearly twice the size.

Tuberous begonias are properly known as B. *tuberhybrida* and, as you might guess, are also hybrids. While they are generally larger plants than the wax begonias, they seem to be more frequently grown in containers, especially hanging baskets, and less often in the open garden. Since all begonias are very frost-sensitive, the only way we grow the tuberous kinds is in containers.

Tuberous begonias are spectacular bloomers, make no mistake, but to start from seed takes even longer than for the wax-leaved types, and a start in January will be necessary for first-year bloom here in the North. A better plan, if you can't bring yourself to buy blooming baskets of the cultivars you want for ten to fifteen dollars (and then keep them over the ensuing winters) is to buy tubers, which will bloom much sooner than seed. The cost difference between tubers and seed, two to three dollars for either a tuber or a packet of, say, fifty seeds, is not that great when you realize that you'd only keep a few plants grown from the seed anyway; you might just as well start off with one or two tubers of the kind of begonias you want.

Tubers should be pressed into the surface of the potting mix in a 3½-inch pot (or as we do, in 18-cell inserts) in February. If you have a spot for hanging baskets and want to start directly in them, put three tubers in a 10-inch basket, or five in a 12-inch basket. Conditions should be the same as for begonia seedlings, and despite the larger size of the plants grown from the tubers they should not be pinched or pruned. After all danger of frost, when nights are consistently in the 60s, the begonia plants can be set out in bright shade (that is, in areas with bright light, but not in direct sun). The soil should be quite rich, and while it should be kept moist (until time for the tubers to enter dormancy in fall), the foliage should stay dry: ground-planted begonias are excellent candidates for drip irrigation.

If you cannot move the containers to a frost-free place for the winter, dig up the tubers and store them until planting time the following spring. You can increase your supply of tubers in the spring by cutting the round tubers into pie-slice-shaped pieces, each of which has a growing point; dust the cut faces with powdered sulfur, and plant as if they were complete tubers.

There are an enormous number of cultivars, and looking for a good, full-color catalog or the actual plants at a garden center is the best way to decide which you think is best for your garden.

## BOLTONIA

A native American wildflower related to the perennial fall aster, *Boltonia asteroides* is a four-foot-tall, rapidly spreading plant that will form a veritable hedge of one-inch, thin-rayed, yellow-centered white daisies in late summer and early fall. An excellent companion to Russian sage or sedum Autumn Joy as well as willing cohort of the asters, boltonia is easy to propagate by the "shovel division" method. The premiere variety is called Snowbank; there is also a pink form called Pink Beauty.

## BROWALLIA

Browallias make nice edging plants or, here in the North, basket plants. The plants are mounding to draping, a foot to fifteen inches tall, with simple, almond-shaped mid-green leaves and two-inch-wide, five-petaled flowers arranged as a blunt blue or white star. Browallias are warm-weather annuals, and cannot be set outside until all danger of frost is past.

Start the seed six to eight weeks before the last frost: Just press the seed into the surface of the soil (it needs light to germinate), water from below, and cover with a humidity dome. At 70–75°F germination should take about ten to fourteen days. Once the seedlings have four to six leaves they can be put into their final containers, three seedlings to an 8-inch basket or pot, or five to a 10-inch. Browallia prefers partial shade and a rich, well-drained soil. As fall approaches, stem cuttings can be rooted to provide winter-flowering house plants. Hanging baskets can be sheared, checked for insects, then brought indoors to regrow and rebloom.

## CALENDULA

Calendulas are an ideal flower for us here in the mountains of Vermont, where the summers are cool. Only recently, though, have the varieties available become interesting enough for them to earn a significant place in our garden plans. The old Pacific Beauty strains that were the mainstay of the home-garden and bedding-plant trade until recently, while consistent, were about as exciting as a marigold. All that has changed now. As we get further into growing calendulas we are finding that the "new" varieties that have made such a change in our appreciation of this old-fashioned cottage garden plant have really been around quite some time, just not available to us.

Calendulas are very hardy, and easy to grow in the right season. Start in plugs eight weeks before the last spring frost, sowing the seed a quarter inch deep and holding in darkness at 70–75°F for a week to ten days. As soon as the plants have four true leaves and the danger of hard frost is past they can be hardened off and set out. Calendulas bloom about two months after seeding and will continue to bloom over a long period of time as long as the weather stays below the 90s and they are regularly deadheaded. For us that is virtually all summer! Warm-climate gardeners grow them in the fall for early-winter bloom or in pots. Garden spacing is one foot per plant for the larger forms; dwarf varieties should do fine with eight inches between plants, whether in the ground or a pot.

Some of the interesting new calendulas we have found over the past ten years are: the Prince series, bred for cutting, which includes a gold and an orange; and Indian Prince, which has a bold orange petal with darker, almost red behind, which gives the blooms depth. Indian Prince like the old Pacific Beauty and Art Shades strains, is tall, reaching two to three feet at maturity. Touch of Red is a group of even more striking varieties with the same motif but the plants are somewhat shorter at about eighteen inches; within the mix there is a buff-colored double flower with a rust red background that has a more open face than most modern calendulas, a vibrant yellow with just a touch of a clearer red, and a deep orange that thickens at the edges into a deep red-orange. All three have deep chocolate centers. Radio is one variety without this center: It is a long-standing favorite of knowledgeable gardeners, bright orange, full-double variety unique for its quilled petals, which make it resemble a dahlia. The plants themselves reach eighteen to twenty inches in height. Another unique strain is Kablouna, which has double scabiosa type flowers that are raised in the center with a background palette of flat, single petals. This crested form combined with the standard range of colors really makes these eighteen-inch plants stand out, and there is a bonus: Kablouna calendulas are the best-tasting of the calendulas—yes, use the petals to garnish salads or herb butters!

For pots, one of the best ways for southern gardeners to enjoy calendulas, try a dwarf strain like Fiesta Gitana, Bon Bon, or Dwarf Gem. If what you'd like is the old-fashioned single form, look for it in the herb section of your favorite catalog under the name Pot Mari-gold or Hen-and-Chickens; the botanic name should be *Calendula officinalis*.

## CALLISTEPHUS

*Callistephus chinensis* is the proper name botanists have decided on for the common annual or Chinese aster. This is a half-hardy plant, able to take light frost when young; it is grown for borders, cutting, and bedding as there is a wide range of plant sizes. There is also a wide range of flower types, from old-fashioned single daisy forms to globular dahlia-flowered forms and even some with long, thin, needlelike petals. Not all of these reflect what I would like to think is good taste, but they do add visual impact to your garden, wherever you come down on the aesthetic continuum.

Asters are easy to grow, though they are prone to a number of problems. One of the most important things to remember, especially if you are growing them for a bouquet garden, is that asters are not cut-and-come-again flowers—once cut, they do not rebloom. What this means practically is that for summer-long performance you will need to sow more than once.

Begin your first set of plants indoors six to eight weeks before the last frost and transplant about four to six weeks later, up to two weeks before the normal frost-free date. Sow the second set directly in the garden at the same time. We put our transplants for cutting a foot apart each direction, and direct-sow three rows of seeds to a thirty-inch-wide bed. In borders, use the arching-row method that is so effective at Kew Gardens: multiple rows are sown in a broad, curving arch relative to the viewing angle from the front of the bed

Annual asters grown for cutting will benefit from support. We use reinforcing wire tunnels because they are quite resistant to wind and the plants quickly hide them. (We have removed a few plants for this photo to better show the caging.)

so that, although the rows are a foot apart, from no single spot can the gap between the rows be seen. For edging and carpet beds, use dwarf varieties and set them only six to eight inches apart each way.

Asters respond to both pinching and disbudding: if you want lots of smaller flowers you will want to pinch; if you want just a few really large ones from each plant you will want to disbud. Pinched plants probably will not need staking, but disbudded ones (and taller varieties generally) likely will; we cage ours. Flowers should be harvested just as the outer petals begin to unfold; plunge them immediately into cool water.

Probably the biggest problem with growing asters is the disease aster yellows. This disease is spread by leafhoppers, one-eighth-inch green insects, which, if you can see them, are identified by the six black spots on their backs. These pests can be controlled somewhat with insecticidal soaps, but probably the best preventive measure to take if you have seen evidence of the hoppers in your garden in previous seasons (leaves are mottled with white and yellow spots and eventually wither and fall) is to cover aster beds with a floating row cover immediately after setting or sowing, and leave it in place until the plants are ready to be staked. This will keep out the leafhoppers until the plants are well established.

As mentioned above, asters come in all sizes. Within the different plant sizes, the flowers can be of many forms, as with chrysanthemums, and the colors cover the full range from blue and violet to yellow, red, salmon, pink, and white. Our favorites are the old-fashioned, single-daisy types with a row of ray petals and a simple central disk; a mix such as Marguerite or Giant Andrella comes in a wide range of contrasting colors and are quite pretty. There are also double forms of the daisy type, and a whole group so fully double they are called pom-poms, or tiger paw asters. Thinner-petaled types are called ostrich plume or quilled asters, and again there are many types, though our favorite is a new series from Germany called Florett. Finally there are dahlia-flowered kinds with tight, short petals that form globular blooms, often with contrasting centers. One series, Contraster, even has petals with contrasting edges, which give the blooms more of a pointillist look.

## CAMASSIA

I forget now how we first got a camassia, but over time it has become one of our favorite plants. It is a native American plant, and the bulbs were widely used by the Pacific Northwest aborigines as a staple food called quamash. Its natural habitat is open, moist meadows, which may be why it has done so well for us! The flowers, displayed on an airy spike three to four feet tall, have widely splayed, narrow petals but, because of their profusion, provide a brilliant overall effect. The color range from species to species (all are quite similar) is from clear sky blue to lavender and darker violet blues. There are white forms as well, and I have heard of pinks but never actually seen one. The common quamash (*C. quamash* or *C. esculenta*) is a smaller plant, with smaller flowers than the other two main species: *C. cusickii* and *C. leichtlinii*.

While camassia can be started from seed, it is usually planted as a bulb. Plant the bulbs three times as deep as they are round at the standard fall planting time in your area (here it is the first of October). You can lift the bulbs every few years and divide any bulbils or offsets that may have formed, and this will maintain the identity of particularly fine plants while allowing their increase. As this is an airy plant for a bulb, plant at least five bulbs at a time, spaced eight to twelve inches apart, preferably in an outer or semiwild border, as the foliage should be allowed to die down naturally. For bouquets, cut just as the flowers begin to open.

## CAMPANULA

This is a huge family of plants and includes annuals, biennials, and perennials ranging in size from six feet tall down to a tiny six inches. Truly fanatic collectors have amassed more than a hundred different types, but we can simplify a bit and will consider just a dozen of the group that will be most useful in American gardens. Another thing about campanulas, generically known as bellflowers, is that they have some of the most outrageously unpronounceable Latin names in existence. We will give those names because it may help in obtaining the precise plant you are after, assuming you take an average interest in the family, but we will use the common names wherever possible.

The main biennial species is *C. medium*, known to most gardeners as Canterbury bells. These are two-to-three-foot plants with the top foot or so supporting inch-wide, two-inch-deep flowers that do indeed resemble bells. The traditional schedule for growing them is the same as is used for such biennials as foxgloves and sweet williams, but all three of these plants now have cultivars specifically developed as annuals, and most of the biennial types can be tricked into acting like annuals if you sow the seed early enough and subject the plants to a properly timed cold treatment.

For plants grown as biennials, the seed is sown in mid- to late summer indoors, then the seedlings are set out in a nursery bed or other protected location to spend the winter. Then, soon after they break dormancy in spring the plants are moved to their blooming location. For plants grown as annuals, the seed is sown in late January to late February, and once the seedlings reach the five-to-eight-leaf stage they are put in a spot where they will be regularly exposed to temperatures that don't rise above 50°F for at least ten days. This "vernalization" will cause them to act as if they had gone through an entire winter, and they will bloom the same year sown. (As mentioned above, some of the newer cultivars will bloom the same year even without cold treatment.)

Because their period of bloom is only a few weeks, Canterbury bells are used mostly in perennial borders and cutting gardens rather than with annuals that have a long blooming season. Transplanted in mid-April at twelve to eighteen inches apart they will bloom in June (somewhat later for spring-sown plants) in a range of colors from white to pink to various shades of blue. Plants are usually removed after bloom, although they can be left to set seed in informal settings.

Culture of the perennial bellflowers will be easier to discuss if we break them into three groups: tall, midsize, and compact. *Campanula lactiflora* and *Campanula latifolia*, despite their similar names, are quite different plants, known by the common names milky bellflower and great bellflower. In both, the flowers are open, with the petals spread into a five-pointed star rather than being fully closed into a tubular bell like Canterbury bells; but the flowers on the great bellflower are larger than on the milky bellflower, a little more closed, and a darker, warmer, almost purple color. The great bellflower generally attains a larger size than the milky bellflower, though both can reach up to five feet in good conditions. Either species can be increased by seed or division, with named cultivars by division. In general the seeds should be sown where they are to grow as they resent transplanting, due to their taprooting habit. Both self-sow readily, and in areas north of the Mason-Dixon line they may spread rapidly unless deadheaded before setting seed. An even better plan is to cut the plant back to half its size or more immediately after flowering to stimulate a second flush of bloom six weeks or so later. In warmer areas, moist partial shade may be a necessity, but in cool summer areas like ours both milky and great bellflowers will do fine in full sun. If yours is a windy garden or you like a more proper appearance, the plants are likely to need support.

Slightly smaller than these statuesque plants—it grows from a foot and a half to three feet tall at most—is the only white-flowered species under consideration here, *C. alliariifolia*, or the spurred bellflower. The name refers to short appendages on the calyx, or flower base, and the plant is easily identified by its long, loosely arched branches with nodding, one-to-two-inch flowers at each axil. Because of its drooping habit, the spurred bellflower takes up more room than other bellflowers and should be planted eighteen to twenty-four inches apart. Because it self-sows freely, like the taller kinds mentioned above, cutting back after bloom will not only control its spread, but improve its appearance and provide, weather willing, a second blush of bloom six to eight weeks later.

The peachleaf bellflower, *C. persicifolia* (say that fast four times!) grows only one to three feet tall but is one of the best of the bunch for cut flowers. Flowering stems arise from a basal clump of four-to-eight-inch narrow leaves that bear no resemblance to peach leaves. The plants increase themselves through new shoots which arise around the periphery of the clump and also by self-sowing. Flowers are about an inch and a half long, equally wide across, and more open then tubular, very much a *bell* flower. Colors run from a purply blue through intervening shades to white. The blooms have a very long vase life if harvested when just the first few buds on the flower stalk have opened and the rest are swollen and colored but not open. Perhaps the most famous cultivar is Telham Beauty, which is three to four feet tall with pale, china-blue flowers.

The clustered bellflower, *C. glomerata*, is more appropriately named than the peachleaf bellflower; its dozen or so flowers per stem are arranged in a tight topknot a foot or two above the basal rosette of relatively broad though pointed hairy leaves. These, too, make excellent cut flowers and can last up to two weeks in the vase if cut at the proper stage (see above) and handled properly. The best cultivars are Superba and Superba Alba (a white).

Among the dwarf campanulas, those less than a foot tall, the largest and best known is *C. carpatica*, the Carpathian harebell, named for central Europe's Carpathian Mountains, which run south from Poland through the Czech Republic, Slovakia, and Hungary, into the northern part of Romania. Climatic conditions there are similar enough to the Appalachian Mountains of the eastern United States that many plants found there also find a hospitable home in America. The Carpathian harebells are mounding plants that reach at most a foot in height and a foot across. The flowers are borne just above the foliage and are about two inches across, blue or white, and upward facing, in the form of open bells. Harebells make excellent edging plants for borders and are good rock garden plants as well, happily increasing themselves in sites where sun and drainage are both abundant. While they like sun, they do not tolerate great heat, and so are primarily northern plants unless you can modify the microclimate of your garden to protect them from the hottest part of the summer. Increase is easy by seed or division.

*C. poscharskyana* is the Serbian bellflower, native to the former Yugoslavia on the Balkan Peninsula. It is not usually as tall as the harebells above, but it spreads more rapidly and is good as a groundcover plant or for rock walls where the eighteen-inch-long prostrate stems can drape over the front of the wall. The upright, lilac-blue flowers are only a half to one inch across, and are much more open than tubular, resulting in a star-shaped bloom. Preferred conditions for the Serbian bellflower are the same as for harebells, and they can be increased by seed or, preferably, by division.

The bluebells of Scotland, *C. rotundifolia*, are only six to twelve inches tall, but like the Serbian bellflower they can be used as a groundcover in sunny, cool spots, quickly spreading to cover significant areas with their basal rosettes of one-inch rounded leaves. The basal leaves often disappear by flowering time, though, and the upright stems that replace them bear masses of one-inch, blue or white nodding bellflowers. Increase by seed or division.

The spiral bellflower, *C. cochleariifolia,* also has nodding flowers, but they are more closed and tubular, maybe a half to three-quarters of an inch across and twice as deep. The color is sky blue with a bit of warmth thrown in, but not lilac or lavender; there is a white form, Alba, but it's hard to find. The plants themselves have spoon-shaped leaves, which at flowering time are virtually obscured by the bloom. The spiral bellflower is another rock garden plant, desirous of good drainage and, in the North, full sun. South of the Mason-Dixon line, afternoon shade will help prolong both the flowering and the overall health of the plants. Increase is by seed or division.

*C. garganica* is the Gargano bellflower, named for Mt. Garganica in Italy, where it was discovered. It grows to about six inches in height and has widely splayed, starlike flowers of blue or white. It spreads readily, even in areas that are warmer than most campanulas will tolerate, and will stand some shade, though its need for drainage is equal to its relatives. Increase by seed or by division.

*C. portenschlagiana*, the Dalmation bellflower, is a mat-forming plant with one-to-two-inch leaves and just above these, inch-wide, upright, bell-shaped blue or white flowers. It makes an excellent edging or wall plant and is also suited for container growing. While hardy through much of the North, the Dalmation bellflower is also much more tolerant of heat than other campanulas and thus is a good choice for southern gardeners. As with the other campanulas, good drainage should be your first concern for the Dalmation bell-flower's success. Increase is by seed or division.

## CATANANCHE

This hardy but unassuming perennial has the charming common name of cupid's dart. The botanic name, *C. caerulea,* tells us that the flowers on this are usually shades of blue, though there are white and bicolor forms as well. The foliage forms a gray-green mound a foot or so high; it is thin-leafed but a bit woolly in appearance, with two-inch daisylike flowers; both the foliage and flowers are reminiscent of bachelor's buttons. The flowers are rather brittle-looking: Ray petals with serrated tips and darker central disk flowers are held singly on wiry stems from two to three feet tall. The blooms are useful for both fresh and dried arrangements and should be cut morning or evening, just as they open.

Cupid's dart starts easily from seed, and if sown early will bloom the same season. Cover the seed lightly, moisten, and germinate at 70–75°F for seven to ten days. Spacing of the plants in the garden is eight to twelve inches between each plant. Particularly choice plants can be increased by root cuttings.

## CELOSIA

This relative of amaranth is widely grown, both for home bedding and for cut flowers. To be honest, though, I had never let celosia into my garden until two years ago when I had the opportunity to see a new form in Holland called wheat straw celosia. This, unlike the gaudy, unnatural-looking celosias more commonly offered, is a fine-looking, tough, easy-to-grow plant.

There are three kinds of celosia. The first, and most garish, is the *C. cristata* type. The large inflorescences (I can't bring myself to call them flowers) look like neon psychedelic brain corals, some of which can reach ten inches across, and they grow on coarse-looking plants two to three feet tall. The color range runs from gross to disgusting, and the only purpose I can imagine using them for is perhaps as a bedding plant at a *Ripley's Believe It or Not* theme park. The second kind, called *C. cristata plumosa,* shares the same awful color range but at least has a more palatable form: the flowers are amaranthlike plumes that can be used fresh or dried for bouquets. Unfortunately, this doesn't help much; they look like the kind of dyed Pampas grass

Quite different from the other Celosia species, *C. spicata* is as attractive in the garden as it is in fresh or dried bouquets.

plumes one can buy at a cheap souvenir shop rather than something you grew yourself.

The third kind, and the only kind I would have in my garden, is *Celosia spicata*. This is an altogether more refined plant, and makes a great show in borders and bouquets. Like its relatives, it also dries well. The plants are three to three and a half feet tall and bear literally dozens of stems, each topped with a pale, silvery pink spike two to three inches long, hence its name Flamingo Feather.

All the celosias should be started indoors four to six weeks before the frost-free date and set out only after all danger of frost has passed. Set the plants of all three types twelve inches apart in each direction in the garden and keep them cut if you'd like the display to last. Wait until the flowers are fully developed before cutting for bouquets or drying, though with Flamingo Feather a slightly earlier cut can help keep the spikes from shattering when they dry.

## CENTAUREA

There are both annual and perennial members of this long-cultivated family of flowers. Perhaps the most widely known of the annual centaurea is *C. cyanus,* the bachelor's button or cornflower. So entrenched is it within human culture that it has its own color, cornflower blue. The flower itself is easy to grow, was bred from the wild and common weed of European cornfields (hence the name), and after its introduction to American gardens has returned to its heritage as a wildflower. Cornflowers now grow along roadsides and in untended fields where pesticide pressure hasn't yet eradicated it along with other traditional—but to production-minded farmers, inconvenient—field weeds like corn poppies, corn marigolds, and wild morning glories (*Convolvulus*), all of which got their common names in the same fashion as cornflowers. Cornflower plants grow to about two feet unless bred to be dwarf, and are slim, svelte, and musty gray-green, with a wispiness that belies their tenacious heritage and their strength in bouquets once cut—for they are excellent cut flowers despite their wild ways and the relatively small size of the flowers, only one to two inches across. The color range of these gems now extends beyond blue to a range of reds, pinks, and whites.

The sweet sultan (*C. moschata*), as might be guessed from its name, is originally from the Far East and, unlike its relatives, is fragrant. The plants themselves are not much larger than *C. cyanus,* but have a more thistlelike appearance, with serrated leaves and a bristly, but soft-looking bloom. The flowers are likely to be a pink or red shade, or even yellow, but not blue, though lilac and lavender do occur.

While the cornflower is native to Europe and the sweet sultan to the Orient, their relative the American basket flower (*C. americana*) is native to this continent and in stature towers over both its Atlantic and Pacific cousins with stems that can reach six feet (though in cultivated kinds four feet is more common). The flowers, too, are larger, up to four inches across, with casual, widely splayed rays surrounding a tight, upright disk. The name basket flower comes from the sepals (flower base), which is made up of a strawlike cup that looks for all the world as if plaited into a basket from which the flower emerges.

All three of these species can be sown directly in the garden at any time during the spring or fall, though it is unlikely the seeds will sprout until soil temperatures are in the 60s. Here in Vermont that will be late May, and the plants will generally bloom by mid- to late July, about a month later than in the Mid-Atlantic and South. Frost-free climates can expect spring bloom by March. Succession sowings and regular deadheading will yield blooming plants throughout the growing season. Garden spacing should be six to nine inches apart for *C. cyanus* and *C. moschata*, while the larger basket flower will do better if given a foot per plant.

Extra early blooms can be had by beginning seeds indoors. Sow seed for all three centaureas a quarter inch deep six to eight weeks before the frost-free date; water well from beneath, and germinate a bit cooler than most other flowers, at 60–65°F. We sow the seeds in a flat with other cool-germination seeds like annual chrysanthemums and stack the flat on top of a flat that is getting the normal 70–75°F treatment. The space between the flats diffuses the heat just the right amount to give the seeds the correct temperature. Once the seedlings are up, keep them spaced far enough apart that the leaves of adjacent plants just touch. Young plants can be set out in the garden anytime after they have four to six leaves, as long as the danger of hard frost is past. For the seedlings spacing in the garden is the same as for direct-sown plants.

Aphids and leafhoppers are the most likely pests to bother your centaureas, though we have never had a serious problem with either one. Leafhoppers may spread aster yellows to the plants if that disease is present in your neighborhood. If you see the symptoms— yellowing plants and flowers that take on something of a green tinge—pull the affected plants and burn them and don't plant centaureas in that area for at least four years. Mildew and stem rot are more likely problems, especially here in the Vermont mountains during a cold, wet summer. Wider spacing among plants, which improves air circulation and drying of the foliage, plus good drainage will make a huge difference in preventing these diseases. If your garden is in a cold, wet spot, choose the sunniest, breeziest spot you've got or consider building raised beds when you prepare the soil each spring (if possible, run them generally east to west; this will maximize the heating of the beds by the sun and get the plants up above the sogginess).

If you are growing centaureas as a border plant, just keep them deadheaded; for bouquets, cut the flowers when they are half open and they will last a week to ten days if plunged immediately in water after cutting. They can be dried fairly easily; tie in small, loose bunches and hang upside down in a warm, dry, dark area. It is not necessary to remove the foliage before drying.

Among the varieties of cornflowers available, my favorite is the Frosted Queen series: traditional colors—blue, pink, and both deep and rich reds—all with a contrasting highlight at the petal end. The Ball series has solid colors on standard size thirty-inch plants while Jubilee Gem is a dwarf strain especially for bedding; slightly larger is Polka Dot, at eighteen inches a good compromise variety with a wide color range. For large flowers, choose Blue Diadem, a striking, classic cornflower blue variety whose blossoms can reach two and a half inches across on thirty-inch plants. Another single color I particularly like is a deep burgundy red that goes under the name of Garnet; similar is Black Ball or Black Boy. Both are exceptional planted with white snapdragons.

The commonly available mixes of *C. moschata* are usually just called sweet sultan or *C. imperialis* (sometimes incorrectly listed as a separate species); single-color strains are available in white and a rich butter yellow. The Bride has thistlelike globular white flowers with a sweet, strong fragrance borne on plants up to two feet tall; while Dairy Maid has rich golden blooms with a raised disk of silky petals surrounded by a fan of open, tubular ray flowers with serrated tips—quite unusual, and fragrant, too. Dairy Maid is sometimes sold as a subspecies called *C. moschata ssp. sauveolens*.

Basket flowers, our only native among the common garden centaureas, are not easy to find. Look for them under the botanic name *Centaurea americana* in specialty catalogs that deal in heirloom flowers, like Select Seeds in Union, Connecticut.

There are three major perennial species of centaurea: *C. montana*, called the mountain bluet; *C. macrocephala*, the Armenian basket flower; and *C. dealbata*, the Persian cornflower. All three are relatively informal plants but beyond that they have a multitude of differences that bear mention.

The mountain bluet is a carefree plant that thrives in full sun on well-drained soils. The gray-cast leaves are deeply lobed and spring early from the soil, followed by loping stems on which are borne small, tight buds whose overlapping gray-green bracts are lined in black. These bracts open to release three-inch, open tubular blue ray flowers with no disk. While there are never many flowers open at one time and their season is short, their profound laxity is endearing; if shorn right after blooming, the plants regrow, and the handsome young shoots provide a good cover around neighboring plants for another month.

The Armenian basket flower, *C. macrocephala*, is well named, both in Latin and vernacular terms. It is indeed a big-headed flower (*cephala* means head), with coarser foliage than the bluet, and a huge, two-inch-diameter bud whose stiffly upright habit and rough-hewn, overlapping bracts make it look very much like a woven basket. Come July (in our garden) the basket opens to reveal a broad, and somewhat fuzzy-looking, massively double yellow flower. At three to four feet, this is not a delicate plant, but it is a striking one and a valuable cut flower.

The Persian cornflower (*C. dealbata*) is midway between the mountain bluet and the Armenian basket flower in habit and foliage, with numerous but small puffy pink to purplish flowers and lobed leaves. A related and often confused species, *C. hypoleuca*, is quite similar, and it is the current home of a valuable cutting and bedding cultivar, John Coutts, which should be sought by name.

All three of these perennial centaureas should be propagated by division every few years, though all will come from fresh sown seed as well.

## CENTRANTHUS

*Centranthus ruber* is known as red valerian or Jupiter's beard, but the foot-and-a-half-to-three-foot, fragrant-flowered plants may also appear in white, as in the variety Albus, or rose, as in Roseus. Individual flowers are only a half inch long, but they are held in striking bunches at the end of each branch, with the overall effect being of large blooms. Centranthus is a naturally hardy perennial that will do well over most of the United States, and is adapted to well-drained stony-to-gravely soils with a high lime balance. It is used primarily as a larger rock garden plant and for cutting, as the blooms are long-lasting in the vase. Centranthus will self-sow, but to preserve the characteristics of choice plants you will need to increase them by division.

## CERASTIUM

There are something like a hundred species of cerastium, but the one we are interested in is the rock garden plant known as "snow in summer." While snow in summer does not do well in southern areas—the heat and humidity cause the center to die out, and the plants look too scraggly to be presentable—it is one of the most valuable plants here in the North for growing in rock walls or between the stones of terraces and paths. While its height is rarely more than six inches, cerastium will quickly cover significant areas with creeping stems clothed in tiny silvery-white leaves that in late spring are crowned by brilliant white half-inch flowers with just a touch of color in the throat. The best variety is one called Yo-yo, a funny name for a very useful plant. Yo-yo prefers a very well drained soil in full sun. If you start cerastium from seed, sow the seeds on the surface of the potting soil and germinate at the standard 70–75°F, then grow cool—in the 50s. Established plants may be divided at any time. Good companions include the creeping forms of veronica and campanula; plants with similar needs or that can be used in similar situations are *Gypsophila repens*, arabis, aubretia, *Thymus spp.*, and creeping phlox.

## CHRYSANTHEMUM

Like campanulas and centaureas, this is a family that includes both annual and perennial flowers that are nearly indispensable in the garden. Annual chrysanthemums are underappreciated plants in America, though, and most gardeners seem only to know of the perennial hybrid types used as fall bedding plants (*C. X morifolium*), commonly known as mums, or the border perennials called Shasta daisies. But the herb tansy (*C. tanacetum*) as well as the pink painted daisy (*C. coccineum*) and *C. cineariifolium*, the Dalmatian insect flower—the source of the natural insecticide pyrethrum, one of the organic flower gardener's strongest poisons—are all chrysanthemums. These (and more) will be dealt with below, under perennial chrysanthemums.

We discussed one of the annual chrysanthemums in *Step by Step Organic Vegetable Gardening*, *C. coronarium*, the edible chrysanthemum of Oriental cooking known as Shungiku. This species also has ornamental forms, which have been selected for the flowers instead of the foliage. There are other annual species: *C. carinatum*, which is probably the most common of the annual mums grown in America; and *C. segetum*, a species which contains many of my personal favorites. Other annual chrysanthemums are: *C. multicaule, C paludosum*, and *C. tenuiloba*, each of which is different in habit and flower, though they all share the daisy form flower and a color range clearly within the yellows and browns (*C. carinatum* also often contains some red).

Although there is a fairly wide range of seed sizes among these different species of annual mums, home gardeners can treat them all pretty much the same. All can be direct-sown or started ahead, though here in the Vermont mountains, direct outdoor plantings on the frost-free date will not flower until late August—just before frost. Like centaureas, they germinate best at 60–65°F, so wait until only two to four weeks before last frost if direct seeding, or begin six or eight weeks before the last frost if seeding in flats. Germination is in about two weeks; blooming is in just over three months. Whichever way you start, protect young plants from hard frost (below 25°F), and plant them eight to twelve inches apart in the garden, depending on the size of the species.

Among the different chrysanthemums, there are some that are compact and uniform enough for bedding and edging, and there are taller species that are suited for informal borders and cutting. Generally, the small types are maintenance-free, but the taller ones, having relatively brittle stems, need support either in the form of surrounding plants, brush, wire, or stakes and string. Most of the taller types will make large shrublike specimen plants if you give them lots of room in the garden, though in that case some sort of support will be essential.

The most commonly available of the annual mums is *C. carinatum*, and most catalogs that list it simply sell a mix called Single Mix, *carinatum dunnetti* (with more doubles), or Court Jesters, which is generally considered the best. The plants have very thin, wispy leaves though they are obviously chrysanthemums—both by appearance and odor—and grow to about two feet in the moist but well-drained acid soils that they prefer. The flowers are a gaudy combination of multicolored daisies with concentric rings of red, yellow, gold, pink, and white surrounding tan to chocolate centers. There are, however, single colors and combinations available if you look a little harder. My favorite is Polar Star which has a deep chocolate center ringed in rich, buttery yellow with the outer inch or so of the petals a clean crisp white. The effect is stunning. In our garden, this nominally two-foot-tall plant often grows a foot taller. A rich, solid yellow is also available, though it is fully double, which makes the flowers a bit too much like your average marigold for my taste.

As I mentioned earlier, *C. coronarium*, the edible chrysanthemum, has some great-looking cultivars as well. My favorite here is Primrose Gem. The plants aren't nearly as large as those of *C. carinatum*, and the foliage is more traditionally mumlike: deep green and lobed. The pale flowers, up to two inches across, are only semidouble, so the butter yellow disk is visible. It is the contrast of disk and ray flowers that makes this plant such a knockout; pale yellow is one of the most attractive flower colors going, and the subtle deepening of color in the center of each bloom only enhances this effect. Golden Gem is also available, but the color contrast is lacking, and so is my interest in it, beyond its use as a solid bloom performer.

The third species that grows tall enough for borders and bouquets is *C. segetum.* My favorite here is one called Eastern Star or Prado. The form is similar to Polar Star, but the plants are a bit shorter, and the flowers are yellow with a chocolate center. Eldorado has a black center, if you'd prefer that combination.

Two good annual mums for the front of the border or for edging and containers are *C. multicaule* and *C. paludosum.* Both are standard daisy-flowered plants that are all yellow or white with yellow centers. They grow eight to twelve inches tall and are long-blooming, trouble-free plants.

The best-known of the perennial chrysanthemums are, of course, the showy mums that are inescapable each year as the days begin to shorten in fall and trigger their bright blooms to splay in incredible profusion above the fragrant-leaved plants. This plant, known properly as *Chrysanthemum X morifolium,* was first brought under cultivation over 2,000 years ago in China, and today the diversity of flower and plant types is, as you might expect, enormous. For our purposes, however, there are three main types: the standard outdoor garden mum; the super-hardy Korean hybrids; and the tender florist's pot mums.

Garden mums come in a wide variety of forms, both in plant and flower habit. Basically, there are dwarf mounding types up to a foot and a half tall, and taller (two to three feet) kinds with more of a vase-type shape. The flower types of garden mums include buttons, which are small, globular double types; daisies with a single row of ray flowers around a contrasting central disk; large dahlia-flowered kinds; and then a catch-all category called decoratives, which includes those with quilled petals, tubular petals, and other outrageous forms. The colors range across the full spectrum with the exception of green and blue.

Care for all the types of mums is essentially the same. Virtually all garden mums are propagated by cuttings or division. Fall divisions can produce material for spring cuttings, but it is better to take cuttings from the new growth on established plants. Take the cuttings in mid- to late spring when the growing tips reach four to six inches, and plant them in 3½-inch pots or 18-cell plug inserts. Once rooted, cuttings can be set out directly in the garden and treated the same as small divisions. Once the plants are growing vigorously, pinch out all the growing points to force bushy growth and more flowering stems. Pinching is usually done twice, once

Take cuttings from fall mums in midspring, root in pots, and then transplant to the garden eighteen inches apart. Once the plants are established, pinch out all growing points two times, a month apart, to produce bushy plants with multiple blooming stems. Fall mums may not bloom properly if illuminated by street lights at night, as their blooming is triggered by long nights.

around Memorial Day, and again just before Fourth of July. The plants are then left to grow.

Mums are hungry plants and want a well-drained rich soil in full sun. Avoid over-fertilizing, though, or they will be more susceptible to insect, disease, and wind damage due to overly lush growth. The major problems that affect mums are aphids, miners, and mites. Aphids and mites can be controlled with insecticidal soap sprays, while miner-infested leaves should be removed and burned. Mums that fail to bloom are not necessarily sick; they may not be receiving the proper light regimen. Since they set flowering buds in response to the longer nights of late summer and early fall, lights that come on in the night, such as security lights or street lights, can upset their internal clock and prevent flowering. Night lights will not bother purchased plants that have already set buds, but they can affect plants you grow yourself. If this is a problem, setting a basket over the affected plants may help—but watch out for rot caused by insufficient air circulation.

The Korean hybrid chrysanthemums developed by Bristol Nurseries in Connecticut during the mid-part of this century are much hardier than standard kinds and should be sought out by gardeners in Zone 4 or colder, where many of the kinds seen in warmer climates will not survive the winter. If you are in a cold area, you can make a difference by keeping your stock plants—those you will use for cuttings in spring to maintain your collection—next to a wall where the drainage is likely to be good: The plants will collect snow by the wall, and they will be protected from harsh winter winds. Even better, move one or two of each kind of mum to a cold frame for the winter.

Only one comment is necessary about the florist's mum: If you want to keep the plant you received as a gift, do so, but only as a greenhouse plant—it isn't likely to flower well outside. Over the years, commercial growers have selected the kinds of mums that take ten to twelve weeks of short days and long nights to start blooming for the florist trade so that they have as much flexibility as possible in timing the plants' bloom. These kinds of mums won't bloom outside until so late in the fall that the flowers are quite likely to be harmed by frost.

*Chrysanthemum X rubellum,* the so-called red chrysanthemum, seems not to be well known outside northern areas, though it is reputed to survive the hot, humid summers of the South well. Gardeners at the northern fringe of where fall mums will survive have long seen it even if they haven't known its identity; once the frost hammer comes down it is one of the few garden flowers that still looks good. While not quite as spectacular as its better-known cousins, varieties like Clara Curtis still provide a good show of two-to-three-inch, single pink daisies with yellow centers on plants that under good conditions will reach three feet in height. It blooms slightly before fall mums, and the fragrant flowers are good for bouquets. Culture is the same.

The classic perennial border daisy is more properly called the Shasta daisy, *C. X superbum,* and was developed by the famous California plantsman Luther Burbank at the end of the last century. Despite its Mediterranean background, the Shasta daisy is a very hardy plant and has never had winterkill in our gardens, despite our regular −30°F winter temperatures. Cultivars range from the foot-high dwarfs like Little Miss Muffett, with masses of two-inch flowers, to large three-foot plants like Polaris and Starburst that are capped with spectacular six- and seven-inch-diameter daisies. Silver Princess, like Miss Muffett, is a compact Shasta that is not only sufficiently uniform to use for edging and bedding, but is easily grown from seed and blooms only three months after sowing. Other Shasta daisies, both tall and small, come in double forms as well, some with yellow on the ray petals as well as the central disk. Some of these special cultivars come true from seed, but they should still be propagated by division and will benefit from lifting every three years or so, even if you just give away the divisions.

Less carefree in our gardens but still worth having for its colorful pink and red blooms, which make excellent cut flowers—and are a source of the botanic insecticide pyrethrum—is the painted daisy, *Chrysanthemum coccineum*. The painted daisy is a much different plant in appearance from those we have discussed thus far, bearing its bright blooms on wiry stems above finely divided, feathery leaves. If cut back immediately after flowering, painted daisies will rebloom. While easily as hardy as the Shastas, the painted daisy is more likely to need support and requires more frequent division to maintain its vigor. It does not do well south of Virginia. It comes easily from seed sown indoors at 70–75°F.

The fragrant and hardy—but hardly showy—herb feverfew (*Chrysanthemum parthenium*) has been widely and successfully bred into a spectacular border and cutting flower without losing either its charm or its vigor. The foliage is deeply divided like the painted daisy, but the blooms, primarily in white, with some creamy yellow, are more like the smaller, button-flowered mums. At first this was a small plant, but breeders have produced some varieties that stand two or three feet tall, with long stems perfect for cutting. While technically perennial, this fine plant (also known as *Matricaria capensis,* and I am not going to get in a fight with the botanists over which name is correct, but rather state the names under which a gardener may find it listed) comes easily from seed sown indoors in early spring at 70–75°F, and so can be grown as an annual north or south of the midlatitude climate it is best adapted to. If not deadheaded, feverfew will self-sow.

## CIMICIFUGA

This is a tall, stately perennial for the woodland edge or the back of a shady border. Massed in the distance, or placed in a clump of three to five plants to form the visual end of a garden backed up against overarching trees, the tall, sentrylike presence of this native American (also known as fairy candles, snakeroot, and bugbane), adds a feeling of watchful security. Cimicifuga prefers a rich, moist soil in partial shade. The early-blooming varieties have a noticeable and not overly pleasant odor, so background placement is best—this is not a problem as the scale of the plants lends itself to viewing from a distance.

The primary species used is *C. racemosa,* which grows six to eight feet tall, of which the top two feet are creamy white spikes comprised of a multitude of tiny flowers. Two smaller, closely related species, *C. simplex* and *C. japonica* have received more attention from nurserymen, and thus there are fine cultivars available, some of which are Acerina, Elstead, and White Pearl which has bright white flowers. All grow about three to four feet tall.

Cimicifuga will come from seed, but unless sown immediately after ripening in a spot where it can spend the winter it will likely need a cold treatment before sowing at 70–75°F. A better way to increase your plants is by division in spring or fall, though you should wait until the plants are well established, and even then proceed gently.

## CLEOME

This wild and woolly annual, like cosmos and lavatera, becomes a large shrub by summer's end and along the way provides a wonderfully loose and colorful backdrop for smaller statured plants in an informal border. Its common name is spider flower, earned by the way that the widely splayed flowers at the tip of the blooming stalk are followed as they climb by thin seed pods held horizontal around the axis of the terminal shoot. By the end of the season this main stalk of seed pods may extend a couple of feet, with the blooming ring as a crown. Beneath the pods are rough compound leaves in the form of a star, three to five inches from tip to tip. Cleome is a coarse plant, but its ability to fill in a bed makes it quite useful.

The best cleomes I know are in the Queen series: white, pink, red, purple, and lilac. Start the seed a month before the last frost, and set out the plants after the last frost. Give each plant a foot square minimum in the garden, where they like a dry soil in full sun.

## CONSOLIDA

Larkspurs were long called annual delphiniums, and indeed larkspurs and perennial delphiniums are closely related, but botanists recently gave the hardy annuals their own genus. Traditionally both the annuals and the perennials were called larkspurs because the flowers have a spur, or tail, that swoops gracefully back from the main blossom, giving individual blooms the appearance of the swooping or diving lark. The spur is most apparent on the bush flowering forms, rather than on the spectacular but more common columnar types, which have the tall, tightly packed flower heads so treasured by flower arrangers.

Annual larkspurs can be grown anywhere in the United States, but for good results two key points must be remembered: First, the seed germinates best in relatively cool soil (below 55°F); and second, the seedlings require a cold period when young to produce strong plants with abundant bloom. This is no problem here in Vermont if the seed is direct-sown in early spring, as soon as the ground can be worked. In areas south of USDA Zone 5, though—which means south of a line that runs from Boston to Pittsburgh, Kansas City, and Santa Fe, and then up the inside of the Pacific Crest—a fall sowing is best. The proper time for sowing ranges from early September in New York to mid-November in Arizona and California. Basically, the young seedlings need a month and half of temperatures in the fifties after sprouting to grow at their best.

You can start larkspurs indoors four to six weeks before setting out time—soon after the garden is ready to plant because they need that cool spring weather—but chill the seed in the refrigerator for a week before sowing. Sow in peat pots or, better, 50-cell plug inserts and do not put the seeded flat on the heating mat. We simply water the flat and put it on the floor of the potting area where it will stay cool until the seeds sprout and then move it to a far corner of the greenhouse where it will stay relatively cool, as the seedlings need to stay below 60°F, just as they would if planted directly outdoors.

Once outdoors, plant spacing can be as close as six to eight inches in dry areas with well-drained soils, but in a humid climate like ours a foot apiece is better to avoid leaf spots, root rots, and mildew, all of which are made worse by close spacing. If any of these diseases show up (a description of the symptoms is in the cosmos entry) remove and burn the plants to halt its spread, then be sure not to replant susceptible plants in that spot for a season or two. If you are growing larkspur in its own bed for bouquets, it will require support. The same kind of string and stake arrangement that works for other cut flowers will work for the columnar types; the simpler wire quonset will suffice for the bushy *regalis*-type larkspurs. For maximum life in the vase, cut the blooming stems when a third of the flowers have opened; for drying, a bit more finesse is required because the last flowers on the stem should be open, but the first not yet fading. Larkspurs can be air-dried if you have a month of temperatures in the seventies or above left in the season. Hang the stems in a dark, airy place in small, loose bunches.

The standard larkspur among commercial growers is Giant Imperial, but we have found that the more compact King Size series is more wind-resistant and so are less likely to need staking. Other types available include the Messenger series, which at three feet is taller than either, and tallest of all, a hyacinth-flowered mix, which can reach four feet. There is also a dwarf form of this type that grows barely two feet tall.

Our favorite larkspur, though, is a *Consolida regalis* variety called Blue Cloud, which is radically different from all the others. Instead of tall columnar flowers, it produces a billowy, baby's breath type of plant covered with small pale blue flowers. Its airiness and charming blooms make it a fantastic plant either for cottage garden borders, where it will interweave with other plants, or for bouquets, where it makes a great filler plant to give body to your arrangements.

## CONVALLARIA

Lily of the valley—what a joy to have a plant that spreads so freely and brings such sweet fragrance and visual delight! This is a woodland groundcover that will grow happily unattended for as long as you leave it, blooming each spring just as the wild, roadside apples show their best blooms and the last of the spring bulbs are passing. Native—or at least prehistoric—in most of the Northern Hemisphere, lily of the valley is a small plant, only six to twelve inches tall, with simple, broad, bladelike leaves that embrace branched stalks of the same height from which dangle fragrant, quarter-inch white bells. There are, however, some pink and double forms in cultivation. Propagation is by "pips," small rhizomes that can be lifted and separated anytime here in the cool parts of the North; it's best to restrict division to spring and fall in warmer climes.

## COREOPSIS

Bred from a native American wildflower, most perennial garden coreopsis are very hardy, and some forms are downright aggressive, spreading quickly via underground stems (though it is hard to mind, given their contribution to the summer garden). These are plants for a sunny, well-drained spot, and they will bloom for literally the entire summer if kept clean of spent flowers.

Two of the most widely grown, *C. grandiflora* and *C. lanceolata*, are somewhat similar plants one to two feet tall, though the former is more of a clumping plant than its brethren, with leaves that are deeply notched. Both plants should be diligently deadheaded to keep them blooming, and both have a decent variety of forms, both single and double, with plant habits from compact to gangly. The flowers are almost always yellow, though there is a cultivar of *C. lanceolata* called Brown Eyes that has a concentric brown ring around the disk which is reminiscent of the annual species. Briefly, the best edging variety is Early Sunrise, which in 1989 won an All America Award, while the premiere cutting variety is one called Mayfield Giant—the tallest we have grown—though the two-foot cultivars Sunray and Sunburst can also be used for bouquets.

Threadleaf coreopsis (*C. verticillata*) differs from these two species, in that the foliage (as you might guess from the name) is very finely divided, like cosmos, and in that it spreads rapidly by underground stems to form thick clumps, especially in the slightly moister soils that it prefers. Nonetheless, it is a wonderful-looking plant and we'd never be without it. The major cultivars are Golden Showers, which grows to two or even three feet and bears bright yellow flowers more than two inches across; Moonbeam, which is similar in stature, but with smaller, more muted yellow flowers that combine well with many others; and Zagreb, a dwarf form that reaches only a foot and has deep yellow blooms. There is a form called *rosea*, which has pink, inch-wide, starlike flowers and brighter, slightly wider leaves. It grows eighteen to twenty-four inches tall and just as wide. There is said to be a white form as well but I have not seen it.

All the species of perennial coreopsis come easily from seed and most will bloom the first season if started indoors, at 70–75°F about ten to twelve weeks before the last frost. Plants can be set out as soon as the danger of hard frost has passed. Particularly fine specimens, however, should be increased by division spring or fall (here in Vermont, we can divide most at most any time).

Annual coreopsis (*C. tinctora*) is a carefree and casual plant barely in from the wild, and suited to use in an informal border. Direct seed outdoors in midspring, sowing the seed sparsely, a quarter inch deep, in arching or meandering rows eight inches apart. There is no need to thin and, in fact, the plants prefer a bit of crowding as it spurs them to greater flowering. The inch to inch and a half mostly yellow daisies top two to three foot plants and have purple centers with variable brown or purple bands around them; sometimes the petals are puckered or ruffled. The long, wiry stems make annual golden coreopsis a cheery cutflower. The seed is sometimes sold as *Calliopsis*, its previously assigned name.

### COSMOS

There are two kinds of cosmos, and both are mainstays in our garden. Bedding types are well-mannered, uniform plants that stay put, while the taller kinds virtually epitomize the casual, cottage garden feeling that many gardeners seek out. Our classifications are different from the botanists', which divides the genus into two major species, *C. bipannatus*, and *C. sulphureus* (see below).

Both the bedding and tall cosmos types are tender annuals that grow easily from seed and will thrive in any average, well-drained soil. In fact, the larger garden cosmos should not be fertilized beyond the general requirements of the overall garden as overabundant nitrogen makes them grow too tall and increases their need for support. Full sun, dry soil, and lean nutrition grows the best plants and will help avoid disease. Good air circulation will also help, but avoid windy sites if possible.

In all but the coldest climates, cosmos can be direct-sown on the frost-free date for bloom two months later. While the plants will bloom until frost, deadheading or harvest of the flowers for bouquets will increase the density and length of bloom. If you will be growing cosmos strictly for cutting, plant a new crop every two weeks, as blooms from succession-sown plants are usually superior to those from cut-over plants.

Final spacing of the plants in the garden should be eight to twelve inches apart for dwarf cosmos, and twelve to as much as twenty-four inches for the larger cutting types. In our cut flower beds we plant two rows evenly spaced in a thirty-inch-wide bed, then after the plants are well up, we run string on stakes around the bed to keep the plants within bounds. In the informal border, clear an area three to four feet across and sow the seed in a series of arcs a foot apart, with the smaller types in the front and the larger in the back. By using arched rows you prevent viewers from sighting along any of the rows (which would destroy the informality of the design), and care is easier than if the seed had simply been broadcast.

Cosmos can be started in plugs four to six weeks before the outdoor planting date. Because the plants are fast growing, use a 50-cell plug insert. If space is at a premium, the seed can be germinated in 20-row trays, or in a pinch in an 18-cell plug insert or 3½-inch pot, and then potted up once they have their first true leaves. Cover the seed lightly, water the container from the bottom until the mix is thoroughly wetted, then place on a heating mat set to 70–75°F. Germination should occur within a week. As a rule we place two or three seeds in each plug cavity to be sure of getting one seedling.

Once the plants are up, they should be grown under cool, dry, lean conditions. Temperatures should be 60–65°F if possible and if it becomes necessary to slow their growth, temperatures can be lowered another ten degrees or so. Bright light is a requirement, particularly at higher temperatures, or the plants will become tall and limp. If this happens, they can be pinched back once they have six to eight pairs of leaves. The plants may benefit from a light misting with liquid seaweed. Cosmos is a daylength-sensitive plant, but this sensitivity can be somewhat overcome by application of growth hormones, and these are present in small quantities in seaweed preparations.

Transplants should not be set out until after danger of frost, and planting depth should be the same as in the container. If you will be supporting the plants somehow, now is the time to erect the framework, though any finishing touches can be added later, after initial cultivation.

Bedding and border types should require no further attention beyond basic maintenance. In wet seasons or poorly drained, too-rich soils with insufficient sun and air, there are a number of diseases than can disfigure cosmos, but there is really little cure for them. Prevention is the key—avoid those conditions if possible, and remove any plants that begin to show symptoms of disease. Burn infected plants; don't put them on the compost pile as the disease organisms will infect the compost, and don't replant any member of the same species in that area for at least four years so the disease doesn't get a new lease on life.

Canker shows up as a graying of the stems. If plants yellow and eventually collapse, the cause is likely bacterial wilt or one of the three or four common root and stem rots. Remaining plants can be sprayed with a fungicide like liquid sulfur or copper, but this is not a long-term solution. Stunted plants with distorted stems or foliage may have aster yellows or curly top virus. Both of these diseases are spread by insects, so, again, spraying can offer some control, but is only a stop-gap measure.

Cosmos grown for bouquets should be cut just as the flowers open, before the petals have flattened out. Vase life is up to a week. If you want to dry the flowers wait until the flowers are open fully and dry in silica gel or borax; the blooms are too delicate for air drying.

Of the two main species of cosmos, *C. sulphureus* (yellow or dwarf sulphur cosmos) usually has smaller flowers in shades of yellow, orange, and warm red. Garden cosmos (*C. bipannatus*) is a large plant with lacy foliage and a pastel color range from white to pink and magenta red (except for the new dwarf strain, Sonata, which won a Fleuroselect Award in 1992 for its compact, wind-resistant growth habit—it grows only thirty to thirty-six inches tall).

The smaller varieties of yellow cosmos are used as bedding plants, and the larger, more informal kinds for a mixed annual border or wild meadow garden. The old-fashioned Klondyke cosmos grows to six feet tall, with yellow flowers, and has been gracing American gardens at least since the turn of the century. Other tall types of note are Diablo, with brilliant scarlet-orange blooms; Lemon Twist, with pale yellow semidouble flowers; and Bright Lights, a mix of yellow, gold, orange, and red. Newer strains are usually much more compact. Two of these, Sunny Gold and Sunny Red, grow one to two feet tall and are strikingly floriferous. Smaller still at ten inches high is the Ladybird series, available in gold, yellow, and red, or as a mix.

Garden cosmos is equally effective in an informal border, but is perhaps at its best in a cutting garden, though it will need to be staked for best results. The Sensation series, introduced more than sixty years ago, is still the standard tall cosmos. The flowers of Purity are pure white; those of Dazzler are a bright crimson red; those of Radiance are also crimson red, but with a rose blush around the periphery; those called Pinkie are a clear rosy pink. All of these flowers are three inches across and are borne on vigorous, lace-leaved plants that will grow four feet tall in average soil. Similar in habit, but with more unusual flowers, are Daydream, with white blossoms that have a deep, rosy pink blush ring around the yellow center disk; Picotee, which has a similar color balance, but the pink outlines the edge of each petal; and Candy Stripe, where rose, pink, and red splash freely across the background white to create an effect that some find charming and some find garish. Without a doubt the most unusual of all is Seashells, which bears solid-colored, tubular petals displayed around a yellow center.

For the largest flowers, try the Versailles series, which is a tetraploid and has blooms four inches across in the standard shades of white, pink, and red, as well as some interesting intermediate colors. There is even a partially double cosmos, called Psyche, which grows to three feet and has the standard color range. The most popular dwarf form of garden cosmos is Sonata, introduced in 1991, which is similar to the Sensation series, but only thirty to thirty-six inches tall and thus much more wind-resistant. Its white form won a Fleuroselect Award in 1992.

## CREPIS

Hawk's beard (*Crepis rubra*) is a too little grown annual slightly less than a foot and a half high, with toothed foliage. It might look like a dandelion if not for the fact that the leaves do ascend the stem a bit, and the inch-and-a-half pink flowers are not nearly as fully double as a dandelion. Once hawk's beard goes to seed, however, the likeness to a dandelion increases as the fluffy seed chutes unfold. Both the standard form of hawk's beard and its white variant Alba increase easily from seed sown directly in the garden in midspring and thinned to six inches apart. For an early start, sow indoors six to eight weeks before the last frost. Hawk's beard prefers a dry soil; high fertility is not necessary, but sun is important.

## CROCUS

Harbingers of spring and second of the after-melt bulbs to bloom (after snowdrops), we use crocuses primarily as woodland edge plants and to line the walk up to our front door (so they will be there to remind us that the snow will soon be gone even from the deep drifts beneath the eaves of the house). They will do well in grass as well; just be sure not to mow them before their leaves have begun to yellow or you will starve them out, and the colony will deteriorate rather than improve. This need for neglect means crocuses are better off in an outer lawn or meadow area that is not kept quite so proper.

Because of their small size, crocuses should always be planted in groups of at least a dozen, preferably more; bury the corms four inches deep and four inches apart in the fall, about the time of the first actual ground freezing frosts. By putting some of the corms in sunny, well-drained spots that warm early and others where shade and snow retard the advance of spring you can stretch what is otherwise a fairly short season of bloom. Crocuses naturalize easily and will form abundant colonies even if left alone; to help them along, lift the corms during their dormant period and split off the small cormels that form in a ring around the base of the mother plant.

While there are few diseases or insect pests that bother crocuses, rodents love the corms, so keep an eye out for signs of their depredations and control them immediately if signs of damage appear. Our primary control is named Fluff, but we do a fair amount of trapping as well.

## DAHLIA

Dahlias are long-cultivated plants with such an enormous range of plant and flower forms that the only way to simplify things is to throw out both the botanical classifications and those of the various societies, and group the different plants purely on how they are used. That said, we will consider two basic kinds: tall and small. You have a choice of growing any type of dahlia from seed or starting with established tubers.

Seed dahlias should be started eight to ten weeks before the last frost for setting out after the weather is fully settled and warm, as they cannot take even a hint of frost. As dahlias are hot-weather plants, maintain a germination temperature of 80–85°F if you can manage it, and the seed will germinate in about a week. It is a good idea to transplant even the smallest seedlings, as the best colors in a mix often come from them. Garden spacing is eight to twelve inches apart for bedding types and eighteen to twenty-four inches apart for the tallest cutting dahlias. All dahlias prefer a rich soil that is well drained and in full sun.

Cutworms may be a problem for newly set seedlings, but they can be controlled with collars set in the ground an inch or two outside the stems. A three-inch-long section of toilet paper tube works well, slipped down over the seedling and pushed an inch into the ground. Slugs love dahlias, too; the best control for them (aside from the preventive measure of avoiding mulch, where they can hide) is to put a flat stone or a length of lumber near the plants. Each morning, flip the board or stone over and crush the slugs that have congregated on its underside. As mentioned, slugs will climb into half-buried containers of beer and drown, but it is a waste of beer when a little foot action can do the job. Unmulched plants will need more attention paid to irrigation. If Japanese beetles become a problem, control them with traps or hand picking (see "Controlling Pest Damage" again).

Cutting dahlias will almost certainly need some form of support, as the large flowers present a considerable surface to the wind and rain. Pinch out the growing point on half the seedlings once they are well established: You will have some early blooming plants from the unpinched half, and you will raise the number of flowering shoots on the later half. Dahlias will respond to disbudding by producing larger flowers; left to themselves the flowers are often in clusters.

Cut the blooms only after they finish opening, as they will not progress any further after cutting. Also, unlike many cut flowers, they prefer warm water to cold while waiting to be set in the vase, where they will last four to six days.

At the first frost, gently dig tubers of any plants you wish to save and remove all but a half inch of the tops. The tubers should be dusted with sulfur, then stored in sand or sawdust, only slightly moist, at 45–50°F until early spring. At that time, you can pot up a few of the tubers, force them into growth on a windowsill or in a greenhouse, and take cuttings; or you can simply wait until the frost-free date, then cut apart the tubers (so that each piece has an eye, or piece of the crown), and reset them in prepared soil for another season's bloom.

While seed-grown dahlias will produce tubers, it is often easier to start with the tubers themselves. They are widely available from mail-order houses and garden centers, and the variety of types available is too staggering to cover here. Your best source of information is the four-color catalogs from mail-order specialists.

Seed-grown dahlias need high temperatures to germinate promptly. Once transplanted, pinch, then protect with cutworm collars and support for tall, cutting types. Cut blooms only after fully open. Come fall, dahlia tubers can be dug and stored for the winter, then replanted the following spring.

## DELPHINIUM

I first got to know delphiniums fifteen years ago when my then-new wife, Ellen, and I moved from my grandfather's cottage to our own place, and my Aunt Sally suggested that before leaving Big Sam and Mamie's we dig up a few of Mamie's favorite perennials so as to keep them in the family. In those early days our gardens were very temporary, and we were always moving beds around as more and more ground was brought under cultivation. At first we had Mamie's delphinium in what is now our display garden area, at the time just a small holding bed surrounded by the remains of a recently cut-over hillside that had spent twenty years growing up to hardhack, pine, and pin cherry. That was no problem for Mamie's delphinium, though, which thrived like the wildflower it almost was (though none of the common delphinium species are listed in *Hortus* as native here, they are native to places with similar climates).

Early one spring, in the course of expanding our greenhouse space to accommodate growth of the nursery business, we unknowingly built on top of this family heirloom. We only discovered this after the plant, spurred to early growth by the presence of a greenhouse above its crown, grew out from underneath the wall—a good six inches—and then straight up, reaching a height of almost four feet. The blooms that year were as good as ever, a deep Vermont October sky blue, and we not only took seed, but after the plant had gone dormant that fall, dug under the greenhouse and moved the crown of the plant to a place of honor in our main border.

That blue, even aside from the spectacular scale of delphiniums, would be enough reason to grow them. Blue is a treasured color in the flower garden, and delphs have it, big time. From the palest to deepest, sometimes even within the confines of a single petal, delphiniums bring blue to the border with a flourish that few other plants can hope for, with individual flowers that reach two to three inches in diameter and are stacked columnar in tall spires of two, three, even four feet.

The major garden delphiniums are hybrids, and these fall into two categories: *D. elatum* hybrids are four to six feet tall and have tightly packed flower spikes in a wide range of pastel shades from white to pink, lavender, and lilac; while the *D. X belladonna* hybrids are two to four feet tall and have wider, looser spikes primarily in shades of blue. Related species types native to California can even be yellow (*D. luteum*) and red (*D. cardinale, D. nudicaule*), and breeders are now working to cross these with the existing garden hybrids to further widen their color range. All make excellent cut flowers, though the hybrids are by far the most spectacular. There is also a small, thread-leaf species, *D. chinensis*, which grows only twelve to eighteen inches tall and has diffuse bloom rather than flowers arranged in spikes; they currently exist only in blue—or, rarely, white—and are short-lived, usually grown as annuals. Nonetheless they are charming plants for the front of the border. Look for names such as Blue Elf, Blue Mirror, or Blue Butterfly.

Delphiniums are not hard to grow in cool, moist summer climates, even if the winters are bitterly cold as they are here in Vermont. Under these conditions delphiniums are long-lived perennials, but in hot or dry summer climates they are generally sown in fall for late spring bloom as annuals, then discarded.

Unless sown immediately after harvest from your own plants, delphinium seed benefits from a cold treatment. In February we roll the seed in a moist paper towel, insert that into a plastic sandwich bag, which is itself put into a canning jar, and then place the jar in the refrigerator for three to four weeks before sowing. Once sown, the flats are set on the heating mat at the standard 70–75°F temperature and will begin to sprout in two weeks, with stragglers breaking ground over the rest of the first month. Once up and growing, we move the seedlings to 50-cell plug inserts to finish their four to six weeks indoors before setting out in mid-May, after the danger of hard frosts. Grow the plants cool, in the fifties, for best results. Southern growers should start seeds in July, not March.

Established plants can be divided in spring or fall where they persist as perennials. It is also possible to take cuttings from new growth in spring, or from divisions potted up in fall and held over the winter in a root cellar or cold greenhouse. The cuttings should be taken when shoots are four to six inches long and potted immediately in 18-cell plug inserts or 3–4-inch pots, then grown on until fully rooted before setting out in the garden.

Whether grown from seed or cuttings, set the plants out a foot apart in each direction if they will only be grown for one season; if you want to keep the plants as perennials, they will need a foot and a half for small strains and up to two feet each for really large strains. The plants need rich, well-drained soil and full sun, though some protection from wind is quite beneficial.

Support is recommended as full-grown, flowering plants are liable to blow down in a gale, and the simple weight of rain on the larger flowers during their peak period is enough to knock them down. Tall delphiniums are usually staked, with a single upright stake per flower stalk placed on the windward side. We use bamboo, sunk a foot into the ground and reaching about two-thirds of the way up the flower. Tie a loose, double-wrapped figure eight around stem and stake to secure it. The smaller *belladonna* types may not need staking but, to be sure, you can give them a wire quonset through which to grow and that should be sufficient.

Whether you are growing the plants for cut flowers or not, they should be cut back immediately after blooming so that the crowns can produce another flush of bloom at the beginning of cool weather in fall. If you cut just as the last flowers have opened, and have a good location, it is possible to dry the flowers, though you will lose a week or two of display in the border. If you are using the flowers for arrangements, they should be cut when a quarter to a third of the flowers on the stalk have opened.

While the plants do need sufficient water, be careful about using overhead irrigation after the flowers are cut as the hollow stalk bases that remain can collect water and lead to stem rots, especially in poorly drained acidic soils like ours or where the crowns were set too deep at planting time. The major problems for delphiniums here, beyond stem and crown rot, are spider mites and slugs. Control of these two insect pests has been covered under "Controlling Pest Damage." Mildew can also be a problem in crowded beds; the best control is prevention—give the plants enough room to grow.

As mentioned above, the hybrid delphiniums are classed here primarily by size, though the botanists maintain an interest in "subtler" distinctions, perhaps. The most famous delphiniums are from England, and in 1949 the Delphinium Society there listed more than 4,000 different hybrids that had been developed by amateur and professional breeders. The premiere strain, of lore at least, is called the Blackmore and Langdon, after the breeders. Unfortunately these majestic plants, with their six-foot-tall spikes of flowers sometimes three inches across, do not thrive in North America except in the Pacific Northwest, a climate quite similar to England's. More suited to American conditions are the Pacific hybrids, which, while not quite as tall at four to five feet, are large-flowered, vigorous, and come in a wide range of colors: from the pale blue Summer Skies, with a white cloudlike center; the pure white of Galahad; the dark blue King Arthur; or the less common, lavender pink Astolat. Smaller strains are Blue Fountains, Magic Fountains, Stand Up, and Connecticut Yankees, all growing two to three feet in a wide range of blue and white shades. One of the most unusual is the strain called Green Expectations, also two to three feet tall with mostly shades of light blue and white and a shading toward green!

# DIANTHUS

The dianthus family is huge, including more than 300 species of annual, biennial, and perennial species, including many of the most popular flowers in the garden: One collector's catalog listed forty-four different species in its 1994 edition, and a Dutch breeder whose listing I checked had forty-six different cultivars of sweet william alone!

The best way for us to make sense of this abundance of pinks—the whole group carries this name not because pink is its predominant, central color, but because the edges of the flowers look as if they have been "pinked" with shears—is to consider them as either bed, border, and cutting plants for the main garden, or as rock garden subjects.

In the first group are the hardy annuals for bedding like *D. chinensis*, the China pink, which will overwinter in mild areas; the mostly biennial *D. barbatus* or sweet william, an old cottage garden favorite that left to its natural schedule blooms in late spring with the lupines and Canterbury bells; the fringe-petaled *D. superbus*, originally found in the northern wilds of the eastern hemisphere, from Norway all the way across Siberia to Japan; the old-fashioned pinks, *D. plumarius*, and some of the modern, or Allwood pinks, *D. X allwoodii*, hybrids named for the English nurseryman who first created them by crossing old-fashioned pinks with carnations. The florist's carnation is also a dianthus (*D. caryophyllus*), but after centuries of selection by growers is now more at home in the greenhouse than in the garden.

The dianthus species most useful as rock garden plants include the alpine pink (*D. alpinus*) from Austria; the maiden pinks (*D. deltoides*) that have naturalized in dry meadows here in the northeast United States, and the Cheddar pinks (*D. gratianopolitanus*), whose common name comes from the limey Cheddar Gorge in southwest England (also home to the sharp cheese so popular here in Vermont) but whose Latin name identifies it as "from Grenoble" in southeast France.

China pinks are technically short-lived perennials, but with early sowing they perform quite well as annuals. The plants grow a foot to a foot and a half, with green to gray grassy leaves above which are held small clusters of flat, slightly fragrant blooms an inch or two across, pinked at the margins, and spreading freely across the white-pink-red end of the spectrum, sometimes with an "eye" of a contrasting color toward the center of the bloom. If kept deadheaded, China pinks have a very long bloom period and, while small, the flowers hold well in the vase. Ellen likes to make small arrangements of just a few sprays of dianthus in tiny, hand-blown Italian jars and place them in out-of-the-way corners of the house, a practice I greatly appreciate.

I have a soft spot for the sweet williams because of their strong scent and bright colors. These are generally larger plants than China pinks, with broader, greener leaves but smaller flowers; once grouped into clusters, as they always should be, the effect of the sweet williams is every bit as bright as the China pinks. The dwarf strains make good bedding plants and the taller types are excellent cut flowers; both have a strong, sweet fragrance. Though technically biennial, sweet williams can be started early for same season bloom—the best strain we have seed for is called Hollandia—and in many climates act as a short-lived perennial.

*D. superbus* is known as the fringed pink because of its deeply cut petals, but it should also be celebrated for its slight fragrance, its relatively tall (twelve to eighteen inches), stately habit, grass green leaves, and the fact that it blooms the first year from seed. Some may find the flowers a bit affected-looking, like a Beardsley portrait of Proust, but they are striking enough in small, simple arrangements that we like them. Perhaps the nicest is a cultivar called First Love, which begins as a pure white, and becomes, over time, light and then deep pink.

The old-fashioned pinks, *D. plumarius,* are also known as cottage or grass pinks and are similar in size to the fringed pinks, but the foliage is much more blue-gray, the flowers less fringed and more fragrant. The species is less common these days, as hybrids using it as one of the parents have become the most popular form of pinks (the modern or Allwood pinks mentioned above). These hybrids vary a lot in habit and flower according to the other parent, but most are blue gray and a foot to a foot and a half tall with double flowers. Some are fragrant, some are not; some are good for cutting, while others are best for bedding, edging, or the rock garden.

The true rock garden pinks are generally less than a foot tall. While there are actually many kinds, most of the garden cultivars in general use are either maiden pinks (*D. deltoides*) or Cheddar pinks (*D. gratianopolitanus*). The two are easily distinguished: the maiden pinks have green foliage and grow in mats, while the Cheddar pinks grow in clumps or tufts and have gray foliage. Also, the flowers of maiden pinks are much smaller but brighter, with some truly electric magenta cultivars such as Flashing Lights and Zing Rose; while the Cheddar pinks have lighter, more subtly colored flowers that are larger, up to an inch across. Maiden pinks will naturalize in dryish meadows here, while the Cheddar pinks really are rock garden plants, adapted mostly to dry, limey areas without immediate, aggressive neighbors.

Most pinks come easily from seed, and the two annuals, *D. chinensis* and *D. barbatus*, are no exception. For June bloom, sow seed in February and germinate at the standard 70–75°F. The seedlings should break ground within two weeks, and by the time hard frost is over they will be ready to plant out. For biennial treatment, the plants can either be sown in place or raised in a nursery bed. Sow in midsummer for following spring bloom. This is an effective schedule nationwide, but is especially good for southern gardeners, as dianthus grows best in cool weather. Provide a well-drained, sunny site, not overly acid or overly fertile. Small kinds need six to eight inches between them when planted out, while the larger types can use a foot each.

Most kinds of dianthus can also be increased by cuttings, and pinks have their own method: Lightly grasp a shoot with two fingers and pull directly away from the plant; the shoot should pull out from the node at its base and thus create a perfectly sized cutting; this cutting can then be stuck in a moist but very well drained medium to root. Some species will also root if long shoots are bent to the ground and covered with bit of soil and then weighted down; nick or bruise the stem just above the buried part to stimulate root initiation.

Single flowers should be cut just after opening, but clustered flowers need to be gathered when no more than a quarter of those in the group have opened to assure a long vase life.

## DICENTRA

Bleeding heart is a quintessential old-time plant, throwing long sprays of locketlike pink or white flowers in languorous arcs out from two-foot-tall clumps of attractive, dusky green foliage. Here in Vermont, where foundation plantings need special attention because of the quantity and weight of the snow that collects beneath the eaves of a house, they are excellent plants for all but a sunny, dry south aspect, where their season of bloom and beauty would be too short. But on the east or north side, shaded part of the day by the house itself, bleeding heart grows quickly in spring to hide that nasty but necessary stone or concrete transition from earth to house, and with sufficient water will bloom long enough to give later perennials a chance to bulk up and take over.

While its commonness might suggest that *D. spectabilis* is native to North America, it is actually from Japan, brought back first to

England in the middle of the nineteenth century. There is a native species, though: *D. eximia* (the fringed bleeding heart), which grows in the dappled shade of the eastern deciduous forests and makes a fine border plant under cultivation. It is only half the size of *D. spectabilis* at a foot or so, but the foliage is deeply cut, and the one-inch pink or white flowers are more abundant. Most important, though, is that the fringed bleeding heart doesn't go dormant in midsummer and is thus a season-long plant for shady spots, even in warm climates.

Flowers of both types make striking additions to a bouquet, but those of the old-fashioned bleeding heart are considerably larger. Increase of favored plants is best accomplished by root cuttings taken in late summer or early spring. If you do have a plant or two dug and stored for spring cuttings, it can be easily forced into early bloom—say for Valentine's Day—by bringing it into a bright, warm place approximately a month before you wish it to bloom. We find that an 8-inch pot is sufficient, and any roots that you need to remove to make it fit the pot can be used for cuttings. After bloom, cut back and replant in the garden as soon as the ground can be worked.

To grow either of these dicentras from seed, sow fresh seed outdoors in a nursery bed as soon as the seed matures in fall. This will allow for the periods of warmth, cold, and warmth (in that order) that it needs to break dormancy. If you are starting the seeds in spring, you'll need to mimic this seasonal cycle by sowing the seed in a warm spot, moving the pot to a cool (forties) spot a few weeks later, and then a month or two later, moving it back to the warmth again.

## DIGITALIS

Important medicinal plants—source of the heart drug digitalis—as well as spectacular ornamentals, foxgloves are mostly hardy biennials though they verge on being perennial here in the cool Vermont mountains. One dwarf strain—Foxy—will bloom as an annual, but all are worth growing, and we consider them a must for any protected perennial border or semiwild woodland edge planting. Foxgloves grow quite well for us even out in the sun and wind of the main garden, but too often a midsummer storm has flattened them just as they reach their peak.

By far the best known species is *D. purpurea*, the common foxglove. The annual strain Foxy mentioned above, which grows only two to three feet tall, is from this species, as are the Excelsior hybrids, which grow to seven feet under ideal conditions—rich, moist, partly shaded soils that don't dry out completely, even in the middle of the summer. Of equal value are the Shirley hybrids, at four to five feet. All have tubular, two-to-three-inch pendant flowers stacked up a one-to-three-foot flowering stem that is nothing short of spectacular; the flowers are pale, creamy white to salmon or pink, sometimes purple, with contrasting spots that while seemingly fanciful, actually serve to lead bees to the pollen-producing anthers deep within.

Once the bees have done their work, all the *D. purpurea* strains will self-sow readily, and this is what gives them their perennial character, though their true nature is biennial. While their pebbled, light green, lance-shaped foliage is attractive before they bloom, many neat gardeners remove spent plants after they have sown themselves to allow growth of the following year's plants. You can control the color balance of naturalized plantings somewhat at thinning time—thinning is a good idea as the seed sets copiously and germinates well—by selecting which plants to keep according to foliage color; in general, lighter leaves mean lighter colored flowers. If you want to start the seed yourself it is no problem, giving the standard warm treatment in midspring.

There are a number of interesting—if less grand—species of digitalis that are true perennials and one hybrid between the wild and tame that will persist two or three seasons before petering out. This hybrid foxglove is *D. X mertonensis*, named for the English town where it was created some seventy years ago. Its common name is the strawberry foxglove in recognition of the color of the flowers. While it grows only half as tall as the biggest strains of *D. purpurea*, the flowers are often larger, and the color is exceptional. It can be maintained indefinitely in cool climates if divided every other year in early spring.

The other parent of the strawberry foxglove is *D. grandiflora*, which grows to three feet and has yellow flowers that, unlike the hybrids, are arranged along one side of the stem. It is a true perennial and, given its understatement, is a striking woodland perennial; one cultivar sometimes offered by nurseries is called Temple Bells. Other species foxgloves are *D. lutea*, with smoother leaves, a smaller habit, and tiny yellow flowers; *D. lanata*, the Grecian foxglove, smaller still at only a foot or two, with even paler yellow, slightly larger flowers; and *D. ferruginea*, the rusty foxglove, which grows as tall as the hybrids, but with a more lupinelike form, and has foliage that spikes out from the upper stem right to the base of the two-to-three-foot flowering spikes which are rust to brick red, an unusual color for shady borders.

## DUSTY MILLER (see Centaurea)

## DORONICUM

Leopard's bane is a hardy perennial that does best in cool northern climates, where it is one of the most treasured early spring flowers. The snow is barely gone when the stout clumps of heart-shaped leaves appear, soon followed by foot-tall stems capped with bright yellow daisies that bring a brightness to both the border and the vase. Leopard's bane is easy to start from seed sown in the normal warm fashion and to increase by division in spring. As the plants go dormant in summer, it is necessary to plan some sort of cover for the bare spots they will leave.

## ECHINACEA

The coneflower is a rangy wildflower gone proper and a valued medicinal herb whose roots are used to make a salve for wounds of all kinds. Just this past winter I had a painful ingrown fingernail which, even after lancing by our local nurse, resisted all medicines aimed at tempting it back to normalcy. All, that is, except the echinacea cream that my herb-loving wife, Ellen, pushed on me. Within three days of dabbing the aromatic paste on my injured digit, the swelling went down and I lost all excuse to avoid the keyboard (which is where I am forced to spend the winter)!

Aside from its medicinal usefulness, the coneflower makes a striking border plant and an excellent cut flower. The plants themselves are rather coarse, like their relatives the black-eyed Susan (*Rudbeckia spp.*), with long, lightly serrated leaves and tough, hairy stems up to three feet tall. Atop the stems are borne large, solitary pink to purple daisylike flowers; the flowers have a single row of ray flowers (petals) that swoon away from the broad, raised central cone of disk flowers that bristle with a greenish hue containing a deeper brown base. Most echinaceas can be grown from seed and will germinate easily under the standard warm treatment as long as the seed is not buried too deeply, as it needs some light to trigger germination.

Special cultivars can be increased by division or by taking basal stem cuttings in spring. Some of the best cultivars are Magnus, which has shorter, more upright ray petals, and Bright Star, which comes true from seed. There are also white forms, with a brighter green central disk with orange undertones. Two of the best here are White Lustre and White Swan.

This dwarf coneflower is right at home in a rock garden situation, and is a long-lived, long-blooming perennial.

## ECHINOPS

Globe thistles grow into large, bushy plants, with soft but bristly looking, deeply cut leaves up to eight inches long. Overall height of the globe thistle can be as much as four feet, and the plant will spread that wide. The flowers are globular, two inches in diameter, and steely to deep blue; they are spiny in the same way as coneflowers, but wholly without ray flowers so that the effect is more like a chive blossom. The most popular cultivar is Taplow's Blue, and it is a useful plant for both the cutting and everlasting garden.

Easily propagated from seed sown in the standard warm conditions, globe thistles can also be increased by division or root cuttings. For division, wait until the plants are old enough that small offset plants appear at the edge of the clump (usually at least three years). We have found that upon moving large, established plants, the roots that had to be severed and left behind will sprout and can then be established as new plants.

## EREMERUS

The tall, imposing foxtail lily is hardy in our garden only in the best of spots: warm but not windswept in summer, well-drained yet snow-protected in winter. But we are quite willing to give the plant its ration in return for its spectacular June display of pale to rich yellow, cream, and pink bloom. Our first plants (and the occasional replacements that have been necessary) came from friends down in what is called the Great Southwestern Valley of Vermont, where the Green Mountains split apart from the Taconics, and the weather is just warm enough for these Asian natives to thrive.

Striking six-to-eight-foot spike-flowered plants, foxtail lilies can be started from seed, but will take three to four years to bloom. To start them from seed, plant the seed immediately upon harvest and cover it thoroughly, as light will inhibit germination. Generally, it is better to buy mature plants. If the plants come as dormant bare crowns, soak them for an hour; then take the large spiderlike roots and spread them across a small mound of sand in a six-inch-deep, eighteen-inch-diameter hole; then firm the soil and water well. Favored conditions for the foxtail lilies are a well-drained but rich soil in full sun; be especially careful that water will not sit around the crown in winter or rot will claim a high percentage of the plants every year. After three to four years foxtail lilies can be increased by gentle division after blooming.

## ERYNGIUM

Sea holly is another thistlelike plant, but much more open and airy than the globe thistle and with a multitude of smaller blossoms halfway between a coneflower and a globe thistle. It is great for mixing into an informal border as one of many surprising here-and-there inhabitants. The best kinds have a charming steely blue color to the coblike flower heads, and grow two to three feet tall with a spread to match. There are, however, other forms that grow from only a foot, up to a towering six feet. Despite the fact that they are relatives of the carrot, the leaves of the sea holly are more thistly than ferny and in some species have intense variegation.

Plants do best and have the most intense color in full sun. They should be increased by division as the seed takes a very long time to germinate and at best sprouts inconsistently. While there are a number of species, we have had the most luck with *E. amethystinum,* the amethyst holly, and *E. planum,* the flat holly. Both make interesting cut or dried flowers for arrangements.

## EUPATORIUM

Joe Pye weed is a common roadside plant in much of the Northeast, and so is often ignored except for the few weeks in late summer when its six-to-eight-foot presence demands attention. I never appreciated it for more than a moment on my morning walks until I visited the once a decade floral exhibition in Holland, Floriade, in 1992 and saw cultivated forms accorded a prominent place in the displays there. Tough stems support groups of three to four somewhat leathery olive leaves, purple at the base, and large flower heads containing fifty or more small purple blooms far overhead. Seen from a distance, colonies of Joe Pye weed do for a sunny spot what goatsbeard (aruncus) does for shady spots. The best method of increase is division, though fresh seed sown in spring can provide larger numbers of plants.

## FILIPENDULA

These interesting perennials combine some of the effects of astilbe and achillea, two plants that would not normally be thought of in the same breath. But there are filipendulas that grow in shade, with astilbelike plumes tossed high above the rather coarse basal leaves, and there are deeply cut, fernlike rosette forms (whose foliage *Achillea filipendulina* is named for) whose small globular white flowers are reminiscent of achillea The Pearl; one species, *F. ulmaria*, could be used where a lady's mantle flower is required but with more height. All in all, this is a genus that helps extend the range of effects possible in a garden where there are many kinds of soil and sun conditions.

The best known of the filipendulas is *F. rubra*, a four-to-six-foot-tall plant—also known as queen of the prairie or false spirea—that thrives in very moist soil on the woodland edge. Its bushy bulk of three to five lobed leaves is topped in early to midsummer with fragrant, feather duster heads of salmon pink to red. Somewhat shorter and less common is a white form.

While germination is rarely perfect, filipendulas can be started with the standard warm treatment in spring. Established plants can be increased by division in spring or fall.

## GAILLARDIA

A western prairie wildflower, the original perennial species *G. aristata* is not much grown anymore, though the seed is available. It has been largely replaced by hybrids between it and the annual form, *Gaillardia pulchella*. The reasons for this replacement are good: The original perennial species is variable in size, habit, and color; takes two years to bloom; needs support to hold itself erect and produce usable cut flowers; and requires relatively dry, well-drained soils to look good in garden settings. All of these limitations have been removed in the *G. X grandiflora* hybrids that now represent virtually all the named cultivars offered. While *G. aristata* can be charming and would make a good meadow planting where the conditions are right, you will likely be more satisfied with the newer kinds.

Both the annual and perennial types can be started by the standard warm treatment in spring. While *G. aristata* will not bloom the first year, the hybrid perennial—and of course the annual—will. These are hardy plants and can be started up to eight weeks before last frost for setting out at four to six weeks old. Spacing in the garden for the bedding type annuals (*G. pulchella*) and the dwarf perennials like Baby Cole and Goblin is eight to twelve inches between each plant; taller kinds will need eighteen to twenty-four inches to avoid crowding. Gaillardias make excellent cut flowers.

## GAZANIA

This brightly colored South African perennial thrives in dry soils and seems to crave neglect, making it an excellent candidate for containers around our place. As gazania is not hardy in any but the warmest U.S. climates, most gardeners will have to grow it as an annual. This is not difficult to do as the seed germinates at a relatively cool 60°F, and young plants grow without hesitation once sprouted. You will need to have a warm, sunny spot, as the three-to-four-inch daisylike flowers tend to close in cloudy, cool conditions and at night, but their bold concentric markings in dark red, rust, orange, and bronze against a cream-to-white background, with gray to green leaves—apparently edged, but actually backed by felty white hairs—are interesting enough to allow them their idiosyncrasies.

## GERANIUM, COMMON GARDEN (see Pelargonium)

## GERANIUM

The true geraniums, or cranesbills, are mostly clumping or trailing perennials useful for lining a walk or draping over the edge of a retaining wall; there are also some smaller species that make first-rate rock garden plants. All the geraniums are easy to grow in most of the United States, and within the genus there are species adapted to sun or shade. The plants are handsome even when not in flower, and the foliage is attractive both summer and fall, when it colors with the trees.

I got interested in hardy geraniums when my Aunt Sally hacked off a piece of a tall one she called "himalayense" (though we have now decided it is the garden hybrid G. X *magnificum*, the showy geranium). Showy it is, when in flower; that one piece has, over the years, turned into hedges of foot-and-a-half mounded plants covered for the stretch of a month in early summer with throbbing magenta blue flowers over an inch across. Cut back immediately after flowering, the plants regrow to provide a vigorous green border that makes an excellent edging for the rest of the summer, dotted with an occasional bloom.

Since that time we have discovered that the varieties and uses of this hardy native plant are nearly endless. One of the best rock garden types is the six-to-twelve-inch G. *cinereum*, of which the best-known cultivar is Ballerina, a plant with leaves that are deeply cut like an aconitum and one-inch pale pink flowers, notched at the edge and veined with deep purple, held in pairs. G. *cinereum* is native to grassy slopes in the Pyrenees Mountains on the French-Spanish border, and so wants a sunny, cool location, and if the winters are cold sufficient snow to protect it. The Dalmation cranesbill (G. *dalmaticum*) is smaller at only four to six inches, but spreads readily, so it can compete against its neighbors. The leaves are rounder, and the flowers, though similar in size, are more open and lack the notched edges and contrasting veins of *G. cinereum*. The conditions it prefers, though, are the same.

The most common hardy geranium in the United States for now is *G. sanguineum*, the bloody cranesbill. There is some question whether the name results simply from the vibrant color of the flowers or the fact that the strong coloring makes them bloody hard to combine with other flowers, but this is a fantastic plant to use for draping over a retaining wall next to a walk. The plants grow up to a foot high in full sun, taller in shade, and the foliage is deeply cut, the flowers lightly notched, an inch to an inch and a half across, and solitary, though numerous. There are pink, white, and rose forms in addition to the standard magenta; one the most attractive of these is *G. s. var. striatum* Lancastriense, which is similar to Ballerina, above. Not easy to find, but best for draping, is the related species *G. wallichianum*, which, though prostrate, can reach two feet in length and will come true from seed.

Next up the height ladder are the *G. X magnificum* mentioned earlier, and *G. endressii*, both of which grow to slightly more than a foot tall in sunny spots. The Endress geranium, named for the collector who originally found it growing in the Pyrenees, has deeply but not finely cut three-to-five-inch leaves and pink to rose flowers an inch across, quite open, slightly notched, and with more depth than many of the other species. This is a vigorous plant with a long bloom period in cool climates and is widely adaptable in terms of light and moisture conditions. The standard cultivar is Wargrave Pink.

The showy geranium and its parent, *G. platypetalum*, both reach one and a half to two feet, have broad, less deeply cut leaves, and bright purplish blue flowers an inch and a half across. These plants should be cut back after flowering unless you have the room and the style that can accommodate their floppy habit. Once sheared they rebound with a solid mass of greenery that stays proper for the rest of the summer and on into fall. Both can also take some shade.

Taller still is the meadow cranesbill, *G. pratense*, at two to three feet a vigorous grower and self-sower that may be too weedy for prim gardens but is nonetheless charming with its inch-and-a-half flowers of purple, silver blue, white, or even pale blue with white veining. There are double-flowered forms of this species—look for those labeled "Plenum." For shadier sites, the wood cranesbill (*G. sylvaticum*) can reach the same three feet in height, but with smaller, more open, upward-facing flowers primarily in purple, but with some pink and white forms available.

Size king of the cranesbills is *G. psilostemon*, the Armenian cranesbill, which can grow to four feet tall. The six-to-eight-inch-wide leaves are deeply but not finely divided, and the flowers are a vibrant, if shocking, dark purplish red with black centers and round, unnotched edges. This is a large plant, best suited for the rear of a border that edges a wood so that it receives dappled sun and can draw on the rich, moist soil of the woodland.

One last, somewhat different species is *G. macrorrhizum*, which grows up to only a foot and a half but has unusual flowers: the base of the flower is puffed up, and extending from the one-inch magenta face of the blossom are the like-colored stamens that arch upward in a way reminiscent of columbines. This is a hardy, sun- and shade-tolerant plant that is good as a low-maintenance groundcover.

All of the cranesbills can be grown from seed, though most of the named cultivars are not likely to come true, and there are some difficulties in getting good germination. Fall sowing of hand-collected seed gives the best results, but beware that many of the species will cross and the resulting plants may or may not be worth preserving. Division in the spring is the more common method of increase, though stem and root cuttings can be taken as well. We prefer division over all.

## GEUM

Popular in some cottage garden situations, this perennial is really only at its best in particular conditions: well-drained but amply moist soil, reasonably cool summers, but not too harsh winters, and a spot that offers some protection from hot afternoon sun. If you have the climate and the soil, geum might interest you enough to grow it, but that does not describe our garden, and for us they have never done very well.

Seed germinates erratically by the standard warm method, but be careful of home-harvested seed as these plants cross readily and are not reputed to improve themselves in the process. A better plan is to increase your plants by division.

## GLADIOLUS

I will have to confess outright that the common garden gladioli, most of which are hybrids of some of the older species, have never interested me. The plants are not reliably hardy here, and so the corms must be dug each fall, stored in scarce root cellar space, and then replanted each spring. For all this care, the flowers are too gaudy for my taste. The wilder species types are hard to find, and as yet I have not spent the time to search them out, though photographs I have seen of them convince me that I might enjoy doing so. Since the wild plants come from warmer climates such as southern Europe and Africa, even these hardier types will likely still need lifting, but at least for the trouble I might get something interesting.

Although gladioli make excellent cut flowers in terms of vase life, bloom size and sheer vibrancy of color, they are just too much for me, and I just can't bring myself to take the space for them. Culture is relatively simple, though the details must be attended to: Plant the corms in groups, approximately six times a corm's thickness in depth, every couple of weeks from early spring on to three months before the first killing frost. This will provide a succession of bloom. Spacing in the garden should be about eight inches between each plant, and extra compost should be added, as glads are greedy plants. When cutting, leave as much foliage as possible to support the corms. At first frost, dig up the corms; dry them for two weeks in a warm, dark place, then dust the corms with sulfur and hold in dry, dark cool storage (40–50°F, as for dahlias and alliums) until the following spring.

## GYPSOPHILA

Baby's breath is to me quite the opposite of gladiolus; it is a plant that it is hard for me to go without. Both the annual and perennial forms are useful for bouquets, and the perennial in particular is useful for a cottage border, with its wide but airy mass of tiny white flowers that provides a visual base or ground for placement of other, more striking plants. These qualities of gypsophila hold true not only in the garden, but in the vase as a cut flower making the plant that much more valuable.

Annual baby's breath *(G. elegans)* is a quick-growing catch crop kind of flower that can be used either to cover over spent bulbs while they fade, or as a filler for bouquets. To plant annual baby's breath, direct seed, broadcasting it or planting it in rows six inches apart every two weeks from the time the ground can first be worked in spring. Plants will bloom about eight to ten weeks after sowing and provide an abundance of eight-to-twelve-inch long sprays of quarter- to half-inch white flowers that are held in branched clusters. Pink and red forms are available but are not as attractive as the white.

Perennial baby's breath *(G. paniculata)* is a much larger plant, easily three feet tall and as wide across. The plant displays across its width a billowing of tiny white, pink, or carmine flowers that seem to float on a wispy frame of gray-green foliage. The large sprays of flowers are equally valuable fresh or dried and should be cut when about two-thirds open (a bit more open for drying). If cut immediately after blooming perennial baby's breath will often rebloom before fall sets in. In the border, the plants serve as a filler for the gaps left by spent poppies, columbines, and bleeding hearts. Fortify the soil with dolomitic limestone before planting and provide support if your garden is windy either in the form of twigs or surrounding plants.

There is a creeping form of perennial gypsophila (*G. repens*) that makes an excellent plant for draping over retaining walls. Culture is the same as for the upright species. Both perennial types can be grown from seed, but trueness to type is not assured for most. Divisions can be made in spring, but must be done carefully as the upright baby's breath resents disturbance once situated. Stem or root cuttings are the best choice for increasing these plants.

## HELIANTHUS

Sunflowers are American natives and a longtime favorite of mine. The towering stalks are sign and symbol of summer while the nutritious seeds, which make excellent bird (and people) food, are a second reason to grow these wonderful plants. As breeders release new varieties that show the diversity possible within such a familiar plant, garden uses are multiplying. Tall varieties are still used to screen a view, but smaller strains have shrunk all the way down to a mere two feet, and the colors range from white and pale yellows to autumnal shades and deep burgundy. Differing flower types have proliferated as well.

Easy to grow in full sun and rich, well-drained soil, sunflowers can be direct-seeded on the frost-free date, four inches apart in rows a foot apart, or as groups of two to three seeds in clumps a foot apart each way. Except for the new cut-flower types, thin to a single plant per foot once the seedlings are well up. All types will benefit if you hill up the soil around their base once they are a couple of feet tall, but this is especially important with tall types in windy sites. Sunflowers can be started ahead if you are in a cold area like ours or if you simply want to grow a champion head. Start the seed in a 3½-inch pot or 18-cell plug inserts four weeks before the last frost, and germinate at 70–75°F. Sunflowers like warm temperatures and bright light. To get the largest plants, fertilize at transplant time and make sure the spot you plant in gets an extra dose of compost or manure during spring preparation. Be prepared to stake giant plants

New sunflower varieties are breaking out of the standard forms. Here, for example, is a fully double cultivar called Teddy Bear.

with a stout wooden pole driven a foot or more into the ground. Smaller varieties grown under normal soil conditions and as part of a mixed border are unlikely to need support, especially if grown in a block, rather than in a solitary row.

For screening, two or three rows are better than one, as the offset of plants from row to row will fully block the unwanted view. In border plantings stagger the types so that the tallest are in the back or in a corner and then work forward and to the sides with the smaller types to provide a visual transition; the ten-to-twelve-foot height of tall varieties is too much of a shock without some form of visual buildup and will look out of place except when viewed from a great distance.

We have had few pest or disease problems with our sunflowers, but they are susceptible to attack by aphids as well as to a range of leaf spots, rots, and wilts, as well as rust and mildew. Aphids, if they become numerous enough to actually pose a problem, can be controlled with insecticidal soap. Most of the disease problems will occur in hot, humid conditions and can best be prevented by assuring good drainage and not crowding the plants. At the first sign of disease remove the infected plant parts—entire plants if necessary—and burn them. Do not replant in the same spot the next year as the disease may persist there.

If you are growing sunflowers for the birds, wait until the petals drop before harvesting, then cut the heads with a foot or two of stalk attached and dry in a warm, dark place. To use the plants for feeding, simply hang the heads outdoors where the birds can get to them. You can also leave the plants in the ground and let the birds find them. For bouquets—yes there are varieties very suitable for cutting—harvest just as the flowers finish opening. Many new varieties bear a multitude of flowers, so keep the flowers cut to maximize the number of ensuing blooms.

Our favorite variety of the classic, tall sunflower is Giant Gray Stripe, named for the markings on the seed; other tall types include Giant Russian and Giganteus. All are listed to grow ten to twelve feet tall, but will surpass that under good conditions. For screening, the best approach is to include in your planting one of the large-sized mixtures like Autumn Beauty, Color Fashion, or Evening Sun. These plants bloom in a rich range of autumnal shades and will also grow somewhat larger than their listed height (six feet) under good conditions. A row or two of a giant type in the back with these more ornamental types in the front will hide just about anything and look great in the process.

Primrose Yellow is a tall (eight feet) sunflower with pale yellow flowers and a standard brown disk. Slightly smaller at six feet but with a similar color scheme is Lemon Queen; its sister strain Velvet Queen has remarkable, deep burgundy petals surrounding a chocolate colored disk—truly one of the most remarkable flowers I have ever seen. At the opposite end of the spectrum is Italian White, with small four-to-six-inch starlike blooms with black centers that are borne in profusion on four-to-six-foot plants. An improved form, Vanilla Ice, has just been released. For a similar flower type with many blooms in classic sunflower colors, try Stella or Piccolo, which resemble very tall black-eyed Susans. There are also double forms of sunflowers: Sole d'Oro is the classic sunflower yellow and about six feet tall, while Teddy Bear is only three feet tall; Orange Sun is a bright calendula orange and will grow to six feet. All have frilly, double blooms.

Perhaps the smallest sunflower is Sunspot, which grows a mere two feet tall, but with ten-inch heads! While not the most attractive plant you can grow, kids will find it fascinating, and it does produce lots of seed in a small space. Zebulon is another small plant—the only sunflower I know with yellow petals and a grayish green disk. The best of the dwarf types, though, is Music Box, a miniature version of the standard Autumn Beauty mix. All of these dwarf types make good container plants, too. Except for Sunspot, these small plants are also suitable for informal borders and cutting gardens.

Sunflowers bred especially for cut flower use include Henry Wilde, which has a particularly clean combination of butter yellow petals and deep chocolate disks on multibranching eight-to-ten-foot plants; Hallo, which is similar to Henry Wilde, but smaller; Sunrich Lemon and Sunrich Orange, two new hybrids that grow about three feet tall and bear single blooms that bloom only slightly more than two months after seeding. Our favorite, though, is Valentine, which produces a multitude of six-inch lemon yellow blooms with black disks atop thirty-inch side stems on bushy five-foot-tall plants. For smaller blooms, plant closer. These can be cut a little earlier—just as the buds are ready to open—and they will open in the vase, prolonging their life as an arrangement to two weeks or more!

## HELICHRYSUM

Strawflowers are grown primarily for use in dried arrangements. This Australian perennial is grown as an annual in all but the warmest, driest climates, where it feels sufficiently at home to establish itself permanently. While strawflowers are hardy enough to survive in the Deep South, the hot, humid summers usually lead to fatal rots and foliage diseases.

Helichrysum seed can be direct-seeded in the garden after the danger of hard frost is past and the soil has warmed up, but in short season areas like ours it pays to start the plants indoors as they are late to bloom. Sow the seeds six to eight weeks before the last spring frost, and transplant in the garden after four to six weeks. If you get the plants in the garden and growing first, they can withstand a light frost. In the garden, helichrysum plants need a foot between each plant and should be planted in raised beds unless the natural drainage is excellent. Very tall types may need support, but there are now many dwarf strains available that will be self-supporting in all but the windiest sites.

Harvest the flowers just as the outer petals begin to unfold and reveal the center, as the blooms continue to open after cutting. Vase life is seven to ten days, but properly dried blooms will last for years. To dry, hang in loose bunches in a dark, dry place.

The standard cutting variety of helichrysum for bouquets is called Monstruosum, available as a mix or by color. The plants grow to three feet and will need support to protect them from wind damage once the two-and-a-half-inch flowers appear. Another well-known tall type is Swiss Giant and there are numerous selections of it offered by different companies; plants are similar in size to Monstruosum, but the flowers are larger. The best known dwarf type is Bright Bikini, which bears full-size flowers on plants only a foot or so tall.

## HELIOTROPE

A mainstay of the old-fashioned fragrance garden, heliotrope also provides striking though subdued blooms for arrangements. A tender perennial from Peru, it is grown as an annual in American gardens. Sow the seed indoors ten to twelve weeks before the last frost at 70–75°F, and transplant to the garden only after the weather is fully settled. Garden spacing is eight to twelve inches between each plant. Use dwarf forms in containers or as an edging; grow the tall strains in a cutting garden, harvesting the vanilla-scented blooms as soon as they begin to open. The standard varieties are Lemoine and Marine, which grow eighteen to twenty-four inches tall. The dwarf forms, at only eight to twelve inches tall, should be sought under the names Dwarf or Mini Marine.

## HELIPTERUM

If you want to grow this charming little flower for drying, you may need to look under three different names, as a few species used to be classified in other families. *Helipterum roseum* used to be known as *Acroclinium*, and *Helipterum manglesii* was know as *Rhodanthe*. Many mail-order catalogs will have listings for helipterum under the old names. Regardless of where you do locate it, sow the seed six to eight weeks before the last frost for transplanting once the weather is settled and warm. Garden spacing is six to eight inches between each plant, and the lithe, wiry plants prefer a well-drained, warm and sunny location. The flowers should be cut after opening fully and gathered in small bunches, foliage intact, then hung in a dark, airy place that is free from frost until the flowers are fully dry.

## HEMEROCALLIS

Daylilies are now one of the backbones of the perennial garden, a solid member of every flower lover's top ten. But it wasn't always so, even though they have been cultivated for at least 2,500 years. Most of today's popular daylilies are hybrids, which now appear at the rate of about 500 new varieties a year, and have grown beyond number— unless you want to count to 40,000 plus. Among their numbers are those daylilies that bloom at every time of the season and just about everywhere in the United States, and we will leave their description to the catalogs, with their full-color pictures and elaborate coding schemes. Two things to remember: If you live in a cold area, daylilies described as "evergreen" are not likely to be hardy, while the so-called dormant types that die back to the ground in the fall protect themselves from subzero weather. Also some varieties are quite fragrant, while others are not.

We will discuss briefly two fragrant species: the Middendorff lily (*H. middendorffii*) and the lemon lily (*H. lilioasphodelus*), both of which are originally from the cold northern fringes of the eastern hemisphere. The lemon lily is the larger and earlier of the two, blooming about the same time as Darwin tulips on three-foot stems with pale lemon yellow, four-inch fragrant trumpets. The plants themselves are adaptable to both sunny meadows and the woodland edge and colonize readily if given the right conditions. The Middendorff lily is slightly smaller than the lemon lily, though its broader, grasslike leaves give it equal substance. The flowers are later to appear but similar in form, smaller and clustered but still fragrant, and more strongly colored, with a play of orange to the yellow. Middendorff lilies are even more adaptable in terms of sun and moisture, needing only a fertile, well-drained soil.

All daylilies (including the species types) are best increased by division in the spring, and in fact will require division eventually if they are to thrive. The time between required divisions, however, varies widely according to the vigor of the particular cultivar. Older, overgrown plants may require a pair of forks or even a sharp spade to separate. A single small tuber with one bud and a snippet of root will eventually grow to be a full-size plant, but for quicker results, larger, handful-size pieces make more sense.

## HESPERIS

This is an old-fashioned favorite known as dame's rocket, and it is widely grown at the woodland edge for its night fragrance. Its flowers have the same, wonderfully eerie feeling as woodland phlox, rising from a distance out of the shadows, but standing themselves as bright reminders of the color that is hidden in all dark corners of the land. Most dame's rocket is a lavender, purple, mauve, or lilac color, though there are some white forms. The plants are short-lived perennials that grow two to three feet tall and a bit ordinary-looking until they bloom. Usually the seeds are started in spring, indoors or out; once the plants have reached manageable size, set them where they can establish themselves and reseed for a perpetual spring appearance, as you would with the wilder forms of foxgloves. Keep in mind that planting dame's rocket in a location upwind of summer evening breezes will bring the sweet fragrance to you.

## HEUCHERA

Another great plant for the woodland edge or semishaded bed, coral bells share the mysterious habit of dame's rocket of producing color from the darkness of shady spots. Coral bells gain their mystery from the fact that the plants grow as a low rosette and then fling their small, arched flowers upward on thin one-to-three-foot stems, creating what many gardeners call a "mist" of color that hovers in the cool darkness. Many of the colors are warm pink and red shades—like Chatterbox (pink), Coral Cloud, and Mt. St. Helens (yes, lava red)—that only enhance the smoldering effect. But there are less-known forms: Green Ivory has pale greenish blooms like lady's mantle, and June Bride and White Cloud produce white flowers. There are also cultivars like Bressingham Bronze and Palace Purple that have ornamental purple foliage.

While many heucheras can be grown from seed (especially the purple forms), divide particular plants in spring or fall to be sure that you maintain their character. Replant the divisions making sure that the small rhizomes are buried completely.

## HOSTA

Queen of the shade garden and backbone of many foliage designs, hostas come in a bewildering array of forms and sizes, ranging from tiny eight-inch variegated varieties like Kabitan that are used for edging, to huge gray-leaved monsters like the four-to-six-foot-tall Krossa Regal, outstanding specimen plants that anchor the corner of a large display. Some hostas even thrive in full sun here in the cool northern mountains, but they are essentially shade plants and look their best in the cool light of a woodland border.

There are easily 500 different cultivars commercially available in the United States alone, far beyond what we can cover here, but aspects of their care are common: Hostas want a rich, well-drained soil, light to moderate shade, and continuously moist, but not wet, soil. As a general rule, those hostas with blue-gray foliage need the most shade, followed by those that have variegated foliage. Thick-leaved types are more drought-resistant than other hostas, while glossy-leaved types are most resistant to the ill effects of dripping from established trees.

Hostas are slow to leaf out in spring, so you may want to combine them with other species that bloom early and then go dormant. Once hosta does begin to grow, the new foliage—especially on soft, glossy-leaved hostas—is very attractive to slugs. Traps are an effective control. Place a large flat stone near where slugs are a problem, and each morning flip the stone over and crush the slugs that have taken up refuge underneath.

Increase is primarily by division in spring just as the plants break dormancy, but most types will not need—indeed should not get—division more than every four to five years, as the clumps take time to fill out and become established. Most unattractive clumps of hosta, and there are many, result from inappropriate siting (in the case of novice gardeners) or too frequent disturbance (in the case of more experienced but overly intrusive gardeners).

## HYACINTHUS

Even nongardeners know hyacinths, the small fragrant bulbs that are shipped by the millions each year from Holland and forced in small pots for spring sales at the local florist and supermarket. While their fragrance does recommend them for late-winter forcing to beat cabin fever, the stiff and all-too-perfect flower spikes that rise top heavily out of the waxy foliage make them much too formal for my garden, even if they are not bedded out in uniform displays. For bedding I prefer tulips, and for naturalizing, something looser and less regimented. Common hyacinths are a tribute to the breeder's skill, but not to his or her art, as there seems to be no art left in them. For a hyacinth with some heart, some expressiveness, look for the so-called Roman, or alpine, hyacinth, a wilder species from the Pyrenees Mountains that divide Spain and France. The Roman hyacinth has open flower spikes, sometimes more than one to a plant, and is more lithe, like a tête-à-tête narcissus, not squat and muscular like common hyacinths. Roman hyacinths are also forced more easily and with less attention than their more cultivated cousins.

## IBERIS

There are both annual and perennial forms of candytuft. The annuals are grown for bedding and for fragrant cut flowers; the perennials are evergreen rock garden plants used for edging or draping over the edge of a wall. Both the annual and perennial plants come fairly easily from seed under the standard warm treatment or can be direct-sown in the garden in midspring. Garden spacing for the annual varieties is about eight inches between plants. Of the two annual types, the rocket candytuft (*I. amara*) is the smaller one at a foot tall, but has wonderful domed spikes of small, white, fragrant flowers. The globe candytuft (*I. umbellata*), grows to eighteen inches and has flat flower clusters in shades of pink, lilac, and red, in addition to the white. It is not fragrant.

The smaller, perennial *I. saxatilis* forms a mat only three to six inches tall, but is covered with a broad-brush sprinkling of half-inch white flowers. A rock garden or wall plant, *I. saxatilis* is suitable for crevices full of well-drained soil. The larger *I. sempervirens* spreads up to eighteen inches in temperate zones, though here in the North twelve inches is closer to the actual mature size. The flowers are domed clumps an inch and a half across. *I. sempervirens* is used primarily as a draping plant for retaining walls, in the same way as *Gypsophila repens*.

## IMPATIENS

Relatively unknown as little as a generation ago, impatiens are now arguably America's most popular bedding plant. When we had our garden center, we started something on the order of a hundred flats each of petunias, marigolds, and impatiens; for other plants we planted ten of this and ten of that. Demand for impatiens increased every year, while for the other plants demand was relatively constant. Why? Impatiens are just about one of the most foolproof plants you can grow. They seem to survive in the most unlikely places with a minimum of care, and they come back from the edge of death (apparently) with little more than a shot of water and a quick shearing. Come fall, you can hack off a branch, root it, and the plants will regrow to flower through the winter on a partly sunny windowsill.

The only problem with impatiens here in Vermont is that they are notoriously sensitive to frost, so they do require some pampering. Oh, and along with geraniums, petunias, and marigolds, you can get a little sick of them because they are so popular. Their popularity is lucky for gardeners, though, because they are not easy to get started, yet are readily available as young seedlings in a wide range of colors and habits.

If you do want to start your own, sow seed on the surface of sterile potting mix—the seeds need light to germinate—ten to twelve weeks before the last frost. Impatiens are very prone to damping off when young, so don't overwater the seedlings and be sure to keep the growing area bright and warm, with good air circulation. At 70–75°F the seeds will sprout in a week or two. If you started the seeds close together, in anything smaller than a 50-cell plug insert, transplant the seedlings to sufficient quarters as soon as they have two or three leaves. Final spacing in the garden should be ten to twelve inches between plants, but put off planting until well after the danger of frost. The slightest nip of frost will set the plants way back, and though they will recover if the frost hasn't killed down below the lowest branches, until they do—probably a month—they'll look awful. Once established however, and free from the vicissitudes of spring weather, impatiens will bloom nonstop till the first fall frost.

Impatiens also make excellent plants for hanging baskets, window boxes, and other containers. Generally the plants are grown at a closer spacing in containers than when garden-planted: The rule of thumb is to plant three plants to an 8-inch pot and five to a 10-inch pot; a two-foot-long window box takes five or six. To get maximum bloom on your plants do not overfeed or overwater; allow the plants to almost reach the point of wilting; then soak them, allowing the excess to run out; then hold off watering until they dry completely out again.

Impatiens grown in deep shade may become leggy and less floriferous. The plants can be sheared back, but without an increase in light they will likely grow back as they were. The only answer is to provide a bit more light. When fall frost finally threatens, small stem cuttings will root readily in potting mix and can be brought indoors to bloom through the winter on a windowsill.

Varieties of impatiens are legion. Impatiens are one of the most successful plants you can grow from a mix, but still we prefer to make our own mix of just three or four coordinated colors. Some impatiens have unusual colors, star and picotee patterns, or even roselike double flowers, so read catalog descriptions closely or select plants already in bloom. Impatiens are one of the few plants I will buy in bloom, though I still pinch out the flowers after planting. For large plants with large flowers—up to two inches across—try the Blitz or Showstopper series: They are also especially good for larger baskets and containers, as the longer branches cascade over the sides (an effect than can be enhanced some by extra watering) more than other varieties. The most exotic forms of impatiens are the double-flowered types like Rosette and Duet.

## IPOMOEA

Morning glories epitomize many a gardener's idea of a simple country plant, yet ipomoea is a big, complicated group of plants that encompasses everything from sweet potatoes to the fragrant night-blooming moonflower. We'll skip the complexity and deal with the kinds you'll likely want to grow and just how to grow them.

Morning glories are tender climbers, and some are technically perennial, but all are grown as annuals in northern gardens. The seed can be sown outdoors after all danger of frost, or indoors six to eight weeks earlier. In either case, the hard-shelled seed should be nicked with a file or soaked in warm water overnight before planting. If starting indoors sow the seed direct in 18-cell plug inserts or 3½-inch pots; once growing morning glories do not like to be transplanted. Grow morning glories on the cool, bright side to keep their size manageable. If they start to climb, stick small twigs in the pots for them to entwine; otherwise the seedlings will get all tangled together and be a real mess when planting time comes. If things get totally out of hand you can pinch back the apical shoot, and the seedlings will branch.

Before transplanting time morning glories should be hardened off in the manner discussed in Chapter 4. Hardening off is especially important in cool climates where the sudden shock after setting out the plants can put them back by weeks. These rampant twiners don't need support: They can be left to twine among and climb upon what ever plants you have deigned to combine them with. Plant morning glories on the top edge of a rough stone wall, at the base of picket fence or a rose hedge to provide a platform on which the flowers can be displayed. We have tried and been happy with all of these planting strategies. Morning glories will also climb happily up a more conventional lattice work, and they will provide extra shade (and in the case of moonflowers, evening fragrance) for a west-facing porch or arbor. It is important that the structure which supports the morning glories faces *west*: All the members of the morning glory family love a sheltered, sunny place, and the warm sun of the late summer afternoons here in Vermont is really the only way to get vigorous growth.

Which one to grow? Moonflowers (*Ipomoea alba*), as noted, bloom at night and are fragrant, so the place to put them is near where you sit or where you leave the windows open on summer evenings. We plant a few around our outdoor dining arbor in the corner of the kitchen garden. Moonflowers will grow about ten feet in the course of a temperate summer, though in the tropics they might become four times as long. The broad leaves of moonflowers are large, up to eight inches long, and the flowers are pure white, with a hint of green in the folds, and four to six inches wide—quite spectacular on a moonlit summer night! Cardinal climbers (*Ipomoea quamoclit*) are pretty much at the other end of the spectrum: the three-inch leaves are almost fernlike, and the inch-and-a-half, bright red flowers open in the daytime. The vines themselves are said to climb ten to fifteen feet, though ours rarely make it the eight feet to the porch roof. Among morning glories we like the old standards when we want a particular color: Heavenly Blue (a pale blue), Pearly Gates (white), and Scarlet O'Hara (bright red). Our overall favorite though is Early Call, an early-flowering mix with large four-inch flowers and a wonderfully broad color range—including some darker reds that border on chocolate.

Certainly the most common, and one of the most beautiful, of the Ipomoeas is the Heavenly Blue morning glory, here climbing a post.

## IRIS

Another flower which the breeders have gone bananas over is the iris, especially the Dutch and German bearded types, and there are now enough high-tech hybrids that just listing them would fill a book. Although something like 90 percent of the irises grown today are these mass-market bearded wonders, there are still plenty of very good species types around—ranging in height from six to thirty-six inches in height and with a range in bloom time from early spring to later summer. As you may guess, my taste tends to these wilder, less formal types. As with other flowers that have such variety of habit we will discuss them according to height, bloom time, and/or the conditions they require.

Of the irises we will discuss here Danford irises (*I. danfordiae*) are both the smallest and the earliest, often breaking through retreating snow with the crocuses. At flowering time, before their leaves have fully developed, Danfords are only half a foot high, seeming to break straight from the ground with a one-inch pale yellow bloom. While more compact than many other irises, they still display the classic iris flower combination of standard and fall (upright petals and horizontal or arching sepals). After blooming, the leaves of the Danford iris will grow to as much as a foot tall, then die back. Danford irises like a hot, dry location during their dormant season, so this is a good plant for rock gardens and stone walls. Because of their diminutive stature, it makes sense to put them at the edge of a retaining wall next to a walk so that they can be see close up. They will naturalize, but are grown from relatively inexpensive fall-planted bulbs, so can be treated as an annual. Plant the bulbs four inches deep in the fall; shallower planting encourages them to split into smaller, nonflowering bulbs.

*Iris reticulata* is similar in timing to the Danford iris and only slightly larger in stature; it has more open-faced blooms, in deep-blue violet with gold and white highlights, and a subtle fragrance of violets. Care for *Iris reticulata* is generally the same as for the Danford iris.

Next in size and bloom is the crested iris, *I. cristata*, which beginning in May ushers in the main flowering season in New England gardens. This species is rhizomatous rather than bulbous and will spread rapidly under its favored conditions: moist rich soils high in organic matter, and indirect but bright sun—a good description of a woodland edge or clearing. The thin leaves of the crested iris arch outward directly from the rhizome and reveal blooms four inches across and quite open, dark blue violet with rich yellow highlights.

There are white and sky blue forms as well. Increase by division after flowering is finished.

Two old-fashioned irises with a long history of cultivation and use are the sweet iris (*I. pallida*) and yellow flag (*I. pseudacorus*), the fleur-de-lis. The three-foot leaves of the sweet iris are as much a part of its ornamental appeal as the lavender to lilac flowers that bloom only shortly after those of the crested iris, in May or June. The slightly fragrant flowers are not very dramatic but the plants stay good looking throughout the season, even in drier soils than most other irises. Some cultivars, such as Variegata, or Albo-variegata, have striped leaves, adding further to their visual interest as a foliage plant. Diseases and pests are practically nonexistent, and sweet iris increases easily by division after flowering.

Yellow flag is a large and relatively coarse plant—up to five feet tall, though many garden selections are a more restrained two to three feet—with three-to-four-inch yellow flowers (the fleur-de-lis) that appear in midsummer. Some cultivars, again, have variegated foliage. This is an historic plant long used for food, medicine, and dyes, and it is trouble-free in its favored location at the edge of a stream or pond. Increase by division every three years or so, though seed sown in the fall will provide flowering plants after a minimum of two seasons of growth. There is also a blue flag iris, which has the habit and preferences of the yellow flag, but a flower with more of the coloring of *I. reticulata:* blue-violet with white and gold highlights.

The Siberian iris (*I. sibirica*) is my personal favorite of the whole genus, with a blooming season that spans the gap between the two irises just mentioned, and a trouble-free constitution if provided with the conditions it prefers (full sun and constant moisture but not standing water). Ranging in height from two to three feet, with attractive swordlike leaves and plump clusters of two-to-three-inch, relatively open blossoms in a full range of colors except orange and brown tones, Siberians are easy to increase by division (though they will take a couple of seasons to reach peak bloom again) and are strong natured enough to choke out most competitors once established. Thus, Siberians make a good low maintenance planting, and a large block of them is absolutely stunning in bloom. The only problem we have seen is thrips that attack the blossoms in dry years. Painful as it was, we cut most of the flowers in bud as soon as the problem was noticed and burned them.

Japanese irises (*I. ensata* or *kaempferi)* are unfortunately bothered by thrips as well, and are also a bit more picky about their growing conditions. While they want moist to wet soil during their growth and blooming season, dry feet are necessary for good winter survival, and the soil must be acidic. Since they also can take considerable shade, Japanese iris are well adapted to wet, shady spots along a stream or pond bank—planted low enough to be watered by early season high water, but up enough on the bank to be above the winter water level. They grow about two to three feet tall with very large flowers that, over the centuries of Japanese culture, have been bred to have standards (the upright petals) that are either very small or that lay flat along the falls (sepals) to give a decidedly flat-topped appearance to the flowers. This breeding has, when combined with a rational sense of color balance, resulted in some very striking plants. It must be said that the breeders of Japanese irises have not always shown any more restraint than breeders of the bearded Dutch or German irises.

Though we will leave a discussion of hybrid bearded irises to the big catalogs, a few notes are necessary on their culture. In general, they will be happy in the normal garden conditions: a rich, well-drained soil in full sun to light shade. Irises planted in heavy soils are more prone to rot problems, though there is a need for ample moisture. Physical injury of the rhizome, either during cultivation or at division time, can lead to infection with rot organisms. Dust sulfur powder on all cut or bruised faces of iris rhizomes to prevent infection.

The other major source of infection in irises is borers. Bearded irises have large plump rhizomes, almost like a ginger root, and this rhizome makes a good home for a pest called the iris borer. This pest's eggs overwinter at the base of the foliage and, come midspring when the foliage is about six inches high, they hatch and tiny larvae burrow into the stem and tunnel down into the rhizome. Once there, they feed on the inside of the rhizome and grow into revolting one-to-two-inch grubs. In midsummer, these grubs pupate in the soil to become night-flying moths that lay their eggs at the base of the irises to begin the cycle again.

The best method of control is to interrupt the moth's cycle. Cut off all the iris's foliage during fall cleanup and burn it so that the eggs are destroyed. In midspring, look for leaves that appear water-soaked or that have small, lighter colored traceries (the tunnels) near the base. Locate the lower end of the tunnel and squeeze the leaf to crush the miner in its burrow. Mark those plants where the pest may have entered the rhizomes and, after blooming, dig them up, find the pests within, dispose of them, then dust the wounds with sulfur and replant.

When planting new stock or dividing established plants, note carefully how they grow: Iris rhizomes actually sit on the surface of the

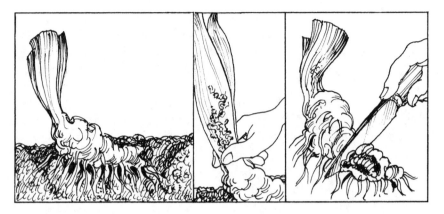

A key point in planting irises is to set the rhizomes so that the top is above ground surface. Iris borers can be found by tracing their tunnels in the base of the leaves and digging them out with a sharp knife. After handling, dust all cut surfaces with sulfur to prevent rot.

soil. When replanted the rhizomes should be set back that way; the roots should be settled down in the soil, yes, but the rhizome should be half above it, as if it were floating on the surface of a pond. Do not mulch over the rhizomes, as sun and air are beneficial to their growth.

## LATHYRUS

In the nineteenth century, sweet peas (*Lathyrus odoratus*) were the plant of choice for the breeding experiments by Czech monk Gregor Mendel on which the entire modern science of genetics is based. Thus, sweet peas are inextricably tied to the history of gardening—indeed to the broader pursuits of horticulture, botany, even the scientific method itself. No one is certain precisely where the species *Lathyrus odoratus* originated, but it has been in cultivation at least since the end of the seventeenth century, and the first commercial variety, Painted Lady, was introduced in England in the first half of the eighteenth century. Painted Lady is still available today.

Aside from all this history, the plants are wonderful garden performers, giving the same kind of informal and playful effect as morning glories when they weave in and among established plants, but sweet peas also provide ecstatically fragrant cut flowers. The plants themselves are quite hardy and in fact require cool weather, so in the North we grow them from a spring planting; in hot climates, fall planting works better. Sweet peas want a moist, cool location, but still with sun; what this means in practice is to avoid those spots that bake, like along a south-facing wall. A spot where the soil is shaded but the plants are able to grow up into the sun is ideal. Add a little extra compost fortified with a bit of wood ash, to provide potassium and some phosphorus, to the planting site. If you don't have access to wood ash, bone meal and greensand or granite dust will suffice. Planting depth for the seeds is an inch, while spacing should be about three inches per plant, after thinning. For best results, soak the seed overnight before sowing, or nick each seed with a file to breach its hard coat and allow water uptake.

If planting among established shrubs, it is a good idea to begin with started plants. Seeds can be started indoors about three to four weeks before the outdoor planting date and then set out in the garden once the danger of hard frost is past, yet cool weather still lies ahead. A minimum 50-cell plug insert will be required to allow the seedlings space to develop. Pinch the plants to about three to four inches tall at planting time, and if the trellis or plant you expect them to climb is more than a few inches away, stick small pieces of brush next to the seedlings to provide a bridge they can follow to their eventual home. Check on the seedlings every few days for the first few weeks to make sure they are heading in the right direction, and if not, gently lift and move the stems so they end up where you want them.

Once up and growing the major problem with sweet peas (as with garden peas) will be in keeping the plants healthy and vigorous once the weather turns hot, and the choice of location will have a large effect on the plant's health. Regular cutting—which provides flowers for the vase—is also a must, as is attention to sweet pea's need for water during sunny, hot weather. Perhaps the best solution to sweet pea's difficulty thriving in hot weather is succession planting: Once the first set of plants is well established and blooming, start another set right at their base. When the first set begins to falter, cut them off at the ground and allow the second set to take over.

There are many, many varieties of sweet peas available today, both as part of mixes and as individual colors. A small strain that has proven itself over the years is the foot-high variety Bijou, which,

Sweet peas seemingly have it all: graceful habit, pleasing colors, and enchanting fragrance; if you have the cool but not harsh climate they prefer, sweet peas will be one of the star performers in your garden.

unlike most other sweet peas, needs no support. Next up in height are strains like Continental; it grows two to three feet tall and is very early, and so is better adapted to areas where summers come early and stay long. Continental also has good fragrance. The standard sweet pea mixes for home gardeners in this country are Royal and Mammoth mix, but you can also find the English Cuthbertson from which they were developed. All are vigorous growers, and while listed at only six feet, can grow taller under good conditions, so be prepared to support them. These are not as strongly scented as the old-fashioned kinds, but they are good for the cutting garden because of their long stems and the sheer quantity of flowers.

## LAVATERA

This hollyhock relative is a shrubby annual two to three feet high and a couple of feet across. The flowers are a bit more like its other cousin hibiscus, though, and it is a good alternative to that plant in the North. Here in Vermont it forms a solid, flower-smothered hedge by early August, just in time to take over from the early summer perennials. Down in the home of the hibiscus, lavatera doesn't do as well, succumbing to the combined persistence of heat and humidity.

Lavatera resents transplanting, so the seed should be sown where it is to grow about two weeks before the last frost. Since the eventual spacing of the plants will be eighteen to twenty-four inches, rather than sowing the seed in a row and thinning the seedlings to their

Lavateras look delicate, but are sturdy, shrublike annuals that can take both heat and cold, and have a long bloom period. Pictured here is the cultivar White Beauty.

eventual spacing, place a pinch of seed in each spot where you want a plant, then remove all but the strongest plants once they are a few inches high.

The most commonly available variety of lavatera is Silver Cup, a metallic pink that is quite attractive with blue companions like *Salvia farinacea*. There is a slightly shorter, white variety called Mont Blanc, but the two lavateras cannot really be grown side by side because of their height difference and mismatched foliage color. A match for Mont Blanc is called Mont Rose; it is difficult to find, and I haven't had a chance to try it yet. For a bicolor scheme, try the more closely matched White Beauty and Pink Beauty. Pink Beauty has a paler pink flower with rose striping that rises from the throat: different.

Quite similar to lavatera, but actually a mallow, is *Malva sylvestris* Zebrina, which grows taller and has white to pink flowers with very deep purple, almost black striations that merge into the throat. They, too, are suitable for cutting and are grown just the same.

## LIATRIS

Liatris is a sturdy perennial bred from the prairie gayfeather, an American wildflower also known by the name blazing star. Liatris is now a staple of the Dutch flower trade and has been vastly improved by breeders, though the original species form is still a charming and reliable performer. The tall, tight flower spikes of liatris are among the minority of garden flowers that open sequentially from the top down, reversing the hormonal trend that most spike flowers show (discussed in Chapter 2). Though it is a member of the daisy family, the flowers seem to bear no relation to the usual composite daisy form, as only ray flowers are present, with the disk flowers entirely absent.

There are two major species grown in American gardens: *L. pycnostachya* and *L. spicata*. *L. pycnostachya*, which comes from the upper Midwest and Plains and is the taller and coarser-looking of the two, often reaching five feet in its second year of growth in the rich, well-drained sunny soils that it prefers. This height is not entirely a blessing despite the plants striking appearance, as it means that the plants will usually need support if the stems are to stay straight. *L. pycnostachya* is generally shorter lived than the smaller, finer-leaved *L. spicata*, which reaches only two to three feet, and is a native of the eastern half of the country.

Both species can be increased by seed, or in the case of named varieties, by division of the tuberlike corms. Seed-grown plants will need two years growth before blooming. For bouquets, cut the white or purple flowering spikes when they are half open.

## LIGULARIA

Not well known or widely grown, this tall, striking East Asian perennial provides a tall yellow accent for shady, moist soils. I first saw ligularia The Rocket in a friend's garden, down at the low end of a large lawn where the grass fades into a brushy woodland border, on the bank of the West River. The Rocket's pointed six-foot spikes of clear yellow visually leapt forward from the dark background of the overstory, and so lent a variability and depth to the lawn edge that only a few other plants like goatsbeard *(Aruncus)* or white monkshood *(Aconitum)* could match. While there are broad-leaved cultivars with more obviously daisylike flowers, we prefer The Rocket, which has deep and finely divided palmate leaves that grow in a large mound three feet tall and as much as six feet across. While fresh seed from existing plants may sprout, the normal method of increase is by division in early spring. Ligularia does not do well in warm climates, say south of a line running from Virginia to Oklahoma.

## LILIUM

The lilies are a huge group of plants that seems to like the cool, moist summers and heavy, acid soils that abound here in the Green Mountains. Unlike some of the other really popular perennials, many of the original species are still widely available, though hybrids are starting to become so numerous as to shove them aside. Not all the traditional kinds can be replaced by somebody's marketing plan, however. The meadow or Canada lily *(L. candense)* is a common wildflower of wet meadows here in New England and will likely be here long after all the current gardens are gone; along with the old lilacs and apples found off in the now grown-up woods, it is more resilient than we are and is sure to survive.

The best way to make sense of the abundance of lilies available to gardeners today is to think of them in terms of their season. The earliest bloom by late June here, and one or another will continue until fall shuts down the show. We will mention the myriad commercial hybrids at their season of bloom, but will concentrate our discussion on the species types.

In the early group are those known collectively as Asiatic hybrids;

and the dark-colored Turk's cap lilies (*L. martagon*) with their nodding blooms; as well as the ancient, fragrant white-flowered Madonna lilies (*L. candidum*). Both Turk's cap lilies and Madonna lilies can grow to four feet, but the Madonna lily is considerably less trouble.

Aurealian and Mid-Century hybrids flower later, in July, as do the Regal lilies (*L. regale*) which can reach six feet in height and bear more than a dozen fragrant six-inch blooms per plant in a range of colors from white and pink to dark red. July is also the time in our climate for tiger lilies (*L. tigrinum*) the widely adaptable and easy to grow orange and black spotted classic that produces up to a dozen and a half eight-inch wide flowers per four-to-five-foot stem. The tiger lily too is an ancient and valuable plant—over the centuries its bulbs have been eaten as if they were artichokes—but it should be kept away from other lilies as it is host to a virus that doesn't affect the tiger lily, but can spread quickly to other more susceptible lilies.

Finally, in August, come those lilies known as the Oriental hybrids and their ancestor the gold-banded lily (*L. auratum*). The gold-banded lily will need extra winter protection north of Zone 5 if you are to enjoy its huge, fragrant white blooms, spotted with gold and red and crowned with red anthers. August is also the time for the speciosum lily (*L. speciosum*), whose white, and, again, fragrant flowers are smaller at only six inches across, but borne in such abundance on the four-to-five-foot plants that a well-grown stem may have as many as two dozen.

This is just a hint of the lilies available from catalogs and from garden centers, but it will give you an idea of the bloom sequence of the different groups. When you go to buy lilies for your own garden be sure to find out which bloom period they belong to so that you'll have a basis for planning. Remember that many strains will succeed in pots if you choose one large enough—say 18 inches in diameter for a trio of large lilies—and plant a small plant like sweet alyssum at their base to shade the roots.

Growing good lilies requires some attention to detail and proper selection of types. A generally accepted rule of thumb is that the Asiatics do better in the East and the Orientals in the West, but that is not to say that both can't be grown in your garden, only that you will have more or fewer problems to overcome. You may just have to go the extra mile. Full sun, protection from strong winds, and good drainage are essential if any lily is to become established as a relatively trouble-free perennial, so choose your spot carefully and improve it as best you can. If your land is unalterably boggy, choose species like Turk's cap and Canada lilies that can stand the soggy conditions. If shade is a problem try Martagon or regal lilies; the wood lily (*L. philadelphicum*) is native to eastern North America, and if you can get it established it will provide a fiery show in the shade.

If you buy plants locally, they will likely be potted up, and planting is simply a matter of setting the plants at the same depth in the ground as they were in the pot. Lilies are sold this way because lily bulbs, unlike tulips or daffodils, have no dried outer scales to protect them from drying out. If you buy your lilies by mail order, they will come mixed in a loose plastic bag with some peat, sphagnum, or moist wood shavings. Open the bag a bit and move the bulbs to a cool, dark, moist place (we use the root cellar) until you are ready to plant, but do not take them out of the bag. Avoid unnecessary handling as the bulbs are easily bruised and the roots broken.

Planting depth, as for other bulbs, is two to three times their diameter (with the exception of Madonna lilies, which need only be set an inch deep) and at least eighteen inches apart. As with other perennials, plant a minimum of three to five bulbs in a group; try to stay with odd numbers so the grouping looks natural. Asiatics may benefit from deeper planting (eight to ten inches) because they root along the stem above the bulb. If mice are a problem in your garden, you may need to surround the bulbs with a tubular cage of wire to prevent the mice from feasting as our ancestors did! A sprinkling of sulfur over the bulbs before covering may have enough repellent effect if the mice aren't desperately hungry.

With a few exceptions, planting depth for lilies is two to three times the diameter of the bulb. If mice are a problem in your garden, slip a tubular wire cage into the planting hole before refilling it. This will keep the mice out but allow the lily's roots to expand.

With tall, large-flowering lilies, set stakes at planting time that are tall enough to support the stem at two-thirds of its eventual height. A small groundcover like sweet alyssum (for pastel lilies) or Gem marigolds (for orange-yellow shades) will provide shade for the bulbs while still allowing full sun to reach the stems. Alternatively, you can mulch the bed; here in the North it pays to wait to mulch until the soil has warmed fully in early June.

For bouquets, cut lilies just as the flowers begin to open, but don't take any more stem than necessary as the stem and foliage are needed to build up the bulb's food supply for the following season. Even if you don't want to bring the blooms indoors, cut the flowers as soon as they pass their peak so that the plant can redirect its energy to the bulb. After frost, cut the stems back to a couple of inches; the stub is left so the location of the bulbs can be determined before they begin to grow in the spring.

Increase of lilies by seed is a complex undertaking best reserved for collectors and hybridizers. For the home gardener, division of bulbils, offsets, and scales are the usual methods. Bulbils are small bulbs that form along the stem and can be removed in midsummer after they ripen. Plant the bulbils in plug trays filled with cutting mix. Keep the trays moist and out of direct sun until the bulbils root. By the following spring the bulbils will be ready to grow into substantial plants. On some species bulbils will form underground, but are treated the same way.

When you plant lily bulbs you may notice that they are made up of layers of thick, crescent-shaped scales; once lilies have become established, loose scales from the outside of the bulb can be removed and planted—like the bulbils—in plug trays filled with cutting mix. On some species these outer scales may start to grow by themselves as offsets; if so, they can be carefully removed as divisions in very early spring. Be delicate or you may hurt the roots on the offset or weaken the main bulb itself. Finally, if you want to greatly increase your supply of a particular variety, you can lift an established bulb just after the plant dies down in the fall, separate it into its constituent scales, dust each with sulfur to combat infection, and plant them as described above. By the following spring they should be ready for the garden though they will need a few years to gain the size of the parent bulb.

## LIMONIUM

Statice is one of the most important flowers for dried arrangements, but also is widely used as a fresh cut flower. *Limonium sinuatum* is a short-lived perennial that blooms the first year from seed; it is usually grown as an annual, and is the statice we most commonly see in the garden.

*L. sinuatum* is available in a wide range of colors and two or three height ranges, but all share a common form: a ground-hugging rosette of lobed and leathery leaves from which rise branched and apparently brittle stems with longitudinal ridges along their length. The flowers, which are in small bunches at the branch tips, resemble small frilled thimbles held open-up. While each plant doesn't seem very bright, they stand out nicely when massed, and when bunched for an arrangement they are striking. The color range is now quite wide, including true blues and yellows through pastel pinks and reds. New introductions even include formerly hard-to-find autumnal and earthen shades.

In frost-free climates annual statice can be sown in the fall for early spring bloom; for most climates in the United States, you should use a spring planting schedule. Statice is strongly affected by both temperature and daylength, and the likelihood of getting a high percentage of the plants to bloom well can be greatly enhanced by how you handle the seedlings. Sow the seed ten weeks before the last frost, covering them lightly or not at all, and placing the flat on a 70–75°F heating mat. When the seed sprouts and the first leaves unfold, the plants should be moved to an area where they will have night temperatures in the fifties (much as is done with tomatoes) for the next three to four weeks. If you are starting the seed in a basement or another place that has no natural light, increase the seeds' exposure to the grow-lights so they get more than thirteen hours a day—up to sixteen is fine. If you are growing the plants in a greenhouse or cold frame, the natural increase in daylength during spring will be sufficient. Three weeks before the last frost, begin to harden the plants off. Set the plants in the garden with two weeks before the last frost and the danger of *hard* frost past. Once hardened off the plants can take a light frost, but the low twenties will kill them. Total time to flowering from the seeding date under these conditions should be twelve to sixteen weeks, but we have had years—before we learned of the seed's need for cold treatment—when we got almost no flowers before frost because we kept them in a warm greenhouse until planting time.

Garden spacing is a foot between plants, and no support should be necessary. Keep an eye out for Japanese beetles, though. Hand-pick the first few to keep them from spreading and remember that if you use a Japanese beetle trap, it should be set upwind of the plants, out of the garden, so that the beetles will leave the garden to get to the scent. Unlike many other cut flowers, statice should be harvested when the flowers are almost entirely open. Cut the stems as long as feasible, remove the lower foliage, and place immediately in water. Blooms should last two weeks without special attention. For drying, hang the flowers upside down in a warm, dark, dry place. Rapid drying and total darkness will help keep the green stem color intact.

The standard varieties of annual statice are the Fortress, Pacific, and Turbo strains. These varieties range from two to three feet tall and come in a wide range of individual colors and mixes tailored to particular color schemes like "Sunset Shades" and "Pastel Shades." A smaller-sized strain is Petite Bouquet, which grows a foot tall.

A true annual statice is *L. suworowii*, usually called Russian statice in deference to its land of origin. It is a striking plant with thin, pink flower spikes curving and twisting twelve to eighteen inches above the plants. The most common named variety is Pink Pokers, though you might find one called Bright Rose. Perennial German statice, usually known as *L. tartaricum*, has shiny, dark green, ovoid leaves that hug the ground and an airy, wide-thrown mist of tiny white flowers. Finally (though there are many more) there is perennial sea lavender (*L. latifolium*), which has an even airier habit, almost like gypsophila, but with a subtle pale lavender color. Though both these perennial statices are listed as hardy to Zone 3, they don't last long in our Zone 4 garden, perhaps because of poor drainage. There is a lot of naming confusion in this genus, so don't be too picky about how a plant is listed by the nursery; go by the description and you will be sure to get the right thing.

## LINARIA

This genus includes both annual and perennial species, but only one of each is much grown in the garden, and neither is common. Toadflax (*L. maroccana*) is a diminutive annual flower (twelve to eighteen inches tall) bearing a rainbow of multicolored half-inch flowers that resemble miniature snapdragons. Toadflax can be used in a rock garden for immediate color or in the cutting garden for bouquets. Sow in sunny, well-drained soil as soon as the ground can be worked in spring, then thin the seedlings to six inches apart for a flush of bloom that lasts until hot weather dries it up. In warm climates annual linaria not only tolerates but appreciates a bit of shade. *L. purpurea* is the perennial species and is larger than the annual both in plant and flower, with thin upward-arching leaves and a six-to-eight-inch spire of quarter-inch flowers arching slightly off its perch. The species is purple, but there is a well-bred cultivar called

Canon Went that is pink; there is also a white form. Perennial linaria is only hardy to Zone 5 without protection, but it self-sows freely and may be started from seed or propagated by root or stem cuttings.

## LINUM

The flaxes are delicate-looking plants and, though not even the perennial types are long-lived, they are quite hardy. The most common annual is *L. grandiflorum,* a slight two-footer available primarily in whites and reds, some bicolored. A related species *(L. usitatissimum)* is the sky blue annual flax from which both linen and linseed oil are made—it grows three to four feet tall. Both *L. grandiflorum* and *L. usitatissimum* should be direct-sown in a sunny, well-drained spot as soon as the ground can be worked in spring. Annual flax will bloom about three months after sowing; for an extended period of bloom, plant in succession as the flowering period is not long.

The two perennial flax species most widely grown are *L. flavum* and *L. perenne. L. flavum* is a foot to a foot and a half tall (though dwarf forms are available) and crowned with primrose yellow, five-petaled flowers an inch in diameter. *L. perenne,* which can be six inches taller than *L. flavum,* is normally a clear sky blue, but is sometimes found at specialty nurseries in white. There are dwarf forms of these species available at times as well. Bloom period of the perennial types can be extended by planting in light afternoon shade, but it will stretch the plants as well, so they should be cut back after flowering to keep them as compact as possible.

All the flaxes will reseed themselves, and the perennials can also be increased by division or stem cuttings.

## LOBELIA

I like lobelias. I don't know why. When Ellen and I were running our garden center, taking care of them was nearly an insurmountable problem. A popular hanging basket plant because of their casual, draping habit, lobelias combine well with other basket plants except that they do not stand dry soil, and if there is one problem with baskets it is their tendency to dry out quickly. Many container plants sit nestled in a corner—hot and sunny for geraniums or dark and protected for impatiens—but hanging baskets have to hang, exposed to the wind if not the sun, and wind dries out plants.

Lobelias in the open ground are considerably less trouble. They are sensitive to frost, and so cannot be set out too early, but they do form a small color-mound that combines with sweet alyssum (*Lobu-*

*laria)* so well that the two have been overdone to the detriment of both. Lobelias are good for combining with other plants because their blues are good blues, their whites are brilliant white, their lavenders and lilacs useful.

Annual lobelias should be started eight to ten weeks before the last frost. The seed is very small, so either sow a pinch in each cell of a plug tray, or use a sharpened pencil touched to your tongue to pick up a few seeds at a time and press them lightly onto the surface of sterile potting mix. Germinate at 70°F, but then grow the emergent seedlings cool and bright: fifties or sixties in full sun. A clump of seedlings in each cell of the tray is alright, but if they start to crowd, thin out the unwanted seedlings with scissors to avoid disturbing the roots of those that remain. Transplant the lobelias to the garden—after danger of frost—six inches apart. If you are in a warm climate, lobelias prefer a spot that is shaded at least part of the day. If the plants falter, shear one-third of their height, and they will bloom again.

Lobelia varieties separate into two classes, bedding and trailing types. Bedding lobelias grow only four to six inches tall, but six to eight inches across in a low mound; trailing types will creep farther and if planted in a container or at the edge of retaining wall will drape nicely. String of Pearls is a good bedding mix, but there are a number of single colors widely grown for bedding: Cambridge Blue is sky blue; while Crystal Palace is deep blue with bronze foliage; White Lady is, obviously, white; Rosamund is a purple-red; Mrs. Clibran is a solid blue with a white eye. The premier trailing mixes are the Cascade and Fountain series. Both contain pastel shades, with some near red.

Two hardy native lobelias from the eastern United States, and a hybrid between them and a Mexican relative, make good perennial garden plants. *L. cardinalis,* or the cardinal flower, grows from two to four feet with intense red flower spikes. *L. siphilitica* is slightly smaller and has blue flowers. The two cross naturally in the wild and in cultivation, and thus there are intermediate forms as well. One particular hybrid, *L. X speciosa,* has been highly developed and is a popular garden and cut flower in Europe, blooming only four months after seeding. All of these perennial lobelias prefer moist, heavy soils and may be increased by seed or stem cuttings.

## LOBULARIA

Sweet alyssum deserves its name, for its fragrance is just that: sweet. Diminutive, hardy, and subtle in its coloring, sweet alyssum

Sweet alyssum (Lobularia) makes a great edging plant as it drapes nicely, blooms over a long period in cool climates and has a wonderful honey-sweet fragrance.

is a perfect annual edging plant. We start our alyssum a full ten to twelve weeks before the last frost, sowing a pinch of the tiny seed in each cell of a 98- or 50-cell plug insert. The seed doesn't need any heat to germinate and once sprouted can grow happily in the coolest part of the greenhouse. Only the hardest frosts bother the young plants, and the only reason we wait until a few weeks before the last frost to set the plants out is so that we can place other, more prominent plants first, and use the alyssum as a base. We also sow some seed directly in the garden where spring bulbs are blooming to help cover their less than graceful exit, and among the stones of our front path to appear as if unbidden. In the garden, sweet alyssum needs six inches in each direction per plant. In our cool climate alyssum blooms happily for most of the summer; if through some neglect it enters a slack period, a quick shearing will restore alyssum to its sweet self.

The standard selections for many years were New Carpet of Snow, a white; Rosie O'Day, rose pink; and Oriental Night, dark blue-purple; now, new blends like Wonderland and Easter Basket have been developed that bloom earlier, with more uniformity from color to color so that mixed plantings look their best.

## LUPINUS

Very few plants have as much going for them as lupines: they are spectacularly beautiful, tolerant of a wide range of conditions, and, as legumes, they improve any soil in which they grow. Lupines are winter-hardy even here in the mountains of Vermont, yet they are able to stand the heat of summer as well, though they may be short-lived south of a line from Virginia out to Oklahoma. Lupine leaves are a fan of ten to fifteen thin, lance-shaped leaflets all radiating from a single stem, with each leaflet veined once in the center. The symmetry and repetition of this arrangement is made even more beautiful in wet weather because lupines share with lady's mantle (*Alchemilla*) the wonderful habit of catching both dew and rain and then holding it, crystalline, on the leaves. The flowers of the lupine are tall spikes made up of one-inch, pealike blossoms in a full spectrum of hues, with some bicolors.

Lupines start easily from spring-sown seed chilled for a few weeks before planting, and they can be grown as fall-sown, overwintering annuals in the South. In spring, seed should be sown eight to ten weeks before the last frost for setting out when seedlings are four to six weeks old. Nick the seed with a file, then soak in water for a day before sowing in a 50-cell plug insert, and then germinate at 70–75°F. Garden spacing should be eighteen inches between plants for large types like the Russell hybrids, which can reach three to four feet tall, or a foot between plants for smaller kinds like the Minarette or Gallery series. Annual lupines like *L. texensis* or *L. hartwegii* can make do with the closer spacing. All make excellent cut flowers.

Most lupines will self-sow in the open garden, though the hybrids will intercross and eventually return to their natural, less vibrant colors. To maintain named cultivars it is necessary to take cuttings or divide the plants—carefully—in the spring. The biggest pest of lupines in our garden is aphids; we cut off affected stems and leaves and throw them in the chicken yard. If you get an aphid infestation and don't have chickens, burning is equally effective. You can also spray with insecticidal soap, or with a harsh stream of cold water, which will sweep the aphids away and stun them.

## LYCHNIS

Closely related to both the annual edging plant silene, or catchfly, and the annual corn cockle, a wonderful cutting flower whose proper name is *Agrostemma*, lychnis itself goes by the common names Maltese cross or rose campion. Maltese cross and rose campion are actually two different species of *Lychnis*, both perennial, though the campion rarely survives more than a few seasons.

Maltese cross, *L. chalcedonica*, is a two-to-three-foot tall perennial native to eastern Russia that has long been grown in American gardens. It is hardy virtually everywhere and easy to grow in a relatively moist but well-drained, sunny spot. The flowering stems arise from the base of the plant, clasped by three-to-four-inch green leaves and topped by a cluster of one-inch, four-petaled, brilliant red crosses. It makes an excellent cut flower.

Rose campion, *L. coronaria*, is even more striking, with gray-green, woolly leaves and glowing rose-red, phloxlike flowers up to two inches across. Like the Bloody Cranesbill (*Geranium*), it is a plant that is hard to work into the border with other plants but worth growing in a bouquet garden. Problems, though, are significant: The plants are somewhat limp; winter survival is spotty; appearance after blooming is less than proper; and campion self-sows vigorously, becoming a problem if not watched over.

Seeds of both lychnis species start easily from seed sown at room temperature six to eight weeks before the frost-free date, for setting out when four to six weeks old. Garden spacing is one foot between plants. Plants can be divided in spring, but growing from seed is the preferred method of increase.

## LYSIMACHIA

I first saw the gooseneck loosestrife at the once-a-decade Dutch flower exhibition, Floriade. It was mass-planted in the display perennial garden, the bed easily six feet deep and fifteen to twenty feet across. At first I thought it was some sort of veronica, but once the marker was located, I found it to be *Lysimachia clethroides*, a hardy perennial that, while restrained here in the North, can be very invasive in the South. Still, the gracefully curved white flower heads and shrublike appearance when planted in masses make it a useful backbone plant for the informal perennial border. The foot-long, arching white spikes appear over a long period from July to September, and the plants come easily from seed, division, or cuttings. Lysimachia prefers a cool, moist soil.

## LYTHRUM

Also known as loosestrife, lythrum is a much different plant from lysimachia—taller, with eight-to-ten-inch magenta-to-purple flower spikes. Most northerners have seen purple loosestrife growing in swampy wastes along the highway in summer, but they may not have known what it was. Lythrum can be invasive, and many people consider it a threat to native species, but where controlled—especially where carefully bred cultivars are used, with their clearer colors and more restrained habit—it is a striking garden plant. Lythrum self-sows freely, but the named cultivars do not usually come true from seed, so it is best to keep the flowers cut and propagate by division or cuttings. The flowers are good for arrangements if cut when only a third of the flowers are open, and then the stems soaked overnight. The flowers can also be used once dry, though they should be allowed to develop further before cutting if drying is your aim.

## MATTHIOLA

A mainstay of both cutting and fragrance gardens, stocks (*M. incana*) are biennials grown as cool-weather annuals. In frost-free areas of the country, stocks are fall-sown for late winter bloom, while here in the North they are planted as soon as the ground can be worked in spring for bloom just before the hottest part of the summer.

There are two kinds of stocks that interest us here. The first is a wispy little plant called evening-scented stock (*M. longipetala*). It would grow to a foot and a half if it were upright rather than sprawling among other plants, and it bears insignificant pinkish-white flowers whose main attraction is their unconscionably strong evening fragrance. The key with this plant—like mignonette—is to sow small clumps of it among other plants growing near a window or where you spend time on summer evenings. Thus placed it will provide a heavenly accompaniment to the soft breezes and the symphony of frogs and lightning bugs that make high summer nights so delicious. All that is required when planting the seed outdoors is to rough up a bit of ground, sprinkle the seed on it, and pat down gently; a bit of water if the spring weather is dry will get things going. Once established evening-scented stock will reseed itself happily. A few small pots full will likewise provide a moveable feast of the olfactory.

Annual or columnar stocks (*M. incana*) have quite the opposite habit: The flowers are showy, but they still have the fragrance of their less ostentatious cousins. In cool climates, plant stocks in the garden as soon as the ground can be worked in spring. Light frost won't hurt them, but they may need a little protection if temperatures dip into the low twenties. The cool temperatures and increasing daylengths of early spring trigger their biennial blooming reflex.

You can get a jump on the season in hot summer areas—which

stocks cannot stand—by starting the seed indoors. Sow the seed on the surface of 50-cell plug inserts, then water from below so as not to disturb them. Stocks will germinate in about a week at the standard temperature of 70–75°F. As with statice, later success depends on how the plants are handled at the seedling stage, so keep three basic rules in mind. First, once the seedlings have their first pair of true leaves, they should be put in a spot where they get bright sun but temperatures only in the low fifties for two or three weeks. This cold treatment, officially known as vernalization, tricks biennials into thinking they have gone through a winter and thus impels them to form flowering buds. Second, if you are starting plants in the basement under lights, make sure that they get at least fourteen hours of light a day, increasing that amount a bit every week, so that the naturally increasing daylength of spring is reproduced. Plants respond to the combination of these two environmental cues much more strongly than to either one in isolation.

Third, if you have a preference for double flowers, select for them during the first few weeks of the cold treatment. Look for differences in the seedlings; the most vigorous, with larger, yellower leaves are likely to be double, while those with more gray-green leaves are likely to be single-flowered. The amount of difference varies among strains, but in some you will even notice a small notch in the seed leaves of the doubles-to-be. The idea is to plant out only those you want, single or double.

Once in the garden, columnar stocks need a square foot per plant. Tall varieties would certainly be helped by some support, but it isn't absolutely necessary. If you cut for bouquets, wait until about half the flowers on a given stalk have opened and immerse the stems in water immediately after cutting, then move them to a cool, dark place. For drying, allow the flowers to open fully, then cut and hang in bunches of only a few stems in a warm, dark, dry place. If dried quickly they will retain their fragrance.

The standard variety of columnar stocks in the United States is Ten Week Mix, named for its bloom time ten weeks after sowing. This is a compact strain twelve to eighteen inches tall, with a relatively wide color range; you will be able to select for doubles. Other varieties that are generally available include the Legacy series, at eighteen inches; the Trysomics, which are especially early and thus good for areas with hot summers; and a two-and-a-half-foot group known as Excelsior or Mammoth stocks; these are big plants and will need support. All are highly fragrant. The small evening-scented stocks are usually sold under the botanic name *M. bicornis* or *M. longipetala*.

## MERTENSIA

Forget the name mertensia, even though it sounds interesting; these are Virginia bluebells, or—as my Bluegrass-bred grandmother taught me to call them—Kentucky bluebells. Either way, they are one of the first and most charming of spring flowers. Our bluebells surround a wild cherry tree and share its light shade with old-fashioned bleeding hearts, sweet violets, columbines, and a mix of small woodland bulbs.

Once established the plants will colonize and can then be divided, or the seed collected and immediately sown where new colonies are desired. It is easy enough to buy a few plants or ask a neighbor for some; then you'll be on your way.

## MIRABILIS

Mirabilis is Latin for "wonderful" and it is an apt name for this tough yet attractive, shrublike perennial that is grown here in temperate climates as an annual. The common name is four-o'clocks as the eighteen-to-twenty-four-inch-tall plants bloom in the late afternoon with fragrant one-to-two-inch flowers in a range of colors from white, to pink, to red, even yellow, and including some bicolors. Whatever the color, it is as unique as the flowers themselves, which are deep-throated like a petunia but not glaucous, and have a luminosity created by a layering of colors in the bloom. As a rule, four-o'clocks are available only as a mix. They can be direct-seeded on the frost-free date for blooms eight to ten weeks later, but we start ours indoors six weeks before that, in 18-cell plug inserts or 3½-inch pots, and then we set these out after all danger of frost. Once frost kills the plants you can dig the tubers that have formed and save those for the following year, or simply start again from seed.

## MONARDA

Also called bee balm or bergamot (and about a dozen other names), monarda is as much an herb as it is a flower. The leaves are used for tea, and their scent is noticeable as soon as you near the plants. The flowers stand atop stiff two-to-four-foot stems but have the loose and jocular habit of the perennial bachelor's button (*Centaurea montana*), in a range of colors far wider: from white to pale pinks, bright reds, dark burgundies, even clear and musky blues to purple. The plant itself is easy to grow, even a bit invasive in the moist, cool soils that it prefers, but a clump will start to die out in its center after a few years and thus needs regular division to keep it looking good. Bee balm is also susceptible to powdery mildew in dry soil, especially if the plants are grown too close together.

There is one good seed-grown strain called Panorama. It grows to about three feet tall, bearing flowers in red, pink, salmon, and white. All monardas are attractive to both butterflies and hummingbirds, and they make excellent cut flowers.

## MYOSOTIS

This is another plant even nongardeners have heard of, but rarely by its proper name: *Myosotis sylvatica* is the Latin name for forget-me-nots, one of the most famous and beloved of garden flowers even though they are not so much grown in gardens as at their edges, where cultivated ground meets a surrounding wood. Given these conditions, or their like, the plants will self-sow prodigiously and will maintain themselves indefinitely, colonizing large spaces with their soft, green, spatulate leaves and fragrant, pale blue (sometimes pink) flowers little more than a quarter-inch across, but densely packed into heads two to three inches across. Direct-sow in early spring; established clumps can also be divided to help the plants find new homes.

## NARCISSUS

Daffodils—they were said in Greek myth to have carpeted the Elysian Fields where those mortals blessed by the gods spent eternity, and thus they were the first flowers that could truly be called heavenly. There is no doubt that after a long New England winter the sight of their bright blooms amid still brown grass reminds one that life does have its eternal aspects and that another flower-filled season lies ahead.

There is an enormous range of types of narcissus; the best way that I can simplify them is as follows: standard daffodils with single flowers and a single bloom per stem (often subdivided into large cupped trumpets and small cupped trumpets); double-flowered daffodils; triandus daffodils with multiple flowers per stem and a pendant habit; cyclamen daffodils with flowers that are upswept like their namesake; jonquils, usually small, multiflowered, and fragrant; tazetta narcissi, including the fragrant forcing kinds known as paperwhites; poeticus narcissi, which have blue-green leaves, contain the only reds in the genus (corona only), and can tolerate wetter soils; and miscellaneous or species types.

Narcissus fanciers make far more distinctions that this and are welcome to; if you'd like to join, there are whole societies to celebrate and study this wonderful plant. Practically though, I would advise consulting a good color catalog to help make sensible decisions about the types you'd like to grow. Most catalogs separate narcissi according to the standard classifications so that you can see how the plants are related and when each type will bloom.

One additional thing it might help to know is how narcissi are sized, or graded. There are two general classes: rounds and double nose; rounds are large single bulbs, while the double nose bulbs have two or even three small bulbs which are attached to one another at the base. Most often they will be classified as DN1, DN2, or DN3 (which is essentially a round). You can expect to pay more for the higher grades, as they took longer to produce and are likely to bloom more vigorously. Still, if you want to buy a large number of bulbs for naturalizing, bargains can be found by purchasing the smaller sizes.

All the narcissi prefer a soil near neutral pH that is well drained. They like full sun but will grow in spots where deciduous trees overhang, as long as the trees do not cast too deep a shade before the narcissi have gone dormant. The south-facing edge of woodlands and rock gardens are both good locations for narcissi. If planting narcissi in the lawn, make sure they are not in a place that will be mowed early. The foliage must be left on the plants to increase the bulb's food reserves until it withers naturally. In the garden this means narcissi should be planted with something that will hide but not shade their dying leaves; some of the best plants for this purpose are daylilies, but there are many other possibilities as well.

All the hardy kinds of narcissus are fall-planted at least one month before the soil temperature drops to 40°F and growth stops for the winter. In warm areas wait until soil temperatures fall below 70°F to avoid risk of bulb rot or fall-emergence of the foliage, which may then be harmed by winter weather. Plant the bulbs at least one and a half times a deep as they are wide, and when in doubt go deeper, as shallow-planted bulbs split and stop blooming sooner.

The most common problems of narcissi—aside from overly zealous lawn mowing—are crown rot and bulb flies, neither of which have ever bothered our plantings. The best control for crown rot is to avoid planting any bulbs which are soft or have obvious bruises that look infected. If you see plants that are stunted and don't bloom well, dig a few of the bulbs and look them over. If the bulbs are covered in white mold, or are soft and brown, dispose of them—but not in the compost pile. Another cause of soft bulbs is the larva of the bulb fly; if you see bulbs for sale with soft spots and small holes near the soft spots, don't buy them. If you have already bought them, don't plant them.

All the narcissi make excellent cut flowers. For bouquets, cut or "pull" the stems to maximize stem length. Pick narcissi just as the flowers are beginning to open. The flowers will last up to a week at the outside. Narcissi stems should be soaked overnight first (they secrete a mucus that is harmful to many other cut flowers) with a change of water during the soaking period, if you are planning to use the flowers in arrangements with other flowers.

Lift and separate narcissi every three to five years, when clusters of bulbs have formed. Dig the clusters after the foliage has died down and allow them to dry in a dark, airy place until the bulbs come apart easily, then separate and replant immediately.

You can also grow narcissi in containers. During the winter months their bright spring colors and—with some types—strong fragrance can take some of the fever out of being cabin-bound. In general it is the tazetta narcissi that force the best, though many of the standard kinds also do well. Check catalogs carefully to see if a particular variety is suited for container growing. Some excellent cultivars include King Alfred or Mount Hood among the large, standard daffodils, and Soleil d'Or or Paperwhites among the tazettas.

You can schedule the bloom of daffodils by storing the bulbs in the root cellar or the crisper drawer of the refrigerator until twelve to fourteen weeks before you want them to bloom. Then plant half a dozen bulbs in an 8-inch-diameter "bulb pan" (which is similar to but a bit shorter than a regular flower pot). Use a standard light potting mix. Water the planted bulbs, let drain, then return them to storage. After ten to twelve weeks back in storage, the bulbs will have formed a substantial root system and begun to sprout. Bring them out into a warm (60–65°F), bright area, and within two weeks they should be in bloom. You can adjust the schedule by altering the temperature at which the bulbs grow once brought out, or by changing the length of time the bulbs are in storage: More time in the cellar and lower temperatures after removal will both lengthen the time until bloom. Once out in the light, the bulbs should be watered only when dry. After bloom they can be planted outside.

The tazetta narcissi do not need any cellar time to establish themselves and can simply be potted up in a bed of pebbles six to eight weeks before you want them to bloom. We half-fill a glass container with pebbles, set the bulbs, then add pebbles up to their necks. Add water up to the surface of the pebbles and replenish it to that point when necessary. Over time the roots will fill the space between the pebbles and the plants will grow. As in the case of the daffodils, blooming can be scheduled by the temperature regime that is followed. Most tazettas are discarded after blooming as they are not hardy outdoors in most of the United States.

## NICOTIANA

When we had our garden center I didn't care much for nicotiana. That was because all I knew was the bedding types. Now don't get me wrong, the dwarf nicotiana that is used for bedding is a relatively carefree plant, blooming easily and consistently till frost, but I just got sick of seeing them (as I did of most bedding plants after years of handling them by the thousands). When I found out about the parents of those high flying hybrids, it was not only my introduction to fragrance gardening, but also to the value of heirlooms. These once popular plants are now out of fashion in favor of more uniform or floriferous hybrids which—this is what turned the corner for me—are too often lacking the soul and spirit of the old-timers. Fortunately for all of us, many of the old-time nicotianas are coming back into favor, and the kinds available through mainstream seed catalogs is on the rise.

All nicotianas require the same culture: Sow the seed six to eight weeks before the last frost, just pressing it lightly into the surface of a flat filled with sterile potting soil mix—the seed needs light to germinate. Moisten the flat from below to avoid disturbing the seed, then set the flat, covered with a humidity dome (or simply a sheet of plastic wrap) in a bright place out of direct sun for the seven to ten days germination will require. If you have room on the heating mat, the normal 70–75°F is just right. Thin the seedlings as they grow or move them to larger quarters; the larger kinds of nicotiana in particular need room if they are to develop into specimen plants.

Set the plants out when all danger of frost is past. Small bedding types need only to be eight inches apart, but the large, old-fashioned kinds—though they can be planted in blocks with a foot between each plant—look best set off by themselves, two or even three feet away from their nearest neighbor. Bedding types will self-clean—that is, deadhead themselves—and bloom till frost. The older kinds will need periodic cutting to maintain their flower power; the cuttings make excellent vase flowers.

The basic garden nicotiana is *N. alata*, also called jasmine tobacco (its close relative is smoking tobacco, *N. tabacum*). In its original form *N. alata* grows three to four feet tall, with relatively large, oval leaves and white, star-shaped, tubular flowers borne on a multitude of branches. The flowers open late in the afternoon and by dark

*Nicotiana alata*, or jasmine tobacco, is a long-blooming, evening-scented powerhouse plant that self-seeds freely and is always welcome in our garden.

release an intoxicating jasmine fragrance that carries on the evening air. Our main planting last year was a good 350 feet from the house, but the scent still presented itself within an hour of dusk, climbing the downslope air that sinks across our hillside toward the town road, where the stately plants had been set to greet passersby.

The first of the *alata* hybrids, still tall but with pastel flowers that open early in the day, was the three-foot-tall Sensation series. Most of the newer hybrids are carefree dwarf bedding plants; in the process of breeding these uniform and reliable bedding plants, most of the fragrance has been lost. The Nicki strain grows eighteen to twenty inches in six different colors; while the Domino strain is even smaller, at only a foot tall, and has nine colors in its range, including three bicolors. Both the Nicki and Domino strains include a lime-green colored form, just as in the older style nicotiana there is Lime Green, thirty inches tall, with an open, yellow-green bloom. A species plant that we like is *N. sylvestris*, a strongly scented and more striking form—the leaves are larger, with the softness of tobacco leaves, and the flowers are four-to-six-inch tubes ending in a flat, fused bell of petals hanging in pendulous clusters from long solitary stems— quite different in presentation from the airy profusion of stems and flowers of jasmine tobacco. Finally, there is an exotic form, *N. langs-dorffii*, with small green, pendulous flowers on three-to-five-foot plants—something of an understatement as far as statement plants go. Like all the nicotianas, it attracts hummingbirds.

## NIGELLA

This is one of the most underappreciated annuals in American gardens, an astounding fact when you consider that it has so many uses. Nigella makes a wonderful cut flower that also dries well, and its airy casualness makes it a perfect plant for an old-fashioned cottage garden. That it was once much more popular is clear from the profusion of names under which it may found: love-in-a-mist, devil-in-the-bush, fennel flower, hair of Venus, even blue beard.

Nigella is grown as a hardy annual, like statice or larkspur. The best plants result from an early spring sowing here in the North or a late fall sowing in mild climates. You can start the seed four to six weeks early indoors, but you'll need to use plugs or peat pots because nigella resents transplanting. Either way that you plant the seed, final spacing in the garden is six to nine inches between plants. If you are growing nigella for the seed pods, which are outstanding in dried arrangements, use the closer spacing because it will favor the flowers produced on the terminal shoots, and they are almost always larger than those on the side shoots. For use in a cottage border, the wider spacing will allow the plants to spread, and this spreading out will lead to a more interesting appearance. Be sure to keep border plants deadheaded to extend the bloom period. For bouquets, cut after the flowers have opened, but before they have separated at the

Nigella "Curiosity" makes an excellent fresh-cut flower (*top center-right*), and later, once the unique "jester's hat" seed pods form (*far left*), a fantastic dried flower as well.

base. For drying, harvest after the pods have bronzed. Small bunches hung in a dark, warm dry place will air-dry quickly.

The most frequently seen nigellas are Miss Jekyll, once just a bright blue but now a whole series of semidouble flowers; and Persian Jewels, a mix of white, rose pink, blue, and various shades between and beyond. Both Miss Jekyll and Persian Jewels grow about a foot and a half tall and are members of the main species, *N. damascena.* If you want a particular color, it would be worth trying some other cultivars: Albion is a pure white; Oxford Blue, very tall for a nigella at thirty inches, is excellent for cutting; and Mulberry Rose has striped seed pods once the flowers have gone by. Other related species are especially good for drying: *N. hispanica* Curiosity grows to a foot and a half and at first seems like a standard blue nigella: Once the flowers fade, however, the seed pods take on the appearance of a jester's hat. *N. orientalis* is even more unusual, in that it has yellow flowers—rare for a nigella—and the seed pod, once formed, looks like an inside-out flower. Both *N. hispanica* and *N. orientalis* are fantastic for dried arrangements.

## OENOTHERA

I love the word oenothera (pronounced *een-o-theer-*a) just for its unexpected look and sound, and I am also fond of its owner, a genus of bright and sturdy plants. My favorite is *Oenothera fruiticosa,* the common sundrop. We were introduced to this cheery edging plant by a neighbor who uses it the way that gardeners farther south might use dwarf boxwood, to provide a low edge for beds of vegetables and flowers. The introduction was short and sweet—she took a shovel and hacked off a piece of the dark green border covered with as yet unopened buds and dumped it unceremoniously into a wheelbarrow. When I got home with the foot-square clump I broke it (not without anxiety—but I was following specific instructions) into dozens of tiny, single-stem divisions, which I planted roughly into a holding bed while I prepared them a permanent place. Within a month, I had a block of vigorous, well-rooted plants each topped with a cluster of sunny one-to-two-inch flowers. Since that time, we have used the sundrop as a neat and floriferous edge to walkways, terraces, and garden beds, and never has it complained about soil, sun, or water. For edging, space the plants six inches apart diagonally in double rows and they will fill in almost immediately. Like sundrops, the showy evening primrose (*O. speciosa*) is a sturdy and self-sufficient plant, even becoming something of a problem in southern areas where, if given rich soil and full sun, it may get out of hand. The flower of the showy evening primrose is white, or in some cultivars, pink to rose, though not everyone is fond of the shade. Propagate oenothera by seed sown in spring or by division as described above.

## PAEONIA

Another perennial in our gardens that first came from a friend was the peony simply labeled "Grandma's Pink." A fragrant and early bloomer, it had been in the Higuera family for over seventy-five years, divisions of the original plant passed down from generation to generation and finally on to the Ogden family, still going strong. We planted the divisions we were given on the windward side of the kitchen garden, where its rich fragrance enriches our late spring work in the vegetable beds.

Like daylilies, irises, and daffodils, peonies are such popular plants that, there are enormous numbers of varieties, and if you want to talk about them you virtually *have* to find ways to break them into manageable groups. The most significant distinction is between herbaceous peonies, which die back to the ground, and tree, or shrub peonies, which don't. We also group peonies by their different flowering times, which are important to almost any gardener. Of course, peonies can also be classified by flower color and type (i.e., single, anemone-flowered, semidouble, and double).

The best way to choose which peonies you would like to grow is to look at them in gardens you visit. If friends have one you like, perhaps they would divide it for you; if they know the name, you should be able to get one for yourself at a local nursery or, if not, from one of the specialty mail-order houses. In any case the catalogs of the specialists offer a showcase of all the different types, often with close-up photos of the blooms and complete instructions on planting and care. The catalogs are well worth the two or three dollars charged for postage and handling.

When you are considering which peonies to plant, keep a few things in mind. One is that this is a northern plant, originally from the Siberian steppes near Lake Baikal east to the Arctic Ocean and south to Mongolia. While peonies will grow in hot, humid climates, blooms will be inferior, stems weaker, and disease more of a problem. Experts recommend that Southern gardeners choose early varieties with single flowers to minimize the effects of heat and humidity, and this is especially important for organic gardeners who wish to avoid the use of sprays.

Northern gardeners should try to stretch the blooming season as much as possible, because most peonies bloom in a short period from late spring into early summer. The Higueras, who gave us our first peonies, have managed to stretch the peony season in their garden all the way from late May into the first week of July. They accomplish this long bloom time by selecting both the earliest and the latest varieties they can find, in addition to midseason types, and then plant them in conditions that exaggerate their seasonality. Thus, the earliest peonies are planted in full sun and light soil, where spring comes first; the relatively warm conditions mean that the peonies don't bloom for very long, but there are others that come along to fill the gap so it hardly matters. Conversely, the latest-blooming varieties are planted in heavy, moist soil on the north side of a grove of maples where the shade retards their development. Again, with the extreme conditions, these plants do not produce as well, but they do bloom, and at a time when all the other peonies are long gone.

Aside from these kinds of extreme cases, peonies prefer a rich, relatively heavy, neutral-to-slightly-acid soil in full sun. They make good hedging plants, and the broadly divided, deep green, slightly glossy foliage is attractive throughout the summer. Most varieties grow to be two to three feet across and three to four feet tall once fully settled, so be sure to allow enough room.

Peonies are generally increased by division in August or September, though as a practical matter they rarely need it. Unless you are actively trying to increase your collection, it is best to leave them alone, as peonies take a few years to reach their peak performance and if well cared for will continue for many, many years. To divide them, dig the plants, hose off the crown (so you can see where the buds arise from the thick root mass), and cut it into pieces with a sharp knife so that each piece has at least three buds, preferably five. Dust the cut ends with sulfur, then replant.

Care in planting makes a huge difference for peonies since they will be left in place for a long time, and if not planted at the correct depth they will not flower properly. Once the spot is selected, dig a large hole—at least eighteen inches across and a foot deep—then remove the worst third of the soil and replace it with compost, mixing thoroughly until the hole is two-thirds full. Add another shovelful of compost to make a mound, and on that place the roots so that the red buds are exactly two inches below the surrounding soil surface; if in doubt place the roots a little shallow rather than a little deep. Settle the roots into the compost, fill around the crown with soil until you reach the level of the buds, and then fill the hole with water. Once the water drains, return the remaining soil to the hole until you have a small mound over the crown of the plant. Press down in a circle around the crown with the palm of your hands to form a shallow, depressed ring; fill the ring with water and allow it to soak in. It's a good idea to remove the flowers before they open the first season unless the division was a substantial one—five buds or more.

Once established, peonies are relatively carefree plants. Each spring, just as the reddish buds break ground, add a one-inch layer of compost or well-rotted—not fresh—manure in a circle around the crown, but not up against it. Once the leaves unfold, some form of support will be needed. Bamboo and twine set around the circumference of the plant will work well, but is less formal-looking than the manufactured "peony rings" sold by many mail-order companies. We actually use large tomato hoops on our plants. Tomato hoops are inverted wire cones that can be inserted into the ground and will provide some structure to the plant, which will grow to hide the hoops. In a windy site, however, tomato hoops will not be able to keep the plants from blowing over. Come fall, cut the foliage back to an inch or so above the ground and compost the cut foliage in a hot pile or burn it. No winter protection is necessary except for newly set plants, but a second application of compost or rotted manure will be beneficial. The plants are unlikely to need irrigation unless a very hot, dry spell immediately precedes flowering.

As mentioned earlier, peonies make excellent cut flowers. While many experts say that a dozen flowers per plant are possible, we have seen many more. Our neighbors the Higueras, using only compost and manure, regularly produce thirty to forty strong stems per plant, and our own, much younger plants have already surpassed the dozen mark. Peonies respond to disbudding, so you can radically

When planting peonies, depth is critically important: the buds should be exactly two inches below ground level. If necessary, place a stick across the planting hole to gauge this; then settle the plant into a bed of compost, water well, and then fill the hole. Peonies also need support to hold their large flowers erect.

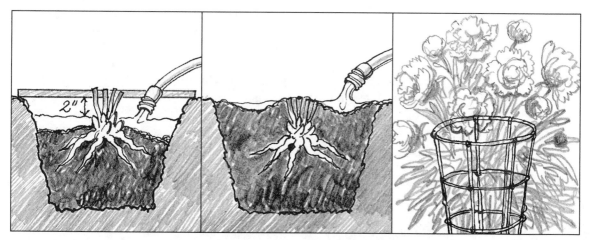

increase the size of individual flowers if you remove all but the terminal buds on each shoot.

Flowers last the longest if cut just as they "break," before the petals have opened. Cut them early in the morning; they will easily last a week in the vase. As a general rule, the doubles will last a bit longer than the singles.

Peonies can be made to bloom early in a greenhouse or sunroom. Dig the plants after the ground has begun to freeze in fall, pot up the dormant crowns, and put them in the root cellar. After a minimum of two months in the root cellar (where the temperature should be 35–40°F), bring the plants out into the light and warmth. Water regularly as you would for any potted plant, and within another two months, you should have full-sized, blooming plants. After bloom they can be moved back to the garden, where they should be left for a few years at the minimum to recover from their exertions.

## PAPAVER

Like chrysanthemums, poppies are one of the plant groups that includes a number of both annual and perennial species I am quite fond of. Perhaps the classic poppy of the late twentieth century is the red Flanders poppy *(P. rhoeas),* and it is this same species that also produced, under the artful eye of the English vicar William Wilkes, the still widespread Shirley poppies, one of the most satisfying annual flowers imaginable.

Both the red Flanders and Shirley poppies spring easily from seed sown as soon as the ground can be worked in spring; warm-climate gardeners can have some by fall-sowing. The plants have glaucous gray-green foliage and branch freely; thinned to eight inches between plants they present quite a show for a period in early summer that can be stretched considerably by diligent deadheading. Cutting is no burden as the flowers are excellent, though short-lived, in bouquets. Treat the red Flanders and Shirley poppies in the same fashion as other poppies, cutting them just as the flowers open and searing the cut end with a flame, then plunging in tepid water. The traditional color of *P. rhoeas* is bright, immortal red, but the Shirley strains are much lighter, pastel shades, often with concentric white rings and deeper centers. The delicacy of the petals only adds to the subtlety of the coloring, and in the cultivars Angel Wings, Fairy Wings, and Mother of Pearl, there is a luminous, smoky undertone that is, without a doubt, one of the most beautiful color schemes I have ever seen in a flower.

Of all the poppies, only the Oriental poppy (*P. orientale*) is best treated as a perennial. The others all bloom readily the same season as sown, and even though they are technically perennial, they are short-lived enough that it makes sense to replace them yearly. Orientals resent transplanting, and can really only be moved or divided during their dormant period in mid- to late summer. Root cuttings take easily if made in late summer though, and the number of plants can be increased quickly. Root cuttings can also be made in situ in early spring by taking a sharp spade and cutting straight down in a circle around an established plant. This will sever the outer tips of shallow roots, leaving them at the perfect depth for root and shoot initiation. Any that sprout can be moved as soon as they have a few leaves, and the mother plant left otherwise undisturbed.

The hen-and-chicks poppy is a member of the species *Papaver somniferum,* and produces an unusual central seed pod (the hen) around which cluster dozens of smaller pods (the chicks). These pods dry easily and keep for a very long time in dried arrangements.

Orientals are large plants when in active growth, so garden spacing should be at least eighteen inches between plants; two feet between plants will allow them more room to develop. The bristly foliage is deeply divided and quite attractive, but you should avoid too large a planting of just poppies, since once they go dormant there will be a gap in the border. Perennial baby's breath and boltonia are often used to hide the dying foliage of Oriental poppies. The six-inch flowers of Oriental poppies are often ruffled or pinked at the edges, many with contrasting colors deep within the center, and they are held atop bare, hairy three-to-four-foot stems; they make wonderful though short-lived cut flowers. Cut in the morning just before buds open, and sear the cut stem ends with a flame.

The opium poppy, *P. somniferum*, is equal in stature to the Oriental poppy, and it is hardy enough to be a short-lived perennial in the Deep South. The leaves of the opium poppy are gray, but smooth, untoothed, and sessile (or stem-clasping). The flowers, like those of the other poppies, are crepelike and, like the Oriental poppy, formed most often into a cup, which may well have ruffled or pinked edges. Reaching three to four inches in diameter and spreading across a color range from white to pink, bright red, lavender, and a host of in-between pastels, most flowers also have black markings deep in their centers; in the light shades these markings may be gray or lavender. Some forms are double, resembling peony flowers, and may be sold as *P. paeoniaeflorum*.

Smallest and hardiest of the commonly grown poppy species is *P. nudicaule*, the Iceland poppy. It is also the only poppy outside the Orientals that has yellow, orange, and salmon shades. These relatively diminutive poppies have toothed but still delicate foliage in a basal rosette. A wiry one-foot stem capped with a two-to-three-inch, open-faced flower, without the darker center ring found in many of the others, rises directly from the base of the plant. Seed should be sown in fall or early spring, merely pressed into the surface of a well-prepared bed, and the seedlings thinned to about six inches between plants. If regularly cut—and Icelandics make one of the best cut flowers among the poppies—the plants will continue to issue legions of short-lived but numerous flowers well into the summer.

## PELARGONIUM

Beginning gardeners will have to forgive me for putting the common garden geranium here where it belongs. As you can tell by the fact that I have placed it here under *Pelargonium,* the common garden geranium is not a true geranium. It is a South African cousin which—given time, care, and freedom from frost—will grow to be a shrub or moderate height groundcover. Pelargoniums are sometimes known by their common name storksbill, while the true geraniums—members of a hardy perennial genus—use the common name cranesbill.

That said, we will call our pelargoniums geraniums and assume you know the difference. Most gardeners—even nongardeners who have walked in a park—are aware of these geraniums, and many gardeners will have bought some over the years from a local garden center. Far fewer will have grown these geraniums from seed or bought mail-order plants started from cuttings, yet that is the best way to get some of the more interesting types.

There are four basic types of geraniums, each with a different type of leaf: the common zonal geranium, which is recognized by its round, puckered leaves with a distinct concentric dark zone ringing the petiole; regal or Martha Washington geraniums, which have slightly serrated leaves and large, azalealike blossoms; ivy-leaved geraniums, which have shiny, point-lobed leaves; and scented geraniums, a diverse group from many different species, most of which have hairy leaves, and all of which exude a strong scent when the leaves are rubbed or crushed. All these geraniums require similar treatment, though there are some minor points unique to the culture of each group.

Until recently almost all geraniums were propagated from cuttings, and for home gardeners this is still a good way to keep a favorite plant around indefinitely. The cuttings root easily, and our grandmothers simply took a three-to-four-inch end section of a nonflowering branch, removed all but the top three leaves, and plunked it in a glass of water until it was half-immersed, then set the glass in a warm but not too bright part of the kitchen for a few weeks until roots began to show under the water. The cutting was then planted like any other tender seedling. This method still works, of course, and for larger numbers of cuttings we apply the same principles on a slightly greater scale. Fill an 18-cell plug tray or as many $3\frac{1}{2}$-inch pots as needed with sterile potting mix, water thoroughly, then stick in the prepared cuttings, making sure that the remaining leaves clear the surface of the mix. You will need to keep the plants at a relatively high humidity during rooting, and any leaves that have contact with the mix create a good place for botrytis rot to set in. Put the pots or flat on a heating mat at 70–75°F, then cover with a dome or plastic tent supported by wire so the plastic doesn't touch the foliage. It should take a couple of weeks for roots to form. Until then, all that is needed is the minimum amount of water that will keep the mixture moist (preferably applied from beneath). As soon as you see new growth move the flat or pots to bright light and start fertilizing lightly with each watering. The time it takes from cutting to first flowers is about three months during the spring, when daylength is increasing; for winter plants take cuttings in mid-August and be prepared to wait longer.

Geraniums grown in the garden can also be dug up and moved indoors. Cut back the foliage at least two-thirds to just above dormant buds, shake off the soil, and put them in what seems too small a pot, as geraniums like to be root-bound. Fill the pot with less-than-richest garden soil mixed with a bit of potting mix, water well, and set them in a semishaded location, free from frost, until they start to sprout, then check carefully for disease or pests (especially aphids) before moving them to their new winter quarters. Come late winter, when their blooms begin to fade, cut the plants back again and fertilize lightly. As the plants sprout, take your spring cuttings. Avoid heavy fertilizing, as soft spring growth is more likely to rot than root. Once the cuttings have been taken, allow the plants to regrow before setting back out in the garden. While I have seen a neighbor's plant that was in an 18-inch tub and more than ten years old, keeping one plant in good condition that long is far more trouble than starting anew from cuttings every year or so.

Regal or Martha Washington geraniums are different from zonal geraniums in that they need a distinct cold period while setting their flower buds. They do not come true from seed, so buy plants with buds already set. If you start from cuttings, be sure to move them to a spot where they will be below 60°F once they root. In most houses these days it is hard to find a room cool enough for the regal geraniums. In the Vermont countryside, where older houses are less insulated or weathertight (we like to call it fresh and breezy), a bright window in an outer room is the perfect place (as it is for rosemary). Once in bloom, regals can be put where you like, though the flowers won't last long in heat, indoors or out.

Ivy geraniums are also more delicate than zonals and should be grown in cooler temperatures and dimmer light. High soil temperatures and low air temperatures, combined with too much available water, lead to a strong uptake of water but little transpiration, and this causes a swelling of the underside of the leaves called oedema. In the worst cases, swollen tissue bursts and calluses form, diminishing the photosynthetic capability of the plant. To avoid oedema and diminished health of your geraniums, water ivy geraniums only in the morning on clear days so that the water and nutrients keep moving. Also, don't place ivy geraniums in harshly sunny areas.

Now that more kinds of geraniums (at least zonals and ivies) are available from seed, geraniums can be grown like any other flower: sown, grown, and set out. Cutting-grown plants will be ready in a shorter time than seed-grown plants unless you start the seed very early.

In the North, to have just-blooming plants in 4-inch pots ready for planting on Memorial Day weekend, you will need to sow seeds the last week in January! You can start as late as the end of February if you are willing to set out smaller plants, however. As the seed is very expensive, we would suggest sowing singly in 98- or 50-cell plug trays. Water the flats from below, cover with a humidity cover, and germinate at 70–75°F. If only some seeds germinate after a week, don't despair; lift those that have germinated as soon as they are big enough to handle and leave the tray on the heating mat. In another week the rest should appear. Most geranium seed available today has a very high germination rate, so it is worth the wait. Once the plants are big enough to handle, transplant to 18-cell plug inserts or 3½-inch pots and treat just like cuttings. Do not overwater or overfertilize at any stage, though, or you will get big, gangly plants. One-quarter strength liquid fish fertilizer, mixed half and half with liquid seaweed at every watering should be sufficient.

When we were in the bedding-plant business there was a certain amount of pressure to turn up the heat and put the fertilizer to our plants to get them growing as fast as possible, but we resisted (partly because of the cost!), and in the end things worked out. The first time a new customer saw our geraniums they might have thought ours small compared to other garden centers (they were), but once they saw how hardy the plants were and how well they took off after transplanting to the less-favored conditions of the open garden, we had regular customers! The state nursery inspector knew, too, and we joked about how there is always a tendency on the part of the grower to produce an oversize, overaged plant in full bloom because that is what most (unknowledgeable) customers will buy, while both grower and inspector know that the best plants are those that are younger and tougher. . . . Nonetheless, if symptoms of deficiency (noted on page 73) appear, don't hesitate to amp up the plants' feeding a little.

Finally, consider growing your geranium as a "standard." With a little bit of work you can create a miniature treelike geranium that can be shaped as a topiary and maintained indefinitely. To do this, insert an eighteen-to-thirty-inch stake upright in an 8–12-inch pot, and stick a new cutting at its base. As the cutting grows, pinch out the side shoots, but keep the leaves. Tie the central stem lightly to

To grow a geranium standard, set the plant in a pot and provide a stake the height you wish the standard to be. As it grows, pinch out all the side shoots so that only the central stem grows, but allow any leaves to remain. Tie the stem to the stake to keep it straight.

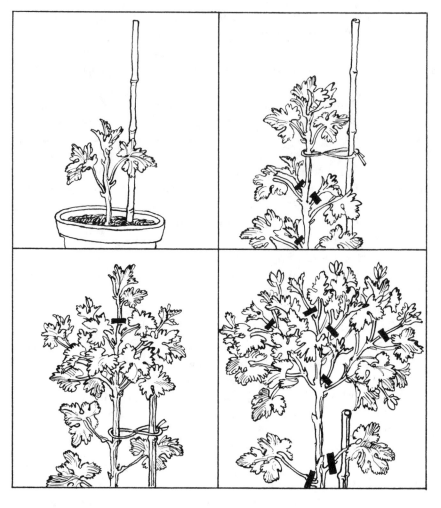

Once the central stem reaches past the top of the stake, pinch it out and allow the side stems at that height to grow enough to form the shape you desire; then remove all the leaves along the central stem, leaving the stem bare.

the stake to keep it straight. Once the stem reaches an inch or two above the top of the stake, pinch out the terminal growth point to force growth to the side shoots. When the side shoots reach four to five nodes, pinch them as well to form a bushy topknot on the central stem. At this point remove all the lower leaves to reveal the bare, upright stem tied to the stake. You will now be able to shape the top. For best results, choose a variety with interesting leaves: With all the pinching the plant may not bloom. Scented geraniums make especially nice standards.

Geranium varieties are nearly endless. One specialty catalog in Illinois speculates that there are more than 10,000 cultivars in existence, though they sell *only* 1,100 or so themselves! There are rosebud geraniums; tulip geraniums; carnation- and cactus-flowered geraniums; geraniums with double or bicolor blooms, or with varie-gated or light-veined leaves. There are even miniature geraniums.

To decide which is your favorite, the best option is to visit nurser-ies and greenhouses that have a wide selection and choose from the plants they have, or order a catalog from one of the specialists and use their knowledge. Once you have your first plant, the procedures outlined above will make it possible for you to increase your plants and trade with friends to build a collection of geraniums that suits your fancy. If you'd like to try growing from seed, then you will be choosing from a fairly limited number of different series. The early standard seed geranium was the Ringo series, named for its zonal leaves, but this has been largely replaced by the Elite and Orbit series. Our favorite red in the greenhouse business was Red Elite, but for other colors we prefer the Orbits, especially one called Orbit Appleblossom, which is stunningly beautiful. There are nine differ-ent colors in the series, and plant habit is quite uniform. Since most of the zonals you will see at the average garden center will be either Elites or Orbits, you might as well save your growing space and buy started plants. There are also multiflora and cascading ivy-leaf geraniums available from seed, but the seed costs up to a dollar a seed, so again you might be better off buying plants.

One last pitch: Consider growing scented geraniums or the alpine ivy types. If you have ever seen pictures of some chalet in the Alps with long cascading geraniums hanging from a second story win-dowbox, you have seen alpines. They are ivy-leaved, but can take more heat than regular ivy types and in full bloom are nearly cov-ered with small, radiant single flowers. There are generally three sizes: the Minis, which reach two feet in length; the Decoras, which grow to three feet; and the Balcon series, which, over the course of a summer might stretch to five feet! In general, all the alpine ivy geraniums are shades of pink, with some coral, lavender, or lilac tossed in.

Scented geraniums almost always have interesting foliage, though the flowers are less spectacular than other types. A quick brush or crush of the foliage, however, releases a fragrance that might range from almond to apple, or apricot to attar of roses; the range is literally endless depending on the species and cultivar in-volved. Scented geraniums are generally grown as pot plants year round and moved indoors with the onset of cold weather. The leaves and flowers can be used in the kitchen or as table decorations. Spe-cialists, either retail or mail-order, are the best source of particular varieties.

## PENSTEMON

While there is a large number of species of penstemon, the most frequently grown is *P. barbatus*, the beard tongue, a charming plant two to three feet tall with fairly sparse, lance-shaped leaves, topped with a bare flower stem from which dangle, in acrobatic abandon, up to a dozen long, tubular blooms, usually in bright red, but occasionally pink, purple, or white. The beard of the flower is a series of bristly hairs on the lower petals, like that of irises. Blooms appear June to July, opening from the bottom up to the top and last a few weeks. Penstemon is fully hardy where there is consistent snow cover in winter, and it comes easily from seed. There are mixes available that have a wider range of colors than the species. Named cultivars or particularly choice plants are easily increased by stem cuttings in late summer. Another species, *P. X gloxinoides* (the gloxinia-flowered penstemon) has showier flowers, but is not nearly as hardy as *P. barbatus* and must be grown as an annual outside the South and Pacific coastal regions.

## PETUNIA

Of the big four bedding plants—impatiens, marigolds, geraniums, and petunias—the last is my favorite. Petunias are hardy, look good in containers, and, with proper care, bloom all summer. Given our weather and sour, soggy soil, we have always used petunias solely as a container plant.

There are three basic types: grandifloras, which have large tubular flowers three to five inches across with frilled margins; multifloras, which have more numerous two-to-three-inch flowers and a compact habit; and floribundas, which combine the best characteristics of the other two types. All but the recently introduced floribundas are available with either single or double flowers, in solid colors or various bicolor combinations.

While the grandifloras have showier flowers, they are more subject to problems from disease or the vagaries of weather—easily beaten down by hard rain to leave a limp, brown-centered plant with bruised, molding flowers. In baskets, where they can be protected somewhat from inclement weather and given excellent drainage, grandiflora petunias are hard to beat.

Multifloras also make excellent basket plants, but are even better for pots and window boxes as their mounding habit keeps them tidy looking from above as well as from the side. They are less likely, though, to hide the sides of the container they are in, so, if aesthetics are important, your containers should be made of wire, wood, stone, or pottery—virtually none of the plastic materials looks right.

Floribunda flowers are somewhat larger than those of multifloras, yet the plants are sturdier and more compact, which yields a tidier appearance and better resistance to inclement weather. Floribundas are good for both outdoor plantings and containers.

Petunia seed is very small—from 250 to 400 *thousand* seeds per ounce—so use the wet-pencil method to place just a touch of seed on the surface of flats or pots filled with sterile potting mix, press the seed into the surface, and water from below. On a heating mat set to 70–75°F, the seeds will germinate within two weeks. From the point at which they sprout, petunias can take very cool conditions, though the coolness will lengthen the time until they flower. Grandifloras bloom in as little as three months if grown at 60°F or higher, while multifloras grown at 60°F or below may take as long as four months to begin blooming.

Once started, though, all kinds of petunias will keep blooming until frost if regularly deadheaded. When deadheading petunias, keep in mind that the goal is to remove the flower's ovary. In petunias the ovary extends a significant distance behind the bloom, and in order to be sure you get it, the pinch should be at least a half inch behind the base of the flower. You will find that the downy foliage leaves a pungent yet pleasant sap on your fingers. With a hundred flats of petunias to pinch and three weeks to go before outdoor garden time had arrived here in the mountains, I always found that smell and the moist warmth of the greenhouse a welcome preview of the summer to come.

One last tip from the bedding-plant trade: Make nighttime temperatures where the plants are grown warmer than the daytime temperatures. Let's say you keep your house at 68°F day and night (warmer than ours at night, but then we have a greenhouse for our plants); you could move the plants to a warm spot in the house overnight and then to the coolest, brightest spot you have for just an hour or two in the morning to trick the plants into thinking that the day is cool. (Research has shown that it isn't actually necessary for the whole day to be cool; just a few hours in the morning is enough to trick the plants into thinking the whole day is going to be cool. For bedding-plant growers, this means turning up the thermostat in the evening, then turning it down in the morning before the sun has a chance to warm up the greenhouse.) This trick is known in the trade as DIF (for differential) and will keep plants from stretching, one of the most common problems with homegrown plants, and one which often leads to poor garden performance.

Petunias should be spaced ten to twelve inches apart in the open garden and a bit closer in pots and baskets. The general rule of thumb is three plants for an 8-inch pot or basket, and five plants for a 10-inch pot or basket. A 2-foot window box will require five plants to look full and sumptuous. The plants can be set in their final containers anytime after they have four to six leaves (you will want to keep the containers inside until the last hard frost), but you might want to wait to transplant, as plants in flats do not take up as much space as plants set out in pots or window boxes. With hanging baskets, however, moving the plants to their final home actually frees up space as you get them off the bench and onto a hanger of some sort. One trick to getting a good habit on cascading basket types is to water the petunias with a spray so that the foliage as well as the soil in the pot gets wet; the extra weight will cause the stems to hang naturally down over the side of the basket. You'll need to stop this practice once the petunias bloom to protect the blossoms, and wet flowers and foliage overnight are a sure invitation to disease. Water only in the morning—preferably only sunny mornings—so the foliage has a chance to dry by evening.

Petunias are highly bred and are almost always hybrids these days; they will stay alive indefinitely if maintained. If you want to have containers of petunias blooming at a particular time, you can practically guarantee when they are at their peak through timed shearing. We discovered this one year when, due to bad weather on Memorial Day weekend, we had a dozen baskets left over. Though we tried to keep them looking good over the following few weeks, very few sold. By the middle of June they began to look rough around the edges, and in despair we cut them back. Lo and behold, as Fourth of July rolled around, they looked fantastic, and we sold every one!

Petunia baskets can be made to bloom at a particular time by shearing. Three weeks before you want them to look their best, cut all the stems back to the edge of the pot; then fertilize and maintain the basket as usual. This technique also works with other basket plants.

The following year we applied what we had learned and found that if you take a blooming basket of petunias and shear it all the way back to the edge of the pot or basket, then give it a shot of fertilizer, it will regrow and bloom almost precisely three weeks from the day of shearing. I suspect that after the days start shortening in early August four weeks until bloom might be a safer estimate, but there is no question that periodic shearing will rejuvenate straggly-looking baskets. With half a dozen plants, you could make sure that you always had two or three looking great. The shearings can be rooted if you would like to have more plants; just follow the standard procedure for soft stem cuttings.

As the new petunia introductions from breeders are coming hot and heavy, especially in the new floribunda class, there is not much point in an elaborate discussion of petunia varieties aside from stating a few favorites.

The old standard for multifloras used to be the Resisto series, named for the plants' weather resistance, and suitable for outdoor planting. Resisto has been largely supplanted by newer introductions like Carpet and Merlin, each of which is available in a wide color range, singly or as a mix. Petunias generally have a wide color range; about the only colors not seen are orange and green. Multifloras also come in picotee or star bicolors, and as doubles, though personally I have no use for either. Our favorite is a series called Pearls, which, though the blooms are relatively small by current multiflora standards, come in clear, soft pastels and really do show that petunias can be an aesthetic plant.

Grandifloras come in the same kinds of colors and patterns, both single and double-flowered, as the multifloras. The top strains these days are the Cloud, Ultra, and Falcon series; an older kind is the Flash series; and just now making waves is Countdown, so called because it is super-early to bloom. Our favorite here is the Super-cascades, because of their adaptation to hanging baskets, and their pastel color range. The white, pink, lilac, rose, and blush make outstanding basket plants.

The first floribunda petunia was Summer Madness, and I remember the year it appeared because it was (and is) really striking in baskets and pots. The background color is an intense coral-salmon, with deeper veining radiating from the throat. Our garden-center customers bought them three to one over everything else we had! This ground-breaker was soon replaced by whole new series that blurred the line between the multifloras and the floribundas, and the two types have become almost synonymous. Two to look for are Celebrity and Primetime.

## PHLOX

Phlox is another large group of valuable garden plants and all are native to North America. To discuss them we should separate the different kinds: There is the tall, perennial garden phlox (*P. paniculata*) and its close relative the Carolina phlox (*P. carolina*); the somewhat shorter annual garden phlox (*P. drummondii*); the wilder woodland phloxes, *P. stolonifera* and *P. divaricata*; and the creeping perennial rock garden form, *P. subulata,* also called moss pink (though it comes in a number of pastel colors). These groups all include some wonderful plants, and if you have the room you should certainly have some of each.

Annual phlox, also known as Texan pride because it was first discovered growing wild in the Lone Star state, is an easy plant to grow when direct-sown in the garden as soon as the soil can be worked in spring. Warm-climate gardeners can grow it as a fall-sown crop, and in really cold climates like ours, it can be started indoors four to six weeks before its outdoor planting date. Small kinds like Twinkle can be set only six to eight inches apart, but the larger kinds, which grow more than a foot tall and make good cutting material, need eight to twelve inches between plants.

The woodland phloxes differ primarily in size. *P. divaricata* reaches to slightly more than a foot tall with inch-and-a-half flowers, while *P. stolonifera* is smaller, with flowers only half as large but in similar colors: lavender and light blue to white. Some cultivars are fragrant. *P. stolonifera* is not as vigorous as its brethren, but it is more tolerant of deep shade. Both woodland phloxes spread by rooting on sterile, nonblooming stems and can be divided just about anytime. They make good groundcovers for shady, moist locations that are nonetheless well drained.

Moss phlox (*P. subulata*) is so called because of its propensity for steep banks and rock outcroppings over which it drapes itself with fine-leaved abandon. Up close the leaves are thin and needlelike, though soft to the touch. The plants form thick mats, and in spring are literally covered with one-inch, flat-faced five-petaled flowers from white across pink and red to light purplish blue. Increase is by division or layering. To layer, take a stem without flowers and lay it across a patch of bare ground, weighting it down with a handful of soil. Once the stem roots it can be cut free of the mother plant.

*Phlox paniculata* is a tall, stately plant growing three to four feet tall and crowned with large panicles of one-inch, often fragrant flowers. The stems are simple, rising from the crown of the plant with slender, pointed leaves that unfortunately are often susceptible to mildew, a fungus that whitens and disfigures the plants. Your best hope is avoidance: Never use overhead irrigation on phlox—especially in the evening, as moisture on the leaves overnight is a sure invitation to problems. Many parts of the South and Midwest, where afternoon and evening thundershowers are common, are difficult places to grow garden phlox because of mildew; in those locales, other species that are resistant to mildew should be grown, such as the Carolina phlox. Here in the North, where problems with mildew are less severe, all that may be necessary to prevent mildew is close attention to siting and care. Garden phlox should be placed where there is ample sun and moving air, and vigorous established clumps should be thinned to perhaps a half-dozen stems to avoid crowding. In a pinch, sulfur sprays will help control this scourge that, unattended to, causes affected leaves to drop, weakening the plants. For bouquets, mildew-free stems should be cut when half the flowers in the panicle have opened. Phlox flowers do not dry well.

While garden phlox not only comes easily from seed but self-sows, choice plants and established clumps should be prevented from spreading seed; named cultivars cross readily and the resulting offspring are almost invariably inferior, reverting to the difficult pinky magenta of their wild forebears. Increase of plants is by division or root cuttings. The simplest method of increase is to separate offsets that appear near established clumps and then move them to a new spot as independent plants.

## PHYSALIS

The Chinese lantern is grown for its ornamental seed pods, which resemble paper lanterns when dried. It starts easily from seed and needs to be closely watched, or it can become a persistent weed. Many books list the Chinese lantern as a perennial, and it may be, but we grow the plants as annuals, which makes it easier to control. The Chinese lantern is a member of the nightshade family, like potatoes, tomatoes, petunias, and nicotiana, and it is very closely related to tomatillos and cape gooseberries, both of which make great kitchen garden plants (they have the same nasty habit of escaping from cultivation to become a weed if not promptly cut once the seed pods form). Sow seed on the frost-free date and thin the plants to a foot apart; cut off at ground level once the papery pods form and hang in a dark, dry place to cure.

## PHYSOSTEGIA

Known as false dragonhead or obedient plant, physostegia is an interesting perennial for the cutting garden and border. It grows three to four feet tall, of which the last foot to foot and a half is a showy, tapered spike of upward-arching one-inch tubular flowers in pink, white, rose, lilac, and lavender, to mention just a few of the available colors. It comes readily from seed, and can be maintained from cuttings or by division every two to three years. The name obedient plant refers to the fact that the flowers, if arranged, will stay where they are put; it does not refer to the plants' habits, because, if provided with the conditions they like, the plants do not stay put. They spread, and so require a watchful eye and regular maintenance to keep them in bounds. Favored conditions for physostegia are constantly moist but well-drained soil in full sun; if provided with partial shade, the plants will tolerate drier soils. Numerous well-described cultivars are available from nurseries and mail-order catalogs, and these cultivars vary in size as well as color. Physostegia is an excellent flower for bouquets, but it is likely to need support in the garden. Cut the flowers just as the lowest blooms open.

## PLATYCODON

A great kid's perennial, the balloon flower has buds that seemingly inflate, then burst open at the tips in midsummer to reveal quite attractive four-to-five-petaled flowers in blue, white, or pink pastel; they will please the parents just as much, at least if they are flower arrangers. Plants grow two to two and a half feet tall with an eighteen-inch spread in full sun, though a bit of shade may be helpful from the Carolinas on south. New plants can be started from seed for bloom the following year or increased by careful division just as they break dormancy in spring. For bouquets, cut the flowering stems when the first few blooms have opened.

## POLEMONIUM

These are coarse-looking plants, but they are interesting nonetheless, and they provide a good early season cut flower. The foliage is responsible for the plant's common name, Jacob's ladder. The lower leaves are distinctly fernlike, with up to twenty opposite lobes paired like the rungs of a ladder along the leaves' six-inch length. Higher leaves, partly up the two-foot flowering stems, are smaller, simpler, and held more closely. Atop the whole edifice is a loose, drooping cluster of purplish-blue flowers with yellow-orange centers slightly less than an inch across. There is a white form available, though it is not easy to find. Jacob's ladder will grow in full sun, but prefers a bit of shade from the afternoon sun; I have seen very nice plantings that edged a west-to-northwest wood. While insects do not seem to be a problem, plants should be kept well spaced to avoid mildew. Self-sowing is common, and seedlings are easily moved, or fresh seed can be started indoors in spring. Plants can also be increased by spring or fall division. For bouquets, deadhead regularly to extend bloom and harvest flowers just as the spray begins to open. Flowers should last a week in the vase. There are a number of minor species of polemonium that can be used in the wild or rock garden; check specialty seed catalogs for availability.

## POLYGONATUM

Solomon's seal is an ancient and widely distributed plant long ascribed to have medicinal qualities; even without its medical uses it is a beautiful and useful plant in the landscape. I think of Solomon's seal in the same way as lilies of the valley, though the manner in which they display their flowers and foliage is different. Both plants, however, like the deep shade of a moist woodland edge and will colonize it rapidly if it is to their liking; and both provide small, white, fragrant flowers in spring. Both plants also have foliage that is simple, elegant, and restrained: lilies of the valley have upright leaves and the flowers are borne on upward-arching stalks; Solomon's seal displays its leaves and flowers nearly horizontal to the ground, atop simple unbranched stems and lets its strings of pendant white flowers hang languidly from the leaf axils along the stem. The plants reach from one foot in the lesser Solomon's seal to almost seven feet off the ground in the greater Solomon's seal. Only the two-foot *P. odoratum* has fragrant flowers, so if you want to enjoy the plant's scent, be sure to buy the right species. Solomon's seal is not simple to start from seed, so it is best to begin with a plant and increase your holding by division, which is easy as they have a creeping, rhizomatous habit. Solomon's seal needs shade, especially in the warmer parts of the country, the soil should be well drained, and there should be room for the plants to spread, as they will. It is an excellent plant to combine with ferns and other woodland edge plants.

## PRIMULA

Another woodland-edge plant, but with a much larger roster of developed species, is the primrose. There are many more kinds of primrose than can possibly be covered here, but we will try to bring some sense to the assemblage. I know it was years before I dared try to grow them; I was so daunted by the number that I couldn't decide which to try first. There are two classic yellow primroses: *P. veris,* the spring primrose or cowslip, an eight-inch-tall plant with dark green pebbled leaves and fragrant half-inch open-faced pale yellow flowers with a darker yellow center; and *P. vulgaris,* the common or English primrose, a similarly sized plant that has larger, darker yellow, tubular flowers.

Most of the garden primroses one sees in this country came from hybrids of one of these two species crossed with a tiny, purple-flowered alpine primrose, *P. juliae* (the Julian primrose). The whole group of these hybrids is collectively known as polyanthus primroses. Virtually all of the common types you may be called upon to buy or try belongs to one of these groups. These spring-blooming hybrid primroses come in a veritable rainbow of colors and patterns and are larger both in leaf and flower than any of their forebears, reaching a foot in height, and possessing one or many blooms up to an inch and a half in diameter.

Two more unusual types are *P. denticulata,* the drumstick primrose, and *P. japonica,* the Japanese or candelabra primrose. The drumstick primrose is a diminutive plant less than a foot tall but possessed of globular flower heads perched sturdily above a light green spatulate rosette of leaves. They come readily from seed and can be maintained by regular division. Candelabras are taller, at one to two feet, with large leaves and a striking topknot of flowers in a wide range of colors, many of which will come true from seed if cross-pollination by other species can be avoided. Candelabra primroses need constant, abundant moisture, and they are best grown in cool shade near year-round running water. They are effectively hardy to Zone 5, which translates to a line running from Massachusetts to Iowa and on to Oregon.

## RUDBECKIA

Black-eyed Susans are classic native American flowers, and have long had a place in borders, bouquet gardens, and wildflower plantings. The common annual form has a single row of golden yellow ray flowers surrounding a deep-brown-to-black raised central disk

(Marmalade is one outstanding cultivar), but there are doubles—like Goldilocks, which won a Fleuroselect medal some years ago, and Double Gold, which won an All America Award—as well as those with a bit more color (usually arranged in concentric circles around the disk like gaillardia), or with standard yellow rays but a more columnar disk that can be either golden or, in the case of Irish Eyes, green. All these rudbeckias provide a brilliant display from midsummer through heavy frost.

Start annual rudbeckias eight to ten weeks before the last frost and set out in a month, after the danger of hard frost. While they like warm weather and dryish soils, they can tolerate a lot of cold and so are a good candidate for early planting out to free up greenhouse or cold frame space. Dwarf bedding types can be set eight to twelve inches apart while the larger cut flower kinds will need twelve to eighteen inches between plants.

Perennial rudbeckias come in a wide array of forms from less than two feet to more than six feet tall, but the most universally popular cultivar is *R. fulgida* Goldsturm, which forms a compact, freely spreading but not invasive clump two feet tall and completely covered with brightly contrasting black-eyed Susans. Goldsturm does not come true from seed, but it increases readily from division spring or fall. This is a hardy, carefree plant that should be in every garden that treasures its bold midsummer glow.

While many rudbeckias are of the standard black-eyed Susan type, there are other cultivars as well, like this tall double named Double Gold.

## SALVIA

The best known salvia to most gardeners is the hardy perennial herb sage, whose proper Latin name is *Salvia officinalis*. In addition to being a valuable kitchen garden plant, the leaves and blossoms are also very useful for dried arrangements. Beyond kitchen sage, however, is a huge range of other salvias ranging from gaudy, tender annuals to long-lived subshrubs. Most flower gardeners, though, will want to concentrate on four or five kinds.

*Salvia splendens* is the least hardy and, to me, the least interesting of the salvias. This is the commonly seen blazing red salvia of recreation centers, shopping centers, and centers for the terminally tasteless. It does have merit in its tolerance of hot, humid weather but that is not enough to recommend it in my estimation. Breeders, ever lustful of greater sales, have made it available in such a wide range of colors and sizes that it may one day appear in attractive form. Start seeds indoors six to eight weeks before the frost-free date, germinating on high heat and growing bright and warm. Set transplants in the garden a foot apart in each direction.

*Salvia coccinea* is similar but a bit more restrained, and this more relaxed habit, combined with a generally toned-down color range, starts to make it okay in my eyes. Still, it is not at all hardy, succumbing to any frost even if well hardened.

*Salvia viridis* (also sold as *S. horminium* or annual clary) is the virtual opposite of the two salvias above. It is as easy to grow as herb sage, is completely cold-hardy, and the flowers (actually bracts) are subtle pastels atop attractive eighteen-to-twenty-four-inch plants with interesting gray-green pebbled foliage. This is a true annual— quick to grow and bloom—and once planted will self-seed at the base of the plants if not deadheaded, which is fine with me as I never resent the free supply of seedlings.

*Salvia farinacea* is a classic half-hardy plant, able to take some frost after diligent hardening off. It is perennial in warm climates but grown only as an annual here in the North. The twelve-to-eighteen-inch plants are smooth-leaved and green, supporting slender spikes of tiny blue or powdery silver white blossoms that are equally useful in fresh or dried bouquets. Once started, these floriferous plants will bloom till hard frost fells them.

*Salvia sclarea* is another half-hardy member of the family, much larger than most, and immediately recognizable for its large, fuzzy gray leaves. This is the herb clary, which is partly responsible for the unique flavor of traditional muscatel wines. Properly grown as a biennial, it can be made to bloom the first season if started early and set out twelve to eighteen inches apart after the danger of hard frost is past. The individual flowers are much larger than other sages and are strung along a sturdy spike in cream, white, pink, or lilac shades.

All the sages—with the exception of *S. officinalis* or culinary sage, which is fully hardy in the United States, and annual clary, *S. viridis*, which is a true annual—can be cut back hard after frost, dug, and carried through the winter in the root cellar for increase the following spring via cuttings or, in most cases, division.

This striking variety of *Salvia sclarea*, or Clary sage, bears large numbers of white-to-pink blooms on two-to-three-foot stems. The name is "Turkestanica."

## SCABIOSA

If you don't care for the Latin name, which comes from the word "to itch" and means rough-leaved, consider that one of the common names of scabiosa is mourning bride, so named because of the intensely dark velvet purple of many of its flowers. Of course it is also called the pincushion flower, due to the pincushionlike appearance of the central disk. This flower has certainly not gotten the good press it deserves over the years, but it is a solid garden performer and should, at the least, be included in every cutting garden.

The annual species *S. atropurpurea* is quite hardy and can be sown directly in the garden in early spring for continuous and copious bloom from midsummer to hard frost. For an early start seed indoors four to six weeks earlier and harden off the transplants before setting out after danger of hard frost (below 25°F). Each plant needs eight to twelve inches to itself in the garden. If grown in the border instead of a cutting garden, place the plants behind other vigorous growers to mask the relatively insignificant basal rosettes. In cottage gardens they can be allowed to interweave with other plants, but in more formal or productivity-oriented settings, staking or support with a wire quonset is required as the plants will flop over a bit when mature. The color range is from white through pinks and pastels to a very deep purple that approaches black. Stems can reach eighteen to twenty-four inches, and they present their two-inch domed flowers in a fashion ideal for bouquets. Vase life is a week or more.

*Scabiosa stellata* is a similar plant, with similar needs, but grown for the mature, dried seed heads, which resemble some sort of satellite or a geodesic World's Fair speaker system. The fresh flowers are pale blue. This is an absolutely invaluable dried material and should be in every everlasting garden. Culture is identical to *S. atropurpurea*.

*Scabiosa caucasica* is the only perennial member of the genus widely grown and it is fully hardy here in the North, though it suffers in the heat and humidity of the South. The eighteen-to-twenty-four-inch flowering stems arise from a rosette of gray-green, lance-shaped leaves and bear open, flat-faced blooms comprised of a row of ray flowers around the characteristic pincushion central disk. *S. caucasica*'s natural color is pale blue with a white disk, but some white cultivars have been developed and many of the blues now have a lilac or lavender blush. The flowers are long lasting in bouquets and arrangements if cut just as they open.

Perennial scabiosa can be started from seed using the standard spring warm treatment. Spacing in the garden should be twelve to eighteen inches between plants. Particular plants can be increased by division or by stem cuttings taken in spring.

## SEDUM

The common name lives forever might give you a clue to one of the endearing traits of this large family of succulents. But just to know that they are hardy would not clue you in to the incredible diversity within the sedums. Many of the most widely grown of the sedums are rock garden and groundcover plants that creep only a few inches off the ground but can colonize large areas while surviving on just a pinch of soil—one of their common names, in fact, is stonecrop. Two of the best of the groundcover sedums are dragon's blood (*S. spurium*) with glowing red flowers, and *S. acre* Elegans, with silvery foliage and tiny yellow flowers. Both of these sedums are plants that are suited for growing among pavers and stepping stones. Both are unkillable in the North, though the heat and humidity of the Southeast may be too much for them to take.

While we have some of the creeping types around our place, our favorite is the taller *Sedum spectabile* hybrid Autumn Joy. This is a magnificent if somewhat alien-looking plant that grows to two feet in our gardens with pale, whitish buds that turn first pink, then a strong bronze, and open like a giant, flat-topped broccoli. (Before you recoil, I have to say that I consider broccoli a very attractive-looking plant, if a bit plainly colored.) The flower heads hold well into the fall and will stand the winter until heavy snow breaks down the stem.

Sedum "Autumn Joy"—a fantastic garden performer.

Autumn Joy is a plant for full sun and well-drained soils though it will survive just about anywhere; in shade or overfertile soils it may simply require support to avoid toppling under the weight of its flowers. Increase is by division or stem cuttings and is quite simple. My first piece came as a "shovel division" from my Aunt Sally.

## SOLIDAGO

We all know this plant; it is goldenrod. Before you skip to the next section, though, please consider two facts: Goldenrod is not really the culprit hayfever sufferers once believed, but simply has the bad sense to bloom so visibly at the same time as ragweed. Also, plant breeders have spent considerable time improving this already hardy and vigorous plant so that its positive traits have been made stronger, while those things about it that might cause it to be less loved have been de-emphasized.

Most of the kinds you will want to try are hybrids of the native American and European species. The most commonly available seems to be Golden Fleece; at eighteen inches it is much more restrained than the wild species. Others you may be able to find include Cloth of Gold, which is about the same size; the tiny Golden Thumb at only one foot; or the giant Golden Wings, which can reach five to six feet.

All solidagos do best in moist, sunny spots and can be increased by division or stem cuttings.

## STACHYS

This is one of my favorite plants, and has the charming common name lamb's-ears, which perfectly describes the texture of the leaves, if not the color. Like the annual dusty miller and the perennial Silver Mound artemisia, it has pale gray foliage that functions well to separate and mellow groups of other, brighter plants. An especially good combination, to my eye, is gray-leaved pinks just in front of tall *Stachys byzantina*. The larger and brighter flowers of the dianthus help bring out the inconspicuous blooms of the lamb's-ears, which, in most gardens, would be regularly cut out to leave only the foliage. If you don't want to bother with the blooms, though, look for the cultivar Silver Carpet, which doesn't flower at all. Increase is easy by division in spring.

## TAGETES

The common name of tagetes will likely be much more familiar to most people: America's almost national flower, the marigold. Like most "sophisticated" gardeners (and this includes many new to the art but already ripe with opinions), I paid very little attention to marigolds, having seen them lined up in parks and shopping centers throughout my childhood. But when it came my time to be the supplier of those public plantings through our garden center, I found that within the orange and yellow tide there was actually more diversity than first meets the eye.

There are three major kinds of marigolds you might be likely to grow. The first is the tall, so-called African marigold (*T. erecta*), which despite its name is, like all marigolds, from Central America. These are tall plants with coarsely divided but not unattractive foliage, easily three feet tall in our garden, with large, three-to-four-inch, fully double, almost globular flower heads in orange, yellow, or, if you will have them (I won't), near white. If you were to use a marigold as a cut flower (I don't), this is the type to use, cut just as the buds open.

Second are the dwarf, or French marigolds, *T. patula*, which come in a wider range of types and sizes, though all are less than eighteen inches tall. There are doubles like those of the African type, usually in solid colors or with contrasting highlights; crested or scabious types (named for their similarity to scabiosa flowers), which have a prominent, raised central disk and rows of (often) contrasting or bicolored ray flowers; anemone types, where the disk is not raised but there are multiple rows of ray flowers; and singles, where a simple, central disk is surrounded by a single row of rayflowers, these, too, often of a contrasting color. The color range of French marigolds includes autumnal near reds, but none of the near white of the African types. Their dwarf mounding habit, healthy green foliage (though like the Africans, a bit coarse), and ability to flower over long periods in harsh summer conditions has made the French types nearly ubiquitous in the mass public plantings that you see in places like Disney World in Florida. The flowers used to be much smaller than the Africans, but now breeders, working to improve both, have brought them more together: the Africans are becoming smaller, more compact in plant habit, and the French are becoming larger in bloom, now from two to three inches across.

The third kind of marigold is the Pumila or Gem marigold, *T. tenuifolia* (sometimes listed as *T. signata*), which are radically different than the previous two kinds. The tiny one-inch flowers are single and open, a spare five petals arrayed around a slightly raised central disk (sometimes either brightly or subtly contrasted), and the foliage is deeply divided, beyond ferny to featherlike. The overall habit is that of a mound twelve to eighteen inches across and up to a foot tall. They make exceptional edging plants as the small flowers literally cover the plants, and the foliage is lightly scented of lemon, releasing its fragrance whenever brushed against, as it is when you walk past it on a path it has crept out to embrace. All told, it is by far

Here the Gem marigolds spill from above a retaining wall, where their lemon-scented foliage can be best appreciated. In the background is the new lemon yellow dwarf sunflower Valentine.

my favorite type of marigold, and one that my gardens are never without.

Marigold seed should be sown six to eight weeks before the last frost for setting out at that time. You may as well start out in a row tray or small plug insert, because all but the smallest dwarf hybrids will need to be moved up to a minimum 50-cell plug insert by the time they are ready to set out. Cover the seed lightly, then soak the flat from beneath to thoroughly moisten the soil, cover with a humidity dome or sheet of plastic, and put the tray or pot on a heating mat or warm spot where the seeds can spend the week it takes them to sprout at 70–75°F. Once they have three or four leaves and begin to intertwine their foliage, transplant to the larger plug insert. While marigolds are sensitive to frost and cannot be set out until the weather is warm and settled, they do not need to be grown at high temperatures. French types will bloom in about eight weeks from seeding regardless of daylength, but the Africans will be a week or two later unless you trick them into thinking it is midsummer or later. Commercial growers have to install complex and expensive systems to accomplish this kind of control (mostly used to bring fall mums into flower before their normal October–November blooming season), but for home gardeners with only a flat or so of plants, it is simple. Just move them out of the light at five P.M. or so every day; this will limit their sunlight to eleven to twelve hours and thus trigger their earlier flowering reflex.

Garden spacing for all marigolds is about a foot between each plant. Depending on conditions you may want to put the smallest of the French dwarfs only eight inches apart to fill a bed with color immediately, and the largest Africans at eighteen inches to improve air circulation between them and fight foliage disease. On the whole, marigolds are very forgiving plants and will accommodate each other at most any spacing to give a full effect by midsummer. Most varieties will also bloom indoors over the fall and early winter if you wish. Start new seedlings for this purpose around the beginning of August in the North, later in the less daylength-sensitive South. You can also take cuttings from established plants, carry them through the winter, and begin again with new cuttings, just as with petunias and geraniums.

There are an enormous number of marigold varieties available. In the discussion of types at the beginning of this section I tried to make it possible for an interested reader of catalogs to determine which types are most appropriate for their needs, and from there I will leave it to the copy writers themselves to describe their wares. I do want, however, to put in a plug for those I especially like.

At our garden center the most impressive kinds of marigolds we saw were the French marigold Queen Sophie, only one of a series known as the Queens; the best of the Africans was the relatively compact Inca series. Perhaps these have been surpassed by newer introductions since we last grew them in 1988, but I honestly can't say I know. The only ones we have continued to grow are the Gem marigolds, especially Lemon Gem, a wonderful pale yellow; Tangerine Gem, which is an intense burnt-orange; and Golden Gem. We grow them as much for the wonderful lemon fragrance of the foliage as for the flowers, though they are useful for garnishing with in the kitchen, as well as being charming in the garden. Like many old-fashioned flowers, they seem not to be attractive to breeders and so are safe from the frequent replacement that is such a mixed blessing to more popular flowers. Those of us who are a bit less fashion-conscious often find that those things we like in food, shelter, clothing, and flowers go in and out of fashion so that periodically we find ourselves leading or being left behind—if we bother to take notice.

On that note, there are two other marigolds of value that are rarely grown. The first is a foliage type, so called by me at least, because it only barely makes it to bloom in our climate. Known as Irish Lace, it is the sole cultivated member of the species *T. filifolia*, and it is similar in most respects to the Gem marigolds, but without the fabulous blush of bloom. *Tagetes lucida* is a relatively unimproved form, generally called the Mexican marigold (though of course all marigolds are native to Mexico), and though it is nothing to look at, it is used as a cover crop because its roots release a substance that repels nematodes; thus, it can be used to cleanse soil that is infested with these pests.

## TROPAEOLUM

Nasturtiums are one of my favorite flowers, I guess because they are so easy to grow, so bright and cheery, and so pleasing to my kids and my wife, Ellen, who uses both the leaves and the flowers in salads. There are two basic kinds of nasturtiums in general culture, the large, old-fashioned climbers (listed as *T. majus*), and the newer, dwarf kinds (listed as *T. minus*). Their natural color range is from a pale moon yellow through gold and orange to warm red. The canary bird vine *(T. peregrinum)*, also known as the canary creeper, is a related species, but resembles the regular nasturtiums only a little. The leaves are five-lobed (palmate) and much smaller, but the vines themselves grow up to fifteen feet over the course of a summer, and the tiny one-inch flowers resemble nothing so much as miniature canaries perched at the end of short, arching branches, swaddled in a mass of frilly green.

You can start nasturtiums a couple of weeks before the frost-free date in 50-cell plug inserts or 3½-inch pots, but the simplest way to grow nasturtiums is to stick the seeds, a foot apart and an inch deep, into well-drained soil just after the frost. They prefer not to be transplanted, and it's easy to allow adjoining plants in the flats to become entangled, at which point planting becomes something of a nightmare—the stems are brittle and easily broken. If you do accidentally "prune" the seedlings, you will lose back what you had hoped to gain by starting the seeds ahead.

Climbers will reach eight feet in height and should be sown at the base of the support you want them to climb. Shrubs make an excellent support and, if you know the color of the variety you plant, some combinations can be made that are quite striking. Nasturtiums will also climb strings and latticework, but they may need a little help getting started since they cling primarily by wrapping the leaf petioles around objects, not by twining or grabbing on with tendrils. Dwarf kinds can be direct-seeded along the edge of paths and planting beds or in pots and baskets—though keeping them green and vigorous during the hot part of the summer can be challenging if the container is too small. Intermediate types make an excellent draping plant for retaining walls, as they will hang down a foot and a half or so, providing a real softening effect for otherwise bare walls.

Nasturtiums require little care once planted, but you should keep two things in mind. First, they are strongly affected by soil fertility and sunlight; in low light and rich soil the foliage will far outdistance the flowers, leading to a diminished floral show, while bright sun and a relatively poor soil will produce relatively small plants but a sensationally colorful display. Unfortunately, while nasturtiums crave sun, they don't like really hot or cold temperatures—frost will knock them flat and a string of ninety-degree days will burn them up—so choose your spot with some care. The second tip is to keep a close eye out for aphids: there are few plants they like as much as nasturtiums. If the plants do become infested, insecticidal soap or pyrethrum are the standard cures, but the intruders can be dislodged with a strong stream of water (that will probably hurt the nasturtiums, too, though).

In dwarf nasturtiums, the standard strain is Whirlybird, a deserving group of a half dozen or so colors that has a uniform foot-tall habit and plenty of upward-facing two-inch blooms (it's important in a low plant to have the flowers aimed at the viewer). A new, even more striking strain, though, is Tip Top, which has been bred to hold the flowers farther above the foliage, so that the plants seem almost a mound of flowers, rather than mounding plants with flowers. One step up in plant size and still with a good color range is the intermediate Gleam strain which is suited to baskets and draping over a wall. Slightly larger still and really unique is Empress of India, which has very dark green foliage, and molten, velvet-red flowers on two-foot stems. A number of unnamed mixes of climbing types are available from mail-order companies, and while these are almost certain to please with their casual and colorful vines that carry a hint of the old-time fragrance that gave nasturtiums their name (it stands for "nose twister," a reference to the clear peppery tang that is their attraction to salad buffs as well), we generally grow named, single-color varieties. Moonlight is well named, and grows to a good six to eight feet in height, with pale yellow flowers, while its cousin Sun-gold has rich golden flowers. There is a red type called Spitfire as well, but this is from a related species, *T. peltophorum* (though it is sold by some specialists as *T. lobbianum*), and it's not a true red. The flame nasturtium, *T. speciosum*, is another rare species with blindingly bright red flowers. Finally, don't forget the canary creeper, *T. peregrinum*; we never do when planting time comes around.

## TULIPA

Despite the changes in garden preference over the past few hundred years, tulips seem to have been one of the constants. Even as tastes changed from the rigid and formal bedding schemes of the pre-Victorian ornamental gardens to more casual and informal styles of the cottage and cutting gardens, tulips have maintained their popularity. This is even more amazing when one considers that except in a very few parts of the country tulips do not establish themselves as perennials, but rather must be replanted after two or three years (if not annually). In many other plants this inconvenience, when tied to the expense of the replacement bulbs, would seriously limit their popularity. But not tulips!

The range of tulips available is vast, running into the thousands, and that is exclusive of the many interesting species types carried primarily by specialty mail-order suppliers. We will discuss the standard groupings that were decided upon by a convention of international horticultural societies and industry groups only a few years ago.

The first distinction is between early, midseason, and late tulips. Generally speaking, the earlies bloom from mid-April to early May, the midseasons from late April to mid-May, and the lates from early May to early June. Within these broad-use classifications are further distinctions made on the basis of plant and flower appearance.

First among the cultivated tulips are the Single Early and Double Early types; the former is a cross of two wild species, and the latter is a chance mutation of the Single Early that was preserved. Both of these tulips grow about a foot tall, give or take a few inches, and are available in a wide range of colors. Shortly after these come the Mendel, Triumph, and Darwin hybrids, which are each somewhat larger in plant and flower than the Single Early and Double Early tulips, with a size range from fourteen to twenty-eight inches. The season is rounded out with Darwin tulips themselves; the Cottage tulips from which they were developed (sometimes called Single Late tulips); and the Double Late types; as well as those with unusual flower types like the Lily-Flowered tulips; the multicolored Rembrandt; and the fringed-leaved Parrot or Orchid types, which were once called (appropriately, I think) Flamed and Feathered Bizarres. The general size range within these tulips is from eighteen to thirty-two inches, all with relatively large flowers.

The last category of tulips is made up of the various wild and nonhybrid species types, and there are many of them, some very close to the cultivated types, like the *T. fosteriana, T. greigii,* and *T. Kaufmanniana.*

We plant our tulips in October. The few colder zones can start in September, but it is important to wait until soil temperatures are 40°F or below so that the bulbs don't initiate any top growth before the onset of winter. Farther south, this could mean waiting until November. If you live in a climate where temperatures are only below freezing for a short time, make sure that the bulbs you buy have been precooled, or store them for a month in the refrigerator, as most tulips need cold weather to stimulate flowering.

Planting depth should be two to three times the diameter of the bulb, with the lesser depth in heavy soils and the greater depth in light, sandy soils. Most gardens are in between, and given the size of bulbs generally available, planting the bulbs five to six inches deep is about right. We dig individual holes for each bulb with a bulb planter, a simple cylindrical trowel that removes a three-inch-diameter column of soil six inches deep. The bulb is placed in the bottom of the hole, and then—if the site is not sufficiently fertile—refilled with compost mixed with a bit of bone meal.

While full sun is best, tulips will do well at the edge of deciduous woodlands, where they bloom before the trees have fully leafed out. Don't forget that after blooming, the tulip foliage will take a while to die down, and during that time it is hardly attractive. Either resign yourself to treating tulips as spring-blooming annuals and cut them down right after blooming or plant them in relatively small, tight groupings so that their dying foliage can be hidden by later, larger plants. In a flower border this is done by planting five to eleven bulbs in a tight, irregular pattern, in an area only a foot or so across at its largest dimension.

Tulips make excellent cut flowers if harvested just as they open, but of course to do so robs the border of its beauty. The solution of course is to plant tulips in the cutting garden as well as in the border. In the cutting garden, a standard row or hex-bed pattern will be most efficient for easy cultivation. After cutting the plants can simply be removed and the space turned over to other crops.

## VENIDIUM

Venidium is a South African native like gazania (the treasure flower) and is desirous of the same conditions—a well-drained sunny location and not too much rain or humidity. There are two varieties available: the species *V. fatuosum*, with four-inch, daisylike flowers in

To bloom properly and on time, bulbs should be planted at specific depths in well-prepared soil.

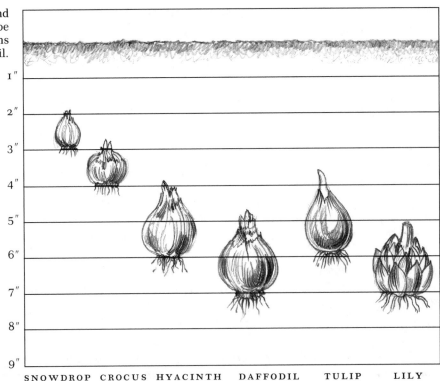

SNOWDROP   CROCUS   HYACINTH   DAFFODIL   TULIP   LILY

deep gold-orange with a dark sunflowerlike disk surrounded by a narrow filagree of velvet-brown; and Zulu Prince, which has pale yellow, almost white petals. Both plants are two feet tall (when they stand erect) and have—again like gazania—grayish, woolly foliage, though the foliage of the venidiums is larger and serrated. If supported to keep the stems straight, and with the cooperation of the weather, these striking plants will produce good cutting flowers. Start seed six to eight weeks before the last frost. Sow the seed on the surface of well-watered 50-cell plug inserts and germinate at the standard 70–75°F. Set the plants out in the garden after danger of frost, allowing one foot between each plant.

## VERBENA

There are a number of forms of verbena. The relatively common garden verbena, V. X *hybridus,* is a tender perennial grown for edging, bedding, and containers; there are both compact and spreading forms. Less known, but interesting as an accent plant or as part of an informal cottage garden, is the four-foot, airy *Verbena bonariensis,* which, though naturalized as a perennial in California and perhaps some other frost-free parts of the United States, is grown as a half-hardy annual in most of the country. In longer season areas it will self-seed, but cold climate gardeners will likely need to replant every spring. *Verbena rigida* grows only a foot or two, but it forms tubers that can be dug in fall and carried through cold winters in the root cellar.

Garden verbenas do not come easily from seed, and so it may be best to either purchase plants, or to take cuttings from overwintered plants. If you do want to start from seed, the key to good germination is to moisten (not soak) the potting soil a couple of hours before sowing, let it drain, and then sow the seed and cover the flat. Do not water after sowing until the seed sprouts, and keep the flat a bit cooler than others, perhaps by stacking it on top of a flat that is directly on a 70–75°F heating mat, which should provide just about the 65°F that is ideal for verbena. Even so, plant enough seed so you will be able to have the number of plants you want from only 50 percent germination. Growing time to transplanting is ten to twelve weeks, and the plants should not be set out until the frost-free date. They will occupy about a square foot each at maturity and prefer a relatively dry, sunny site.

The two species verbenas start more easily, under the standard treatment, though some gardeners chill the seed for a few weeks before sowing. The taller V. *bonariensis* should be pinched once during the seedling stage both to keep the transplants a manageable height and to force base branching, which causes the plants to give a better show once out in the garden. Both plants stand, or rather even prefer, a moister soil than the garden verbena.

As to varieties, with the exception of the new All America and Fleuroselect winner Imagination, which is a glowing violet-blue, I am going to leave you to the descriptions of the catalog merchants and your local garden center. Just be sure to note whether those you buy are the compact or the spreading type, depending on the use you have in mind. Particularly with the garden center, your best bet is to choose particular plants that you like from those available, and then take note of the variety. Once you have a few plants you like, you can maintain them year-round; just take late summer cuttings, which root easily, and overwinter them in containers indoors. They may not look like much by spring, but fresh cuttings taken then will return to their former garden glory.

With the species types, you buy the seed by botanic name. *V. bonariensis* has very thin yet strong stems, very little foliage, and sparsely held, flat, clustered blooms made up of tiny lavender flowers. As mentioned earlier, this plant works well as an accent, planted alone in large blocks of other flowers, or simply tucked into an informal border where its small flower heads can punctuate a casual design with an occasional surprise. *V. rigida* is an edging plant like its hybrid garden cousin, and though it is limited in color solely to a deep violet, the one-to-two-foot-tall plants are far more mildew-resistant than the common garden verbena. Both of these are perennial in the Deep South and California.

## VERONICA

This is a large family of plants with casually arching, pointed flower spikes in shades of blue, white, and pink. There are some rock garden forms that creep, but our concern is primarily with border and cutting kinds. Veronicas come in two sizes: twelve to eighteen inches and eighteen to thirty-six inches roughly speaking, though the botanists seem to be constantly rearranging this whole group of plants, and the actual size depends a bit on both the climate and the conditions.

The larger of the two is usually sold as *Veronica longifolia* and blooms in late summer, while the smaller *V. spicata* blooms two to four weeks earlier. Both make excellent cut flowers that will last up to a week in the vase if cut just as half of the flowers are open on the foot-long spikes of bright blue, white, or pink.

Specific cultivars range in height from twelve to forty-eight inches tall. Among the better kinds are: Icicle, two feet tall, which blooms virtually all summer; Foerster's Blue, which has similar stature and flower power, but deep blue flowers; and Minuet, which is fifteen-inches tall and pink with gray-tinged foliage; Red Fox is a darker rose color; Sunny Border Blue, a deep blue eighteen-inch plant introduced way back in 1946, has maintained its popularity to such an extent that in 1993 it was voted Perennial Plant of the Year. All these veronicas are widely available at garden centers or by mail from specialty catalogs.

If you want to start from seed, your best bet is Sightseeing, a mix of all three colors that grows eighteen to twenty-four inches tall and provides plenty of cutting. Seed is small and so should only be lightly covered, but otherwise it responds to the standard warm treatment. Established plants can be increased by division or by cuttings. For the greatest longevity, site veronicas in sunny, well-drained but moist soils. Standing water in the winter can be disastrous.

## VIOLA

Viola is the family that includes not only the wonderful old-fashioned violets and Johnny-jump-ups, but also the garden pansy. All of these plants are extremely hardy and self-sufficient perennial plants, yet most can be grown as annuals, given the proper scheduling.

We are mainly concerned with two kinds of violets—the so-called sweet violets, *V. odorata*, and the horned or tufted violets, *V. cornuta*—though botanists recognize many more. Both *V. odorata* and *V. cornuta* prefer the same general conditions and are equally hardy, but there are a number of differences between them. The flowers and the plants of the tufted violet are larger, though their broad but pointed leaves are smaller than the round-to-kidney-shaped leaves of the sweet violet. Also, though both are vigorous, sweet violets spread more quickly, because they put out runners which quickly root at the tips. Color range in sweet violets is relatively small, mostly violet or white, with an occasional pink, while tufted violets have a broad range that includes just about every color in the spectrum.

Both the sweet violet and the tufted violet can be started in early spring from seed, covered lightly and kept relatively cool (60–65°F) until germination, then grown even cooler (55–60°F), and set out after the danger of hard frost. Late summer plantings will need to be set out at least a month before hard frost in the fall to become established. Tufted and sweet violets can also be increased by division or cuttings in early spring or fall.

Johnny-jump-ups *(Viola tricolor)* are charming little plants that can—but rarely do, in our garden—reach up to a foot tall. The three-quarter-inch flowers are a wonderful combination of two purple petals behind a trio of butter yellow petals highlighted with white and purple. This hardy plant naturalizes easily in uncut lawns and at the edge of cultivated gardens, wherever it is allowed to escape unnoticed during its nonblooming season. Once in bloom, few would pull out this small but beautiful flower, so it survives. A traditional use for Johnny-jump-ups is as a groundcover in beds of spring-blooming bulbs. They can be grown from seed using the same method as for the tufted violet.

Pansies *(V. X wittrockiana)* are one of America's most popular bedding plants for cool weather. As they are fully hardy, they can be sown in fall for spring bloom or in very early spring for summer bloom. All pansies will grow into plants about a foot tall and a foot across over time. As with violets, seed should be barely covered, and then germinated cool (65°F maximum). Sow the seed in late summer for early spring bloom, move the plants to a nursery bed, or transplant to 3½-inch pots, and store for the winter in a well-mulched cold frame. (Hint: Keep the newly sown flats in a cool garage or basement until they germinate if your summer weather is sultry). Transplant to their final location once the danger of temperatures in the teens has passed. Spring sowings should be made three months before the last frost for transplanting after the danger of hard frost (25°F and below). Garden spacing is six to twelve inches between plants, depending on how long the plants will be left in the garden. In cool climates like ours the spring-sown plants will bloom all summer, and thus will need wider spacing; but farther south the heat and humidity are likely to do the plants in by midsummer, thus, they are planted closer.

The classic pansy of my childhood had velvety petals with bold blotches of color intermixed; today these so-called "faced" pansies are still popular. Swiss Giants, Majestic Giants, the Roc and Maxim series; all are big sellers, but I, for one, prefer the simpler and subtler solid colors and pastels. At first I had to settle for a few particular colors within the popular and widely adapted Universal series—the white, yellow, orange, blue, and purple—but now whole series are available: Crystal Bowls; Clear Crystals; and perhaps best of all, a series called Watercolors, which is mostly single colors but with some bicolors, that have a subtle shading rather than a sharp delineation between the colors.

## ZINNIA

Last but certainly not least, given its wide popularity, is the zinnia, named for Johann Gottfried Zinn, a German botany professor who lived in the early eighteenth century. Zinnias are the quintessential high-summer flower, blooming in a wide range of colors that includes just about everything but blue and black. Though once a rangy Southwest American wildflower, over the years breeders have produced an incredible range of plant and flower types, from one half to four feet tall, with single and double, solid or variegated flowers, only an inch across up to monstrous, cactus-flowered types measuring a full six inches in diameter.

Zinnias are warm-weather plants, and given that warmth, they grow fast. The best culture is to sow them where they will grow shortly after the frost-free date once the soil is at least 65°F, for late summer bloom. The larger types of zinnias make excellent cut flowers and if grown for that purpose, successive plantings will yield the best blooms; sow every two weeks and harvest once the blooms are fully open.

Though they resent transplanting, earlier blooms can be had by starting zinnias four to six weeks ahead, indoors; just keep a few key tips in mind. First, start in the final container, and to make sure they germinate quickly (and thus avoid rotting in the moist soil), give them high temperatures: minimum 70–75°F (80–85°F is even better) for four to seven days. For example, sow two to three seeds in a 50-cell plug insert, and once the seedlings are up, cut out—don't pull out—all but the strongest ones. Second, grow out the seedlings in the warmest, sunniest spot you have; they will only be there a short time, but even a minor chilling will set them back. Third, you can trick zinnias into flowering up to three weeks ahead of normal by subjecting them to a short-day treatment when they are young. To do this, simply move the flats to a dark spot every day around five P.M., and bring them back out in the morning, so that the total daylight they receive is around twelve hours daily. Once you start to harden them off for transplanting, allow them the full daylength. In areas south of Virginia, where the days don't stretch as much in the spring, this treatment will be less effective.

Once the weather is fully settled and the soil is warm (right at the same time you direct-sow in the garden), set the plants out a foot apart in each direction. With cutting types, we pinch out the terminal shoot to force branching and make for bushier plants, but you can also treat zinnias the opposite way, taking off all side growth to produce single, supersize blooms on the terminal shoot. This would be especially effective with the naturally large flowering types, of course. Generally no support is necessary for any of the zinnias. Bedding and edging zinnias don't need any pinching, nor do those grown in baskets or pots.

The best soil for zinnias is moderately rich, yet well-drained and in full sun. Good air circulation will go a long way toward preventing mildew, which is brought on in climates like ours by the warm days and cool nights that are typical of August—just as the plants are approaching their peak. As with phlox, avoid overhead watering, especially in the evening. Choose naturally resistant varieties like the cheery, single Pinwheel series, the large, double, open-pollinated State Fair or the newer hybrids like the Ruffles series. In severe cases, spraying with an organic fungicide like sulfur or garlic juice will also help. Aphids and Japanese beetles both seem attracted to zinnias, but they can be controlled with soap and water—the beetles by knocking them into a bucket of soapy water early in the morning while they are lethargic, and the aphids by spraying with specially formulated insecticidal soaps. If nematodes are a problem it may help to grow your zinnias where the marigolds were the year before, as marigolds seem to be repellent to these noxious soil-dwellers.

The types of zinnias are legion, and we will discuss them by size, as there are small kinds suitable for pots, planters, and edging, mid-sized kinds that are suited for bedding and cut flowers, and then taller kinds that make a strong statement in borders and bouquet gardens. The smallest in flower are the linearis types, members of the species *Zinnia angustifolia*, which have narrow, straplike leaves and two-inch daisylike flowers in white, yellow, and orange, all with orange disks. These make wonderful basket and edging plants with their low, eight-inch height and broad, informal spread. They bloom freely from about eight weeks after sowing until frost cuts them down, and they need no deadheading. Larger but with the same kind of simple flower—and simplicity is important with flower species that have been a bit overbred for eye-popping bedding schemes—is the Pinwheel series, a member of the *Zinnia elegans* species. The plants reach a foot tall with a spread of eighteen inches, yet the stems are long enough to be useful in small arrangements. The three-inch single flowers are white, salmon, rose, orange, or cherry red, each with a raised golden orange disk. All are very mildew-resistant and long-blooming, and the flowers even dry well, unusual for a zinnia. To my eye, this is one of the best zinnias.

Smaller in plant habit, but with two-inch fully double flowers is Thumbelina, a dwarf mix that blooms in only fifty days and is perfect for container plantings or tight bedding schemes. Perhaps the broadest wave of new zinnias has been in the compact but not tiny class—compact plants that grow a foot tall and bear masses of uniform, double-flattened to pom-pom type blooms three-inches or so across. Among this group are the Dasher, Peter Pan, Dreamland, and Small World hybrids; all are available in a wide variety of individual colors or as formula mixes.

Aside from the open habit linearis and Pinwheel types, my favorite zinnias are the larger, cut-and-come-again types. We like the old-fashioned, open-pollinated Pulcino or Pumila mixes that have a wide variety of both color and flower type, and the new hybrid Sunbow and Ruffles strains which have standard flattened to pom-pom type flowers and long enough stems to serve as accent blooms in large, fresh arrangements. We also like what is called the Scabiosaflora mix, a mouthful of a name, but one that is descriptive of the flowers, which, with their raised central disk and predominately single ray flowers, resemble scabiosa flowers, though the colors range across the whole zinnia palette.

The real giants are among the cactus-flowered zinnias like Zenith or Giant Cactus; I don't have much use for them, and even less use for the garish and gaudy bicolored Whirligig and Peppermint Stick types, though if your tastes or needs run toward the shocking, you might want to give them a try.

# Gardens for Flowers

In Chapter 2 we discussed general garden care, without going into many specifics, and in the last chapter we discussed individual flower species in some detail, but without much talk about how they combine with each other in actual gardens. One of the ways in which flower gardening differs from food gardening is that flower gardens exist in a wide diversity of forms and in a wide range of conditions, while most food gardens are designed—where they are designed at all—with the same basic principles in mind no matter what the vegetables grown. We arrange our food garden in regular rows or beds for ease of cultivation and harvest and give it our deepest soils and sunniest location. With some flower gardens there may be the same needs to be met, but not with all, as a particular flower bed is not so easily categorized.

In this chapter we will look at different kinds of flower gardens, from the rigidly formal bedding schemes of parks and highways to the practicality of the flower arranger's cutting garden and the seemingly wild abandon of a managed patch of wildflowers. Each of these gardens has a different culture, from the preparation of the site and sowing of the seed to the final enjoyment of the results, whether that enjoyment is something as simple as a pot of geraniums on an apartment balcony, a collector's hillside rock garden, or the mysterious and sensual pleasures of a nighttime stroll through a garden of fragrant plants. All these gardens—as different as they are—require care and attention to succeed, and for each a specific kind of care determined by its own dynamic.

—Hugh Johnson,
*The Principles of Gardening*

## ANNUAL BEDDING

Formal beds of the type that were popular 150 years ago—when private estates had the time, money, and labor to put out large, immaculately maintained beds of annuals—have never really regained their former glory. Today the only places one is likely to see such displays are in public parks and highway medians—or office parks and shopping malls—which I suspect is not quite the same.

The key element in annual bedding is uniformity, with compact plant habit not far behind. The aim is color—usually bright color, but sometimes (rarely) subtle color. One of the classic if overused schemes is the patriotic planting of red, white, and blue beds; another bold favorite is bright yellow, true blue, and white; gaining in popularity now are subtler pastel schemes in various shades of pink, blue, and white. While I won't recommend particular colors, I will say that to my eye the best results come from using 50–60 percent of one anchor color, with the remaining 40–50 percent split among two or three others in proportionate but unequal amounts. At times the pattern you have chosen will dictate the precise proportion of plants in each color, and if so, this model should be followed.

However designed, the aim of formal bedding is not diversity and continuity as much as a feeling of stability and impact. In a mixed border or island bed (see below) the effect we try to create is a sort of managed nature, which ties diversity into a coherent whole and choreographs its change over the season. This is a very British concept, dating back to the Victorian era and the influence of gardener-writers like William Robinson and Gertrude Jekyll.

Annual bedding seeks a different ideal, in which the garden is brought to a particular state and then held there. Bold, sometimes geometric, patterns of color are created and then maintained as is until the season brings the display to an end. To see the garden today or next week is to see much the same garden, with much the same feeling and much the same effect. This formal approach, as opposed to the English border or cottage garden, is a very French idea of gardening, and is perfectly suited to the very highly bred annual bedding plants available today.

As mentioned above, uniformity is the key to a good display when working with formal beds of annuals. This is true both for the plants themselves and for the design and planting of the bed. Thus, not only is it important for the plants used to be uniform in plant habit from color to color within the range of shades available, but they should all be raised under the same conditions, that is, planted on the same date, given the same temperature, light, and fertilizer, etc.

The pattern in which bedding plants will be set should be carefully marked out so that all plants are the same distance from their neighbors; in geometric patterns it is important that lines curve smoothly with edges straight and parallel. This is not difficult to accomplish, even in round or oval plantings, with the use of stakes and string. For concentric circular rows, set a stake with a nail in its top at the center and run a string out to a marking stick at the diameter of the circle to be planted. Then simply rotate the marker around the center stake, making a small furrow as you go. For the next circle, adjust the length of the string and repeat.

Oval patterns are created by using two stakes equidistant from the center and a loop of string tied loosely around the stakes. The marker stake is pulled outward until the loop of string is taut and then used to drag a furrow. As primary tension in the loop of string shifts from one stake (called a focus) to the other, it deforms what would otherwise be a circle into a flattened ellipse; the farther apart the stakes for a given length of twine, the flatter the ellipse.

To keep bedding plants as compact as possible, grow the seedlings under the brightest, coolest conditions you can manage, and if possible use the warm night/cool day trick we discussed in Chapter 3. Make sure all the seedlings get identical treatment during transplanting, which should be done all at once rather than spread out over a number of days. Consistent cultivation is also important for formal beds, and it will likely be necessary to cultivate at least once even if mulch is used; you must wait until the plants are large enough so that the mulch won't hide any of the leaves. Mulch applied too early can slow down some of the plants and affect the bed's appearance. Remember, the appearance of stability and permanence in a formal bed is purely for the viewer; for the gardener the bed is constantly changing and it is absolutely necessary to observe closely and act promptly to maintain that viewer's illusion.

One of the most popular forms of formal bedding uses spring bulbs, and their normal uniformity certainly lends itself to this kind of use. The principles of design and layout are the same, though many gardeners mark the patterns with bone meal rather than just a stake on the theory that the bone meal will boost performance of the bulbs. More important to my mind—in terms of the display—is that the bulbs be set at a uniform depth so they emerge concurrently. Given proper timing, a spring bed of bulbs can be followed immediately with summer annuals for a continuous display from frost to frost.

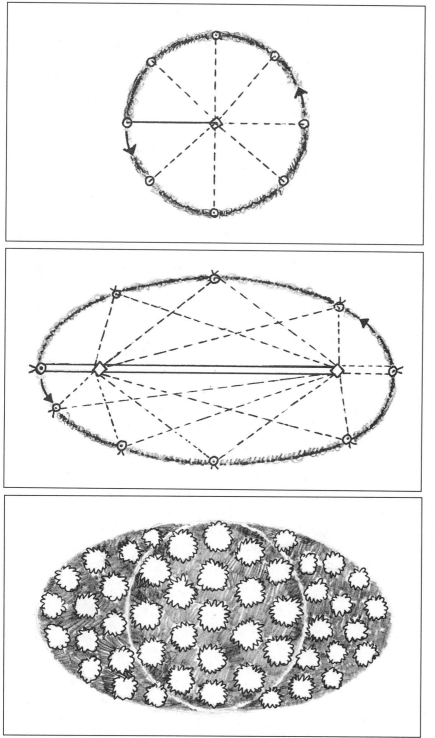

To make a circular bed, set a stake and attach a piece of twine as long as the radius desired with a marker stick at the end and rotate it around the stake.

To make an ellipse, set two stakes in a line and use a loop of twine slightly larger than will encircle the stakes. Pull the twine loop taut with the marker stick and then rotate it around the two stakes; an ellipse will result. The longer the loop of twine, the fatter the ellipse will be (more like a circle).

When planting be sure plants are evenly spaced, as uniformity is important in bedding schemes.

## MIXED BORDERS

The mixed border, brought into fashion by the garden enthusiasts of Victorian England, is quite opposite to the brilliant but static display of an annual bed. Managing a mixed border is an art that requires a subtlety that, when well done, hides its extensive planning behind a facade of seamless succession. The kind of experience that leads to a summer-long border show can only be gained outdoors, close to the plants, but a few rules of thumb will certainly advance the rate at which an amateur can accumulate the familiarity with plant combinations that is the mark of the accomplished flower gardener.

**Design**    The basic design concept of the mixed border is variation among the plants, with subtle transitions among groups—precisely the opposite of formal bedding, which seeks absolute uniformity and sharp, crisp edges. This variation necessarily occurs over time as well as among plant types, with different parts of the bed progressing through their seasonal pattern of growth, bloom, and senescence at different times.

Before we discuss the ordering of plants within a border to take advantage of these changes, we need to discuss the border itself: Where should it be, and what size and shape? The question of where is determined by the plants and the site. If you have only a shady lot, then the site rules, and you will want to design a garden for shade-loving plants; on a rocky, barren spot, you will do best to choose from plants that thrive in those conditions. Some of these special situations are discussed later, but let us assume for now that you choose the plants—rather than the other way around—and that you will find or make the conditions they need somewhere on your property. What then of the size and shape?

A good design will still be constrained by the site, as you should strive first to work with your surroundings, rather than resist them. Thus if your house and grounds are modern and formal, or strongly suburban, on level ground, with crisp regularity to the placement of driveway, walk, terrace, and pool, say, then the beds may look best if regular and geometric. But in rural or hilly settings where straight lines can't be found, then they shouldn't appear in the flower garden either; borders and beds should follow the contours and fill irregular spaces created by the permanent elements of the landscape.

Whatever the shape, borders should be at least four feet across at most points to allow sufficient visual depth for arranging different height plants in a tiered arrangement front to back. In island beds, which can be viewed from all sides, twice this width is a good rule of thumb, with tall plants in the middle and a height decrease toward the edges. Length will be entirely determined by the site, but it should be also at least four feet wherever possible.

Regardless of the bed's size or shape, the plants within it should be arranged to vary in height and habit. Plant in clumps so that the flowers appear to have sprung up in groups throughout the cultivated space (even in strictly geometric beds). A corollary of this principle is that single plants should be avoided except in special circumstances. If the border contains more than a few plants, single specimens, unless very large, get lost visually. Also, the groups of plants should be odd-numbered—three, five, seven, and so on—so that the group will not look too regular once set in the bed.

A well-designed bed will have variation not only in the height of plants from front to back, but variation along the back and along the front, so that the visual texture is complex and no grouping is too small to create its own visual space. Real experts, with sure eyes and a detailed knowledge of the plants, sometimes violate these rules specifically to create interest, but it's best to start with beds that mimic the ideal before tinkering with the formula.

Managing the succession of bloom color, form, and season is the true challenge of perennial gardening and of the mixed border. One of the major practical differences between annuals and perennials is that most annuals, once they bloom, continue until frost unless something goes wrong. This is rarely the case with perennials, which have a specific bloom time, rarely longer than a month. Thus it is possible to have a mixed border that looks radically different in June and in August.

Let's take a simplified example to see how this might be done. Given a bed five feet by twenty-five feet, we would first decide on the color schemes and bloom times. Let's say that on the left, where there is a bit of shade, we will put plants along the pink, red, and white spectrum that bloom in early summer, and on the right, in the sun, plants on the blue, white, and yellow spectrum that bloom in midsummer. We would place the largest plants first: a group of foxgloves in the extreme left corner, in the center rear a block of delphiniums, and at the right-hand end, some tall white garden phlox. Not precisely centered between these three, on the shady end we would then set some goatsbeard (*Aruncus*), and at the sunny end a clump of globe thistle (*Echinops*). Just in front of these clumps, which now fill the back of the border, we could arrange a crew of Shasta daisies and tall yarrows like Coronation Gold or Moonshine, plus some yellow daylilies and blue veronica. If strong oranges are appealing to you, there are some striking Oriental poppies. At the shady end you could add white or pink bleeding hearts, astilbes (which come in a wide range of colors in the red to white end of the spectrum), and coral bells. At the edge of the shade, columbines or various sizes of campanula would thrive and provide a transition from the pink to the blue and white. Along the front of a border like this would go primulas and woodland phloxes at the shady end, and at the sunny end white harebells or dianthus, and (if the drainage is good) some aurinia. There are also dwarf cultivars of the plants farther back in the border.

This quick sketch uses only perennials, which limits the border's possibilities; the addition of annuals into the plan will open it up immensely. Given the chance, I would edge the bed mostly in annu-

A bed with single plants popping up willy-nilly and no transitions from front to back looks disorganized and messy. Well-designed beds *(below)* rise in height from front to back, using masses of single plants so that each element of the bed creates its own visual space, but with the overall effect being one of natural complexity. By choosing groups of plants that bloom at different times, you will get a bed that remains interesting throughout the season.

als. Sweet alyssum (*Lobularia*) is very adaptable and could, just in its normal color range, serve as an edging over the whole length of the bed; or Gem marigolds at the sunny, yellow end and impatiens at the shady, pink end.

Of course edging is not the only place for annuals in a mixed border. Some perennials, like bleeding hearts and Oriental poppies, die out after blooming and leave large holes in the display. Well-chosen annuals that grow to substantial size—like cosmos and asters and zinnias—can grow into these spaces, cover the dying foliage, and then replace the plant after it is gone.

Keep in mind that if you leave space in the right spots, the colorful season of a border like this can be further stretched by the inclusion of bulbs, both the standard spring sorts like daffodils and tulips (with front edgings of the minor species) and the summer-flowering alliums. Just be sure to plan for their neighbors to hide their foliage once they go dormant.

## BOUQUET GARDENS

At the other end of the spectrum from annual beds and choreographed borders is the cutting or bouquet garden. For all the appeal of beds and borders, they are not very interactive—too much picking ruins the show. While spent flowers need to be removed, we don't want to pick those which are just opening, yet these are the ones best for bouquets. So if you love cutting flowers or arranging flowers, it's best to have a separate section of the garden where you can ignore aesthetics and concentrate simply on producing as many blooms as possible for the vase or drying rack.

One of the often overlooked beauties of a separate bouquet garden is simply the lack of forethought design. A lively jumble of have-what-may stuck randomly in blocks at transplant time sometimes produces, at bloom time, visual surprises that too-cautious good taste prevents us from trying out in beds and borders; it thus keeps our eyes awake to new possibilities of color and form for future years. And one of the great pleasures of a cutting garden is wandering like a bee through the beds, going wherever a bloom catches our eye and adding it to the bouquet in hand, creating it as we go.

There are a few things to consider in making a bouquet garden, all of which are based on the simple practicality of the mission. First, we classify the plants solely as annual or perennial; small, medium, or large; and direct-sown or transplant. Perennials are stuck in the back of the plot, whatever its shape or size, out of the way of annual preparation, and left to themselves. Spring bulbs go immediately in front of these, with the daffodils at the rear where they can remain undisturbed and tulips in front. The transplants go in next, large first, at eighteen inches between plants; then the medium, at twelve inches between plants; then the small, at six inches between plants. Biennials are treated as annual transplants in this scheme, since they will bloom the year they are moved to the cutting garden. In the front part of the plot, where they are easily accessible, are the rows for direct-seeding, and there, too, large plants are put to the rear, medium next, then small, with the rows spaced the same as for the transplants; when we thin, we leave the plants closer together in the row than is the space between the rows. Those plants like asters, annual baby's breath, and Shirley poppies, which need to be planted more than once for a full season's bloom, are just sown in the next available space as needed, with no concern to order.

Care of the cutting garden is the same as that given to the garden generally (discussed in Chapter 2), though there are a few things you should be sure to do. Most annuals should be pinched at the time they are transplanted so that they will produce more flowering stems; keep in mind that you can also do the opposite—removing side stems to produce a single, larger flower on the central stem.

The second thing is that virtually all the plants except bulbs should be supported in some fashion, though the supports need not be fancy. We grow our cut flowers in regular beds thirty inches across by twenty-five feet long, and this modular arrangement, along with the separation of the plants by height, makes support easy to provide.

We use a kind of heavy-duty metal mesh—available at most building supply stores—that masons use to reinforce concrete, and tomato growers use to build cages. This mesh comes in a roll six feet wide, with a welded six-inch-square grid pattern, and it can be cut with a stout pair of wire or sheet metal shears. The rolls are very heavy, but once rolled out on the ground and cut into six-foot lengths the material is not hard to handle. This yields pieces that are six feet square, but due to the natural curl of the roll, what you get is quonset-shaped mesh tunnels thirty inches tall and thirty inches across.

By cutting out the cross pieces of the mesh on both sides where it touches the ground, we create built-in pins by which these tunnels can be anchored over the beds. Flowers that grow to three feet or less can be amply supported by simply placing one of these "tunnels" over the bed; for taller plants like cosmos, drive stakes into the ground at the four corners and attach the corner legs of the tunnel to the stakes at the height necessary. In time, the plants grow up through the mesh and partially hide it; given its natural, rust-aged look, what isn't hidden blends in very well.

The vase life of cut flowers is strongly affected by the care they receive immediately after cutting. There are an enormous number of details (mentioned in Chapter 5 under the individual flower headings), but virtually all cut flowers last longer if they are cut in the early morning or late afternoon and placed immediately into a bucket of cool, clean water. As soon as you are done cutting, move to a cool, dark place to do any further preparation. We like to assemble our bouquets in the garage, with the door open.

A bit of extra equipment will make handling flowers easier and keep them in top shape. The flower shears mentioned in Chapter 2 hold the cut stems after cutting, which makes for easy handling, and a pail or bucket with a handle that allows you to carry it with one hand is an additional help. Last, get some floral preservative. We prefer to use the Ro-Gard brand, which is clear so it doesn't stain glass vases.

A garden grown for dried flowers is treated just the same as one for fresh bouquets, though the timing of harvest is different in some species, and the blooms, once cut, are treated differently. Easy species like statice or yarrow can just be gathered into small, loose bunches and hung upside down in a dark, dry, airy place. Some, like love-lies-bleeding (*Amaranthus*), whose stems need to be held upright so that the natural draping habit of the flowers is preserved, will need special attention. This is noted where necessary in Chapter 5.

**Everlastings**

Suitable places for drying are attics, barns, and above-ground garages with finished floors (dirty or dusty places don't work well because the flowers may pick up the dust while drying and lose the brightness of their colors). We now dry our flowers hanging from the rafters of our woodstove-heated post and beam home, which provides just the right conditions as well as great ambiance, but when we had our farm market, we rigged up a drying area in a neighbor's barn using black polyethylene sheeting taped on horizontal wires to simultaneously block out light and provide protection from a hundred years of dairy dust. Commercial growers often replace the clear plastic on an inexpensive greenhouse with black poly and keep the ventilation fans set to a low temperature so there is good air flow; a situation like this is nearly ideal and can dry a large number of blooms very quickly.

If all you have is a dusty barn or garage, the bunches can be held within paper bags that are loosely tied around the base of each bunch. You might consider turning over a cupboard or closet to drying, though. All it takes is a small, electric fan-heater combo and a way for the hot air to get out. Quite a few blooms can be fit into a small area by rigging wire or clothesline in tiers and filling the space with bunches two or three layers deep.

Even difficult flowers can be dried if you are willing to spend the money on desiccants. The most effective of these is silica gel, a porous, colloidal form of the common mineral compound silica. This fine powder soaks up moisture by providing a surface area of more than five acres for every ounce, and flowers that would never dry successfully in air can be immersed in it and dried in less than a week. After use, the silica gel itself is redried in an oven, then stored in airtight containers until its next use. Some inexpensive but less effective materials are powdered Borax and clean builder's sand.

## THE COTTAGE GARDEN

Somewhere in-between the well-planned diversity of the mixed border and the practical but prosaic beds of the cutting garden lies a relaxed and happy medium in which favorite flower combinations and whimsical discoveries exist side by side. This easygoing style is called the cottage garden.

In the classic cottage garden annuals, biennials, and perennials are grown along with fruits, vegetables, trees, shrubs, and vines; all are equal and romp freely across whatever path or pergola, bench, or bower they encounter. Monet's gardens at Giverny epitomize the style in my mind because his garden is organized—but not straitjacketed—into beds, and the feeling is one of overwhelming abundance.

In the casual world of the cottage gardener, a new acquisition will be put where there is room and, if not pleasing will be moved, eventually finding a home. If a perennial, it may stay in that spot for many years; if an annual, it may self-sow and spread. In either case, it will make peace with its neighbors or be gone. Practically, this is the way most of our gardens function, but we must learn to recognize that fact and relax; the common sense of it makes good design sense, too.

## THE FRAGRANT GARDEN

A moment's thought will tell us that most flower gardens are designed for enjoyment by the eye, but there is one kind that only reaches its true art through another sense—that of fragrance. Our human prejudice toward sight over touch, taste, sound, or scent is not shared by many other creatures who may not see in color—or not see at all by our standards—yet who perceive much about their environment using the other senses. Because of this profound sensual difference, a fragrance garden needs a whole different set of design principles in addition to the conventional concern with appearances.

Airflow is of critical importance, because fragrances drift and are delivered on air. Thus, the location of a fragrance garden should be upwind of where it is to be enjoyed, and distance is important because some plants spread their scent much farther than others. It is also wise to consider the effect of time: night-scented plants like moonflowers or nicotiana should be near the spots where you spend time on summer evenings. Other plants release their fragrance only when brushed, and so should be used as edging plants for paths and walks. We have tried to note these differences in the individual entries of Chapter 5.

## WILDFLOWERS

Wildflower gardens are the ultimate in a free and natural approach. They are attractive to many people as an easy, low-maintenance way to provide both viewing and cutting flowers, but of course the low-maintenance part of the deal only comes about if care is taken at the beginning.

There are two ways you can put in a wild garden. One is to prepare the entire area you wish to plant as if you were putting in lawn or a border, then sow it with an appropriate mixture of seed, and nurse it through the first season. For any large space this process is not only time-consuming, but expensive. Even with good preparation, an appropriate choice of plant species is necessary for success.

The second way to go is the cluster method. The whole area is again prepared, but instead of broadcasting flower seed, you sow noninvasive grasses and legumes, then establish clumps of transplants and let them spread on their own. The trick is to choose the right plants for your conditions and then grow large numbers of relatively small plants in plug inserts (see Chapter 4) so that clumps of good-sized plants can be scattered at frequent intervals throughout the meadow or glade-to-be.

We find that a 50-cell plug insert is a good size, because the re-

*Two ways to plant a wildflower garden:*

One is to prepare the entire area as if you were going to plant a lawn or border and then sow it with a mixture appropriate to your region and nurse the plants through their first season, removing any unwanted invaders.

The second method is to sow a noninvasive cover crop—leaving some patches unsown—and then fill those patches with large blocks of transplanted wildflower seedlings. Given a good mulch, these colonies will spread on their own to fill in the meadow. This second method, while a bit more work, gives much more control over the general color scheme of the planting.

sulting transplants are just the size of the point on a standard iron bar of the type used as a rock pry. Planting is simple: You jam the iron bar into moist ground (immediately before or during a rain is perfect) and stick the plant firmly into the hole. A practical minimum size for the clumps is five or six plants but a dozen is better, because the young plants will protect each other.

Annuals, whether direct-sown or cluster-planted, should be established early enough to guarantee that they will set seed before fall, while perennials need sufficient time to grow large enough to survive winter. Over time, the pasture grasses will thin out, and if all goes well, the wildflowers will spread into some of their ground, leading over two or three years to a good mixed planting. The meadow should be mowed high once a year, after most of the plants have matured their seed, to prevent entry of shrubs and trees.

## CONTAINER GARDENS

With container gardens we come full circle to an even greater form of control than annual bedding, though the feeling one can get from container gardens can be as relaxed as the cottage garden. Whether as simple as a window box full of petunias, or as complex as a city rooftop or backyard garden constructed of built-in planters, whenever plants are grown in containers a whole new set of considerations arises. Some of these are the same as for bedding plants, but there are additional concerns.

Container plants need to be compact, but they also need to be tolerant of wildly variable conditions because there is a relatively small volume of "soil" in the container, and often there will be a daily (or weekly) cycle of very wet and very dry conditions, with similar variation in soil temperature (as the sun heats the sides of the pot and then later, when the night air cools it). All this variation in environment means that container varieties need to be exceptionally resilient plants.

While the freedom to move all but the largest containers does make it possible to adjust the growing conditions in a way not possible with plants grown in the ground—say, moving a pot of sun-loving gazanias out from the shade of the house—the best-looking container gardens usually involve a diversity of pots whose locations are well set and rarely changed. This is because we want the plants to adjust to their home and fill out the rigid, architectural forms of the containers and soften them.

Whenever a plant is moved and is faced with a new orientation to sun, shade, and other plants, it takes a while for the foliage to fill out its new space. Also, the pots themselves, especially if made of clay or other porous material, develop a characteristic patina that is itself a design element. Mosses may grow around the base, and rock or crevice plants growing through the cracks of the steps, deck, or terrace on which it sits develop in specific relation to it. Once the pot is moved, this symbiotic relation is disturbed, and the result is a raw look.

So think about a garden in containers just as you would a garden in the open ground; that is, conceive of its basic structure first, and place the visual "anchors" (in this case the pots, both large and small) that will give it its overall form, and then choose the appropriate plants to fill out the vision of how you want it to look. Begin with the largest containers and work your way down, and once they are sited, consider the plants by size as well. Just as in an open ground garden, it makes sense to vary the depth of the planting to

Garden design becomes more important as the space becomes smaller. The size, shape, and placement of potted plants determines the structure of a container garden and should be carefully considered. The best plan is to create multiple spaces, or "rooms," with tall plants or built-in planters.

give a feeling of flow and to force visitors to walk around some of the bigger plants to discover what is hidden behind.

Within this structural design, the form of the plants themselves will need to be considered as well. The proportions of various containers should relate to the spaces in which they sit and the habit of the plants they contain. For example, a narrow passageway between house and garage may demand a tall, thin pot capped with a draping plant like lobelia, while the windward side lattice work of a sunny deck may be more appropriate for a box planter full of morning glories with a lone, fragrant moonflower to scent the evening air.

Mature plants and their needs will (or should) affect your choice of containers for them to grow in. There are any number of materials available, and their choice should be given a fair amount of thought because it affects not only the ambiance of the garden, but also the care they will require once planted, and in the off season if you live in a cold climate. There are also resource and pollution concerns.

Terra cotta—simple unglazed red clay—is the classic material for flower pots, used since time immemorial. It is not only good-looking, but healthy for the plants, as its porosity allows the plants' roots to get the air they need. This porosity also means that terra cotta pots dry out more quickly and will need, on average, more attention than similar-sized pots made of glazed clay or other materials such as painted wood, metal, and plastic. Terra cotta also needs protection from the worst of winter weather because pots left out in the elements can, when a rain that soaks the clay is followed by very cold weather, freeze and crack. Its vulnerability, at least to sharp knocks or wind-driven tips onto a hard surface, is terra cotta's biggest weakness.

**Clay**

Because they can be cast and molded as well as thrown, clay containers can be made in many shapes, sizes, and forms: from as little as two inches across up to huge, four-foot tubs and planters. Interlocked, stacking modules can be used to create large, tiered planters with a modern feel, and thick-walled hand-thrown tubs with ornate classical filagree can be set about as stately accents with an ancient ambiance. Old terra cotta planters can sometimes be found at dealers or at sales, but they are no less expensive than new ones, and the expense often runs into hundreds of dollars for a single piece.

Terra cotta containers come in many sizes and shapes, each with a different aesthetic, and each appropriate for a different planting.

**Wood**    Wood gives a soft, comfortable feeling, but is really only suitable for large containers as the relation of its thickness to its strength makes it impractical for anything less than, say, four square feet of planting space. Wood is light, though, which can be an advantage in some locations, and it allows a lot of creative freedom in making the container part of the design of the garden, as the exterior trim of the container can repeat architectural elements of the house or of garden trellising and lattice work. Wooden containers can even become a structural element of the garden, for instance, as a wall surrounding a private terrace from which flowers can drape. This is one of wood's greatest design virtues, and should be considered, especially in small spaces. Unfortunately, wood rots unless you use relatively scarce and expensive woods like cypress and redwood, or wood treated with preservatives (inappropriate for containers that you may grow food in) which create pollution problems when they are manufactured.

Perhaps one of the best wooden containers is a recycled wine barrel. With a half dozen inch-wide or better holes drilled in the bottom, these make good-looking, long-lasting, nonpolluting containers that work well for a wide variety of plants and are not expensive in relation to their capacity. They are widely available at garden centers.

**Concrete, Stone,**    I am not normally a fan of concrete, but in the casting and creating
**or Brick**    of large, ground-level containers for plants it not only has a number of structural advantages, but can be made to look quite attractive through the addition of material to the mix while it is being formed. For example, very small, rounded pebbles of the kind used for paving can be embedded in the surface of concrete to give it a rough-textured, subtly multicolored surface. Though the paintlike colors of hardware-store concrete pavers are too unnatural-looking for my taste, more natural colors in the form of sand, clay, or cinders give concrete a cast that fits in with the local geology and thus looks more at home than many other kinds of containers. If the molds used are consciously irregular, the finished containers will, after a few years of weathering, look almost like stone.

Stone itself can be used to make containers, and while a few hardy souls might actually take a chisel to choice stones and hollow them sufficiently to hold plants, a more likely course of action is to mortar them together to make a planter of the type that can be made with brick. Both brick and stone can be used in the same way as wood to form a major structural component of a garden, enclosing it at the same time that planters are created. Because of the weight involved, these kinds of construction are necessarily at ground level, and the relatively great expense—likely in the thousands of dollars—is not to be ignored. They are also, once built, immovable.

On occasion, old stone sinks and troughs are available at auctions or barn sales, and if you have the means to transport them home, they make excellent containers and offer a real look of permanence to a garden.

**Metal**

With the exception of window boxes (see below) most of the metal containers around these days—and they are few—are not particularly attractive because they are made solely for commercial use and thus the aesthetics have been largely ignored. But often the most interesting large recycled planters one sees are metal objects retired from some previous use and reborn as home to a group of plants. Some examples: old zinc or copper troughs and sinks, iron boiler jackets, industrial ladles, even carts or dollies. Once they have a thick patina of age these objects can become very attractive and lend the same kind of ancient air as does partially decayed concrete covered with moss and lichens.

**Plastic**

While not the most permanent or aesthetic material, plastic has many advantages, and manufacturers have recently found ways to make it more closely resemble terra cotta. Its two major advantages are light weight and low cost. Like clay, plastic can be formed into a multitude of shapes and sizes and can have any color or finish from (fairly) rustic to glossy and modern. This makes it a good choice for high finish urban gardens, where modular, interlocking plastic planters can be used in many of the ways that wood or brick would, but without the weight, and with the freedom to change the layout fairly easily. For rooftop and balcony gardens, it is often the only reasonable choice.

**A Special Note on Baskets and Boxes**

Hanging baskets and window boxes are often up off the ground, which introduces special problems. The type of hanging baskets you can buy at most garden centers are almost always plastic, and are almost always tacky. The only thing good to be said about them—aside from the fact that they have been carefully designed for easy care—is that they are white or green, and thus quickly hidden by the plants. Until then, though, they are an eyesore.

Far better are the less common and more expensive wire frame baskets. These are substantial, coated metal frames, and at planting time are lined with moss, filled with potting soil, then planted. In addition to the basket's more traditional look, plants can be set directly into the sides of the basket by poking through the moss, which gives the basket additional fullness. Because of the porosity of the moss, however, wire baskets generally need more attention than the same size plastic unit; they also need to be sited where dripping will not be a problem.

Window boxes need to be firmly fastened, or there is a danger of the box falling. For this reason, metal or plastic boxes with specially designed mounts are the common choices. Upstairs boxes also need a catch pan underneath or the overflow will drip on whatever—or whoever—is beneath. Where dripping is not a problem you can buy wire boxes similar to the hanging baskets: once lined with moss, they are quite attractive. Porch boxes, similar in form to window boxes, sit on a wall or the edge of a deck or porch; they can be made quite large and thus can be made from a wider range of materials.

## Care of Container Plants

As mentioned earlier, the limited soil volume of containers places extra demands on the gardener. First off, the soil used for containers must be as perfectly designed for the plant as possible. Commercial potting mixes of the type discussed in Chapter 2 combine the necessary traits of excellent drainage with the ability to absorb and hold significant amounts of water; given their light weight, they are nearly ideal for balcony, basket, and rooftop planters. Pots that will be at ground level, though, can have their soil mix changed either to provide special conditions or to cut down on the amount of peat used.

Rock garden plants will benefit from extra sand, and plants that grow large even in small containers, like common pot geraniums, need the extra weight for ballast. Take the field mix described in Chapter 2—one-third sand, one-third good garden soil, and one-third rough compost—and fill the pot about two-thirds full, then top off with the commercial mix to provide a weed-free surface mulch that doesn't pack down when watered. Really large containers can use a lot of mix, so we save by filling the bottom third or so of our large planters with broken bricks and cinder blocks or stones picked from the garden; then we fill around that with the field mix.

Planters filled with the field mix need little additional fertilizer to support a season's worth of growth, but we add bagged organic fertilizer to pots with straight commercial potting soils. Amounts added range from only a tablespoon for an 8-inch pot up to a double handful for a half whiskey barrel.

Attention to watering is particularly important for container plants as the natural wet-dry cycle is accelerated due to the limited soil volume. With a soil mix of the type already described—field mix below and commercial mix as a mulch layer—most watering can be done from above, either with a watering can or a hose, and there will not be much packing or muddying of the plants. For any containers that are small in relation to the plant they hold—this is most likely with vining plants—very frequent watering may be necessary, and it would pay to consider some sort of automatic system.

Drip irrigation systems for container plants differ from those used for field plants. Most on-ground or in-ground systems use controlled release emitters placed right in the supply line, whereas container drip systems use "spaghetti tubes." These spaghetti tubes are long, flexible one-eighth-inch tubes that branch off the supply line, and they include small plastic stakes to which the end of the tubes are clipped. Over the course of the summer both tubes and stakes will be covered by foliage, but if you want an invisible setup—especially for large, permanently sited pots—experts recommend placing the spaghetti tube at the same time the pot is planted. Enter the planter via the drainage hole at the bottom and snake the spaghetti tube up through the potting soil to the surface of the container, where you can then fasten it. For details on designing and installing drip irrigation systems, see the books listed in the bibliography.

# APPENDICES

# PLANT LISTS

## Plants with Gray Foliage

Artemisia
Aurinia
Cerastium
Lavandula
Stachys

## Long-Blooming Plants

Achillea
Ageratum
Alcea
Allium
Amaranthus
Anemone
Anthemis
Antirrhinum
Aquilegia
Begonia
Browallia
Calendula
Callistephus
Campanula
Celosia
Centaurea
Chrysanthemum
Coreopsis
Cosmos
Dahlia

Delphinium
Dianthus
Dicentra
Digitalis
Doronicum
Echinacea
Gaillardia
Geranium
Gypsophila
Hemerocallis
Heuchera
Impatiens
Ipomoea
Limonium
Linaria
Linum
Lobelia
Lobularia
Monarda
Nicotiana

Petunia
Phlox
Physostegia
Platycodon
Rudbeckia
Salvia
Scabiosa
Sedum
Tagetes
Verbena
Veronica
Viola
Zinnia

## Frost-Hardy Annuals

| | | |
|---|---|---|
| Antirrhinum | Linaria | Salvia (some) |
| Calendula | Lobularia | Scabiosa |
| Lathyrus | Papaver | |

## Frost-Tolerant Annuals

| | | |
|---|---|---|
| Ammi Majus | Consolida | Nicotiana |
| Callistephus | Gypsophila | Nigella |
| Centaurea | Helichrysum | Petunia |
| Chrysanthemum | Limonium | |
| Cleome | Matthiola | |

## Frost-Sensitive Annuals

| | | |
|---|---|---|
| Begonia | Gazania | Pelargonium |
| Ageratum | Helianthus | Physalis |
| Amaranthus | Helipterum | Tagetes |
| Browallia | Impatiens | Tropaeolum |
| Celosia | Ipomoea | Venidium |
| Cosmos | Lobelia | Zinnia |

## Seeds That Need Light to Germinate

| | | | |
|---|---|---|---|
| Ageratum | Begonia | Impatiens | Papaver |
| Antirrhinum | Browallia | Lobelia | Petunia |
| Aquilegia | Helichrysum | Lobularia | Physalis |
| Aurinia | Hesperis | Nicotiana | Platycodon |

## Fragrant Plants

| | | |
|---|---|---|
| Anthemis | Hosta (some) | Matthiola |
| Artemisia | Hyacinth | Narcissus (some) |
| Convallaria | Iberis (some) | Nicotiana |
| Dianthus | Ipomoea (some) | Paeonia (some) |
| Heliotrope | Lathyrus | Tagetes (some) |
| Hemerocallis (some) | Lilium (some) | |
| Hesperis | Lobularia | |

## Draping Plants

Arabis
Aubretia
Aurinia
Campanula
Cerastium
Dianthus

Geranium
Gypsophila
Lobelia
Lobularia

Petunia
Sedum
Tropaeolum

## Bedding Plants

Ageratum
Begonia
Campanula
Celosia
Chrysanthemum
Dahlia

Dianthus
Gazania
Hyacinth
Impatiens
Lobelia
Lobularia

Matthiola
Nicotiana
Pelargonium
Petunia
Phlox
Salvia

Tagetes
Tulipa
Verbena
Viola
Zinnia

## Long-Lived Perennials

Achillea
Aconitum
Artemisia
Asclepias
Aster
Astilbe
Baptisia
Boltonia
Campanula
Catananche
Centaurea

Chrysanthemum
Cimicifuga
Convallaria
Coreopsis
Delphinium
Dianthus
Dicentra
Doronicum
Echinacea
Echinops
Eremerus

Eupatorium
Filipendula
Gaillardia
Geranium
Hemerocallis
Hosta
Iris
Liatris
Lilium
Lythrum
Narcissus

Oenothera
Paeonia
Papaver
Phlox
Platycodon
Polemonium
Polygonatum
Rudbeckia
Solidago
Veronica
Viola

## Low-Maintenance Perennials

Achillea
Anemone
Anthemis
Artemisia
Aster
Catananche
Centaurea

Coreopsis
Doronicum
Echinacea
Echinops
Eryngium
Filipendula
Geranium

Gypsophila
Hemerocallis
Heuchera
Iris sibirica
Lythrum
Penstemon
Physostegia

Rudbeckia
Scabiosa
Solidago
Stachys
Veronica

## COMMON AND LATIN NAME CROSS-LISTING

| Common Name | Latin Name | Common Name | Latin Name |
|---|---|---|---|
| Acroclinium | Helipterum | Coneflower | Echinacea |
| Avens | Geum | Coral bells | Heuchera |
| Baby's breath | Gypsophila | Cranesbill | Geranium |
| Bachelor's button | Centaurea | Cupid's dart | Catananche |
| Balloon flower | Platycodon | Daffodil | Narcissus |
| Basket flower | Centaurea | Dame's rocket | Hesperis |
| Basket of gold | Aurinia | Daylily | Hemerocallis |
| Beardtongue | Penstemon | Dutchman's breeches | Dicentra |
| Bee balm | Monarda | False indigo | Baptisia |
| Black-eyed Susan | Rudbeckia | False Queen Anne's lace | Ammi |
| Blanket flower | Gaillardia | False rock cress | Aubretia |
| Bleeding heart | Dicentra | False spirea | Astilbe |
| Bluebells | Mertensia | Feverfew | Chrysanthemum |
| Bluet | Centaurea | Flag, Blue | Iris |
| Boneset | Eupatorium | Flax | Linum |
| Bugbane | Cimicifuga | Flowering onion | Allium |
| Busy lizzie | Impatiens | Flowering tobacco | Nicotania |
| Butterfly flower | Asclepias | Forget-me-not | Myosotis |
| Candle larkspur | Delphinium | Foss flower | Ageratum |
| Candytuft | Iberis | Four o'clock | Mirabilis |
| Canterbury bells | Campanula | Foxglove | Digitalis |
| Cape daisy | Venidium | Foxtail lily | Eremerus |
| Cardinal climber | Ipomoea | Gayfeather | Liatris |
| Cardinal flower | Lobelia | Geranium | Pelargonium |
| Cherry pie | Heliotrope | Globe thistle | Echinops |
| China aster | Callistephus | Goatsbeard | Aruncus |
| Chinese lantern | Physalis | Goldenrod | Solidago |
| Clary | Salvia sclarea | Gooseneck loosestrife | Lysmachia |
| Cockscomb | Celosia | Hardy ageratum | Eupatorium |
| Columbine | Aquilegia | Harebell | Campanula |

| Common Name | Latin Name | Common Name | Latin Name |
|---|---|---|---|
| Hawk's beard | Crepis | Queen of the prairie | Filipendula |
| Hollyhock | Alcea | Red Valerian | Centranthus |
| Jacob's ladder | Polemonium | Rock cress | Arabis |
| Joe Pye weed | Eupatorium | Sage | Salvia |
| Jupiter's beard | Centranthus | Sea holly | Eryngium |
| Lady's mantle | Alchemilla | Shasta daisy | Chrysanthemum |
| Lamb's-ear | Stachys | Snakeroot | Cimicifuga |
| Larkspur | Consolida | Snapdragon | Antirrhinum |
| Leopard's bane | Doronicum | Sneezeweed | Helenium |
| Lily | Lilium | Snow in summer | Cerastium |
| Lily-of-the-valley | Convallaria | Solomon's seal | Polygonatum |
| Loosestrife | Lythrum | Speedwell | Veronica |
| Love in a mist | Nigella | Spider flower | Cleome |
| Love lies bleeding | Amaranthus | Statice | Limonium |
| Lupine | Lupinus | Stocks | Matthiola |
| Maltese cross | Lychnis | Stonecrop | Sedum |
| Marguerite | Anthemis | Strawflower | Helichrysum |
| Marigold | Tagetes | Sundrop | Oenothera |
| Meadowsweet | Filipendula | Sunflower | Helianthus |
| Michaelmas daisy | Aster | Sunray | Helipterum |
| Monkshood | Aconitum | Sweet alyssum | Lobularia |
| Moonflower | Ipomoea | Sweet pea | Lathyrus |
| Morning glory | Ipomoea | Sweet sultan | Centaurea |
| Nasturtium | Tropaeolum | Sweet william | Dianthus |
| Obedient plant | Physostegia | Thrift | Armeria |
| Pansy | Viola | Tickseed | Coreopsis |
| Patience plant | Impatiens | Toadflax | Linaria |
| Peony | Paeonia | Tobacco | Nicotiana |
| Pincushion flower | Scabiosa | Tree mallow | Lavatera |
| Pinks | Dianthus | Tulip | Tulipa |
| Plaintain lily | Hosta | Violet | Viola |
| Poppy | Papaver | Windflower | Anemone |
| Pot marigold | Calendula | Wormwood | Artemisia |
| Primrose | Primula | Yarrow | Achillea |
| Pyrethrum | Chrysanthemum | | |

## SPECIES AND COMMON NAME CROSS-LISTING

| Latin Name | Common Name | Latin Name | Common Name |
|---|---|---|---|
| Achillea | Yarrow | Centaurea | Basket flower |
| Aconitum | Monkshood | Centaurea | Sweet sultan |
| Ageratum | Foss flower | Centaurea | Bluet |
| Alcea | Hollyhock | Centranthus | Jupiter's beard |
| Alchemilla | Lady's mantle | Centranthus | Red Valerian |
| Allium | Flowering onion | Cerastium | Snow in summer |
| Amaranthus | Love lies bleeding | Chrysanthemum | Shasta daisy |
| Ammi Majus | False Queen Anne's lace | Chrysanthemum | Pyrethrum |
| Anemone | Windflower | Chrysanthemum | Feverfew |
| Anthemis | Marguerite | Cimicifuga | Bugbane |
| Antirrhinum | Snapdragon | Cimicifuga | Snakeroot |
| Aquilegia | Columbine | Cleome | Spider flower |
| Arabis | Rock cress | Consolida | Larkspur |
| Armeria | Thrift | Convallaria | Lily-of-the-valley |
| Artemisia | Wormwood | Coreopsis | Tickseed |
| Aruncus | Goatsbeard | Cosmos | Cosmos |
| Asclepias | Butterfly flower | Crepis | Hawk's beard |
| Aster | Michaelmas daisy | Crocus | Crocus |
| Astilbe | False spirea | Dahlia | Dahlia |
| Aubretia | False rock cress | Delphinium | Candle larkspur |
| Aurinia | Basket of gold | Dianthus | Pinks |
| Baptisia | False indigo | Dianthus | Sweet william |
| Browallia | Browallia | Dicentra | Bleeding heart |
| Calendula | Pot marigold | Dicentra | Dutchman's breeches |
| Callistephus | China aster | Digitalis | Foxglove |
| Campanula | Canterbury bells | Doronicum | Leopard's bane |
| Campanula | Harebell | Echinacea | Coneflower |
| Catananche | Cupid's dart | Echinops | Globe thistle |
| Celosia | Cockscomb | Eremerus | Foxtail lily |
| Centaurea | Bachelor's button | Eryngium | Sea holly |

| Latin Name | Common Name | Latin Name | Common Name |
|---|---|---|---|
| Eupatorium | Joe Pye weed | Lychnis | Maltese cross |
| Eupatorium | Boneset | Lysmachia | Gooseneck loosestrife |
| Eupatorium | Hardy ageratum | Lythrum | Loosestrife |
| Filipendula | Meadowsweet | Matthiola | Stocks |
| Filipendula | Queen of the prairie | Mertensia | Bluebells |
| Gaillardia | Blanket flower | Mirabilis | Four o'clock |
| Gazania | Gazania | Monarda | Bee balm |
| Geranium | Cranesbill | Myosotis | Forget-me-not |
| Geum | Avens | Narcissus | Daffodil |
| Gladiolus | Gladiolus | Nicotiana | Flowering tobacco |
| Gypsophila | Baby's breath | Nigella | Love in a mist |
| Helenium | Sneezeweed | Oenothera | Sundrop |
| Helianthus | Sunflower | Paeonia | Peony |
| Helichrysum | Strawflower | Papaver | Poppy |
| Heliopsis | Heliopsis | Pelargonium | Geranium |
| Heliotrope | Cherry pie plant | Penstemon | Beardtongue |
| Helipterum | Acroclinium | Petunia | Petunia |
| Helipterum | Sunray | Phlox | Phlox |
| Hemerocallis | Daylily | Physalis | Chinese lantern |
| Hesperis | Dame's rocket | Physostegia | Obedient plant |
| Heuchera | Coral bells | Platycodon | Balloon flower |
| Hosta | Plantain lily | Polemonium | Jacob's ladder |
| Hyacinth | Hyacinth | Polygonatum | Solomon's seal |
| Iberis | Candytuft | Primula | Primrose |
| Impatiens | Patience plant | Rudbeckia | Black-eyed Susan |
| Impatiens | Busy Lizzie | Salvia | Sage |
| Ipomoea | Morning glory | Salvia | Clary |
| Ipomoea | Moonflower | Scabiosa | Pincushion flower |
| Ipomoea | Cardinal climber | Sedum | Stonecrop |
| Iris | Flag | Solidago | Goldenrod |
| Lathyrus | Sweet pea | Stachys | Lamb's-ear |
| Lavatera | Tree mallow | Tagetes | Marigold |
| Liatris | Gayfeather | Tropaeolum | Nasturtium |
| Ligularia | Ligularia | Tulipa | Tulip |
| Lilium | Lily | Venidium | Cape daisy |
| Limonium | Statice | Verbena | Verbena |
| Linaria | Toadflax | Veronica | Speedwell |
| Linum | Flax | Viola | Pansy |
| Lobelia | Cardinal flower | Viola | Violet |
| Lobularia | Sweet alyssum | Zinnia | Zinnia |
| Lupinus | Lupine | | |

# GLOSSARY

**Acid soil**  Any soil with a pH reading below 7.0 on a scale of 1–14; the lower the reading, the more acid the soil. *See also* pH

**Alkaline soil**  Any soil with a pH reading above 7.0 on a scale of 1–14; the higher the reading, the more alkaline the soil. *See also* pH

**Annual**  A plant that under normal conditions completes its entire life cycle in one season. *See also* Biennial, Perennial

**Anther**  The pollen-bearing part of a flower's male sexual organ. With the filament, atop which it sits, it comprises the stamen.

**Aphid**  A small sucking insect, usually pale green, gray, or black, but also yellow-pink or lavender. They are less than a quarter inch long, pear-shaped, and appear in great numbers at the tender growing points of the attacked plant. They are most easily recognized by the sticky fluid that they secrete, called honeydew, and by the ants that will often be found at the same site, appearing to "tend" the aphids. They can be controlled by knocking them from the plants with a hard stream of cold water or by spraying with insecticial soap.

**Apical**  Pertaining to the apex, or tip. An apical meristem is the growing point of a given plant. *See also* Axillary, Meristem

**Apical dominance**  The tendency of the apical meristem to inhibit the growth of axial buds by the production of auxins, whose strength decreases in proportion to the distance they have to travel. Removal of the apical meristem, therefore, results in increased branching.

**Asexual propagation**  Reproduction without the recombination of genetic material via the mating of male and female sex cells. *See also* Clone, Vegetative propagation

**Auxin**  A plant growth hormone that in low concentrations promotes growth, while in large concentrations it inhibits growth. Cell elongation rather than division is promoted, thus branching is inhibited by the presence of auxins. *See also* Apical dominance, Cytokinin, Rooting compound

**Axil**  The upper or inside angle of the junction of a leaf and stem, or where a smaller stem arises from a larger one.

**Axillary**  Pertaining to the axil, as in axillary bud, a potential growing point located in an axil. *See* Meristem

**Bacillus thuringiensis (Bt)**  A species of bacteria that attacks soft-bodied caterpillars and paralyzes their digestive systems, leading to death. Additional strains of this microbial insecticide have been discovered or developed to attack other pests. Related species of bacteria have been found that attack other pests, such as Japanese beetles and grasshoppers.

**Basal**  In plants that form rosettes, the basal leaves are those that arise directly from the crown of the plant, and which often differ from leaves arising from the stem. *See also* Crown

**Bedding plant**  Any plant used to create so-called bedding displays, which are often geometric and surrounded by areas of lawn or paving. The most important characteristic for bedding plants is absolute uniformity in color, height, habit, and bloom period. The term is also loosely used to apply to groups of plants that are being raised in a greenhouse before being set out in the garden.

**Beneficial insects**  Insects that help rather than hinder our gardening efforts. They may do this by pollinating flowers, by eating harmful insects or parasitizing them, or by breaking down plant material in the soil, thereby releasing its nutrients. Some insects could be considered both harmful and beneficial, e.g., butterflies, which are beautiful in their adult form but destructive when in their larval or caterpillar form.

**Biennial**  A plant that under normal conditions takes two years to complete its life cycle, growing to full size in its first season, then flowering in its second season before dying. *See also* Annual, Perennial

**Biodiversity**  Short for biological diversity. A state in which an ecosystem, whether natural or managed, contains a wide range of species and individuals of diverse genetic makeup in complex relations to one another. It is widely held that such diversity and complexity lends long-term sustainability to the ecosystem and is thus desirable both in nature and in gardens.

**Borer**  A pest that bores into the stems of plants; usually a larva such as a grub, caterpillar, or maggot. Symptoms often include an entrance hole and wilt on stem portions beyond. They can be controlled by digging out the pest, injecting an appropriate botanical or microbial insecticide, or by pruning the plant below the damage and destroying the pruned-off part along with the pest.

**Botrytis**  Also known as gray mold. A fungal disease that is promoted by cool, moist weather. Symptoms appear as water-soaked, blighted areas on flowers, stems, or leaves with a moldy gray growth, hence the common name. Control by removing all infected plant parts and making sure the plants have sufficient room so that good air circulation is maintained around them.

**Bract**  A leaf that seems part of the flower cluster of a plant, or in the case of plants with insignificant flowers, may substitute for it in appearance by its bright coloring. Annual clary (*Salvia viridis*) and poinsettia are two examples.

**Bt**  *See* Bacillus thuringiensis

**Bud**  A dormant, immature shoot from which leaves or flowers may develop. *See also* Apical, Axillary

**Bulb**  An underground storage organ consisting of a thin, flattened stem section surrounded by layers of fleshy and dried leaf bases and roots attached to its bottom. *See also* Corm, Tuber, Rhizome

**Bulbil** Any small bulblike organ attached to a plant, usually on the stem at the apex or at an axil, or produced underground as an offset from a larger basal bulb.

**Bulblet** An underground bulbil. *See also* bulbil

**Callus** The new tissue that grows over a plant wound or cut.

**Calyx** Collective name for all the sepals of a flower, the modified leaves that surround and protect flower buds.

**Carpel** *See* Pistil

**Cell** The basic unit of living matter, consisting at a minimum of a nucleus within a mass of protoplasm that is enclosed by a membrane.

**Chlorophyll** A group of green pigments within the chloroplasts which effects the conversion of solar to chemical energy by the process of photosynthesis. *See also* Photosynthesis

**Chloroplast** The cell organelle in which photosynthesis takes place. *See also* Organelle

**Climber** A plant that climbs on its own, using twining, gripping pads, tendrils, or some other method to attach itself to structures or other plants. Plants that need to be trained to a support are properly called trailing plants, not climbers.

**Clone** Botanical term for plants produced by vegetative or asexual propagation, and which are therefore genetically identical to the parent plant.

**Cold treatment** Subjection of plants or seeds to low temperatures to enhance germination and/or flowering response. This technique is especially helpful in getting biennials to bloom in their first year. *See also* Stratification, Vernalization

**Compost** Fully decayed vegetable matter with the appearance of soil that is used to improve both the texture and fertility of garden soil. Some composts are made with the addition of animal manures and mineral powders like lime, greensand, and phosphate.

**Corm** An underground storage organ consisting of the swollen base of a stem, with roots attached to the underside. *See also* Bulb, Tuber, Rhizome

**Cormel** A small, underdeveloped corm, usually attached to a larger corm. *See also* Bulbil, Bulblet

**Corolla** Collective name for all the petals of a flower, as opposed to the sepals. *See also* Calyx, Petals, Sepals

**Cortex** The usually corky tissue within stems and roots that serves as a storage area for food reserves and provides structural rigidity to the plant.

**Cotyledon(s)** The seed leaves, which are present before germination, as distinct from true leaves, which develop after germination. *See also* Dicot, Monocot

**Cross-pollination** The fertilization of the ovary on one plant with pollen from another plant, producing a progeny with a new genetic makeup distinct from either parent.

**Crown** The base of a plant, where stem and root join, usually, but not always, at ground level.

**Cultivar** Properly, a *culti*-vated *var*-iety of a plant that was developed through horticultural processes, rather than in nature. Its name is not part of the Latin name. *See also* Variety

**Cutting**  A section of stem or root removed from a plant and prompted to develop into a new plant, genetically identical to the parent plant.

**Cutworm**  The larvae of several species of moths that pupate just beneath the surface of the soil. While in the larval stage they emerge at night and "cut down" seedlings, then devour them, leaving no evidence beyond the severed stem. Control by putting one-inch-tall collars around the stem of newly set transplants so that the cutworms can't get to them. In addition, some bran flakes moistened with Bt (make sure the label specifies that the kind you choose works for cutworms) can be left for them to eat instead; this will kill them.

**Cytokinin**  A plant hormone that stimulates cell division rather than elongation. See also Auxin, Rooting compound

**Damping off**  Any of a number of fungal diseases that attack seedlings, causing the stem to wither at the soil line, collapsing the plant. There is no good cure for affected plants, but any remaining plants can be saved by removing all the diseased material and moving the seedlings to a warm, bright, airy location. Proper thinning and avoidance of overwatering, especially during cloudy periods, are the best preventives.

**Daylength**  Flower initiation in many plants is affected by the relation between daylength and nightlength. Those that form flower buds only when the daylength is less than a given amount of time are called short-day plants; those that bud only if the day length exceeds a given amount of time are called long-day plants. The critical length differs widely among species, however, and cannot be specified overall. Day-neutral plants flower after a certain period of vegetative growth regardless of day- or nightlength.

**Desiccant**  A material, such as sand or silica gel, that is used to dry flowers for long-term preservation.

**Dicot**  Any plant that has two cotyledons, or seed leaves. *See also* Cotyledon, Monocot

**Dioecious**  Having male and female sex organs on separate plants. *See also* Monoecious

**Disbudding**  The removal of axillary buds from a plant to force all its energy into the apical bud; usually done to increase the size of the resulting flower for exhibition.

**Division**  The breaking or cutting apart of the crown of a plant for the purpose of producing additional plants, all genetically identical to the parent plant.

**Embryo**  The dormant, immature plant within each seed.

**Endosperm**  The food storage tissue within a seed.

**Epidermis**  The outermost layer of cells in herbaceous plants, equivalent to human skin.

**Fibrous root.**  A root system that branches in all directions, often directly from the crown of the plant, rather than branching in a hierarchical fashion from a central root. *See also* Tap root

**Filament**  Threadlike stem on which the pollen-bearing anther is held. *See also* Anther

**Flower**  Specialized organ of the plant consisting of the male and/or reproductive parts, often brightly colored or strongly scented to attract insects for the purpose of fertilization.

**Foliar feeding**  Fertilization of plant through application of a fine mist containing nutrients directly to the leaves.

**Fungicide**  Any material capable of killing fungi. Sulfur and copper sulfate are two common mineral fungicides.

**Genus**  A group of related species, each of which is distinct, and unlikely to cross with any other. In the standard classification, a group of genera forms a Family, and a group of families an Order. *See also* Species

**Germination**  The initial sprouting stage of a seed.

**Glabrous**  Hairless but not necessarily smooth.

**Glaucous**  Covered with a powdery, blue-gray-green finish.

**Greensand**  A natural mineral material mined for its content of potassium, which is released very slowly through the natural microbial activity of soil organisms.

**Hardening off**  The process of gradually exposing seedlings started indoors to outdoor conditions before transplanting.

**Heeling in**  The temporary burying of the roots of newly dug plants to prevent their drying until the new planting site is prepared.

**Herbaceous**  Dies back to the ground in winter. Generally applied only to nonwoody biennial and perennial plants.

**Herbicide**  Any material that kills plants, generally weeds. Some soaps have herbicidal properties.

**Hirsute**  Covered with dense, coarse hairs.

**Humidity**  The amount of water vapor present in the air. Relative humidity is the percent present in the air relative to the amount that the air could contain, given the temperature.

**Inflorescence**  Collective name for a group of individual flowers. The grouping can take many forms: a *spike*, where the blooms are closely packed along a vertical stem; an *umbel* or a *corymb*, where the blooms form a flattened dome; the complex hierarchical arrangement called a *panicle*, or the tightly packed disc flowers in the center of a daisy, called a *capitulum*.

**Insecticidal soap**  A specially formulated soap that is only minimally damaging to plants, but which kills insects primarily by causing their outer shells to crack, allowing their interior organs to dry out.

**Insecticide**  Any material that kills insects. There are numerous botanical and mineral powders that are toxic to insects, as well as biodegradable chemicals such as soaps.

**Internode**  The part of a stem that is inbetween nodes. *See also* node

**Juvenile**  That stage of development wherein the plant concentrates its energy on vegetative growth rather than on reproduction.

**Latin name**  The international, scientific name of a plant, agreed upon by botanists to apply uniquely to a particular species, and denoting its relationship to other, similar plants. The Latin name consists of two parts: the first is called the *generic name*, as it states the genus to which the plant belongs; the second is called the *specific name*, as it describes the species to which the plant belongs. If there is a variety or cultivar name as well, it follows the specific name. In written form, the generic name is capitalized, while the specific and the varietal name are lower-case; the entire name is italicized. A cultivar name, if used, should not be italic and should be enclosed within single quotation marks. Pronunciation of Latin names varies considerably from region to region around the world and should not be an inhibition to their use. *See also* Cultivar, Genus, Species, Variety

**Lime**   A rock powder consisting primarily of calcium carbonate that is used to raise the pH (that is, to decrease the acidity) of acid soils. *See also* Acid soil, Alkaline soil, pH

**Meristem**   Any growing point of either root or stem on a plant where active cell division is taking place. There are both apical and axillary meristems. *See also* Apical, Axillary

**Mesophyll**   The spongy inner tissue of a leaf, functionally similar to the cortex of stems and roots, where the raw materials—carbon dioxide and water vapor—are held during the process of photosynthesis within the adjacent palisade cells. *See also* Palisade cells

**Microclimate**   In general terms, the character of a particular piece of land as influenced by purely local factors like elevation, direction and degree of slope, nearby buildings, and vegetation such as trees and hedges, etc. Also: conditions right at ground level, out of the prevailing winds and under the effect of the covering plant canopy and the mass of the earth.

**Monocot**   Any plant that has only one cotyledon, or seed leaf. *See also* Cotyledon, Dicot

**Monoecious**   Having separate male and female sex organs on the same plant. *See also* Dioecious

**Nightlength**   *See* Daylength

**Nitrogen**   Major plant nutrient especially important for plants where foliage is the main interest.

**Node**   That spot on the stem of a plant where both leaf and axial buds occur. The area of the stem between the nodes is called the internode. *See also* Internode

**NPK**   Acronym for the three major plant nutrients contained in manure, compost, and fertilizers, and used to describe the amounts of each readily available. N stands for nitrogen, P for phosphorus, and K for potassium (which was earlier called Kalium).

**Nucleus**   The organelle within a cell that contains the cell's chromosomes and thus controls the various other cellular processes, including division into new cells.

**Nutrient**   Any substance, especially in the soil, that is essential for, and promotes growth of plants. Generally applied to a group of a dozen or less common elements, especially nitrogen, phosphorus, and potassium. *See also* NPK

**Nutrient deficiency**   An inferior state of health in any plant brought about by insufficient amount of a given nutrient being present or available to the plant.

**Organelle**   A single-purpose component within the cell.

**Ovary**   The part of a flower containing the ovules that will develop into seeds upon fertilization. With the *style* and *stigma*, it comprises the *pistil*, or female sexual organ. *See also* Pistil

**Ovule**   Within the ovary, the body which will contain the seed upon fertilization. *See also* Ovary

**Palisade cells**   A group of cells, just beneath the epidermis of the leaf, that contain most of the chlorophyll in the leaf and are thus responsible for the bulk of the photosynthesis that occurs in the plant. *See also* Photosynthesis

**Pathogen**   Any organism that causes disease; generally applied to bacteria, viruses, and less correctly, fungi.

**Peat**   Partially decomposed mosses and sedges harvested from bogs and used as a component of soilless mixes. *See also* Soilless mix

**Peat pots**   Planting pots made from compressed peat. These are used for plants that resent disturbance, as at transplanting time the entire pot can be set out in the garden; the young plants' roots will grow through the walls of the pot.

**Pedicel**   A flower stem, as opposed to a leaf stem or peduncle from which the individual pedicels arise. *See also* Peduncle

**Peduncle**   The main stem supporting a cluster of flowers, as opposed to the pedicels, which are the stems of individual flowers. *See also* Pedicel

**Perennial**   Any plant that lives more than three years. In general the term is applied only to herbaceous plants, which die back to the ground each year, as opposed to those with persistent, woody stem. *See also* Annual, Biennal

**Perianth**   A collective term for the external parts of the flower: the calyx, or sepals, and the corolla, or petals.

**Perlite**   Small globules of heat-expanded volcanic rock used to increase the porosity and drainage of potting mixes. Often used in the rooting of cuttings, as it is both inert and sterile.

**Petal**   A specialized leaf that surrounds the reproductive parts of a flower. Often colored to attract pollinating insects.

**Petiole**   The leaf stalk that connects a leaf to the stem.

**pH**   A symbol for the acid-alkaline balance of the soil. The balance is expressed as a number from 1 to 14, with 7 considered neutral. Thus a pH of 6 is acidic while a pH of 8 is alkaline. Higher numbers are more alkaline, lower numbers more acidic.

**Phosphorus**   Major plant nutrient; especially important for plants where flowering is the main interest.

**Photosynthesis**   The process by which the chloroplasts in plant cells use sunlight to combine carbon dioxide from the air with water vapor to form carbohydrates that are used as the basic food stuff for the growth of the plant.

**Picotee**   A pattern of flower-petal coloration in which the edges are a contrasting color to the body of the petal.

**Pinching**   The removal of a growing tip from a stem, which causes any axillary shoots or buds of the stem to develop.

**Pistil**   The female sexual organ of a flowering plant, comprising the stigma, style, and ovary. *See also* Carpel

**Plug tray**   A type of seedling tray in which each seedling grows in an individual, tapered cell, thus reducing root competition with adjacent seedlings and minimizing transplant shock.

**Pollen**   The male sex cells, which are held on the anther for transfer by insects, wind, or some other mechanism to the tip of the stigma where they can then proceed to attempt fertilization of the female egg cell or ovule in the ovary at the base of the style.

**Pollination**   The transfer of pollen to the stigma of a receptive flower. Fertilization does not occur until the pollen actually reaches the ovule at the base of the style.

**Potassium**   Major plant nutrient especially important to the strength of roots and stems.

**Pruning**   The removal of plant parts to improve the health, appearance, or productivity of the plant.

**Rhizomatous**   Having or capable of producing rhizomes.

**Rhizome**   A horizontal stem, usually underground, from which grow both leaves and roots. Usually persistent from year to year. *See also* Runner, Stolon

**Rock phosphate**   A naturally occurring mineral, calcium triphosphate is mined and crushed for use as a fertilizer.

**Root-bound**   A situation where the roots of a plant have completely filled the container in which they grow, with further growth prevented until the plant is removed from the container.

**Root cutting**   Section of root prepared for the purpose of vegetative propagation. *See also* Cutting

**Rooting compound**   Commercial preparation of plant hormones used to promote rooting of stem and root cuttings. Usually available as a powder into which cuttings are dipped before planting.

**Runner**   A horizontal stem running along, but above, the surface of the soil, which produces roots and leaves wherever its nodes contact the soil. *See also* Rhizome, Stolon

**Scarification**   The nicking, sanding, or otherwise compromising of the hard outer coating of seeds to increase their water intake and thus promote quick germination.

**Seed**   The fertilized, ripe ovule that contains the embryo from which a new plant may develop, given the proper conditions.

**Self-fertile**   Able to fertilize itself.

**Self-sterile**   Unable to fertilize itself; requires cross-pollination as the flowers are sterile to their own pollen.

**Senescence**   The aging process; a plant that is old and weak is said to be senescent. Also describes a plant that is in the process of going dormant for the season, though technically only the parts that are dying, i.e., the leaves are becoming senescent.

**Sepals**   Modified leaves that surround and protect flower buds. *See also* Calyx, Corolla, Petal

**Sexual propagation**   Production of new plants by seed, whereby the genetic material from two parent plants is combined, producing a new plant that is distinct from, even if quite similar to, its parents.

**Shattering**   The process by which seed capsules, when ripe, spontaneously break open, scattering their seed.

**Shearing**   Wholesale cutting back of a plant, rather than selective pruning or deadheading. Often used to regenerate plants with many small stems, when deadheading would be too time-consuming. *See also* Deadheading, Disbudding, Pinching

**Soilless mix**   Any potting mix that is made without the addition of soil. Some common components include peat, bark, coconut fiber, vermiculite, perlite, and sand.

**Species.**   The basic unit of plant classification. Plants within a species have several characteristics in common, but most important, they can cross with one another, but not normally with members of other species. The classification of species is quite fluid, with periodic revisions by botanists a fact of life that gardeners are forced to contend with.

**Stamen**   The male, pollen-producing part of a flower, consisting of the *anther* and its supporting filament.

**Standard**   A plant pruned so that it consists of a single, bare, vertical stem atop which is maintained as a shaped mass of foliage.

**Stem cutting**   Section of stem prepared for vegetative reproduction. *See also* Cutting

**Sterile**   Applied to plants: unable to reproduce sexually, i.e., to produce viable seeds. Applied to potting materials: free of disease organisms or pathogens. *See also* Pathogens

**Stigma**   The part of the female sex organ which receives pollen from the anther. Supported by the style, through which it is connected to the ovary. Often sticky when receptive.

**Stolon**   A horizontal stem that runs along the surface of the soil, rooting where its tip contacts the soil. *See also* Runner

**Stoloniferous**   Having or capable of producing stolons.

**Stratification**   The exposure of seeds to moisture and low temperatures to overcome the dormancy of certain species, often from harsh winter climates. *See also* Cold treatment

**Style**   The part of the female sex organ that supports the stigma and connects it to the ovary.

**Sub-species**   A major division of a species, more general in classification than a variety.

**Sulfur**   A mineral element that has fungicidal properties. Sulfur dust is used to prevent many fungal diseases, and also functions as a minor nutrient for plants.

**Tap root**   A thick central root, attached directly to the crown of a plant, that branches little if at all. *See also* Fibrous root

**Terminal bud**   A plant's apical bud. *See also* Apical

**Topdressing**   The application of fertilizer, whatever its form, to the surface of the soil around established plantings.

**Tuber**   An underground storage organ, part of either the stem or the root of the plant. Stem tubers produce multiple buds on their surface, from which shoots may arise the following season, while root tubers will sprout only from the point at which they were attached to the stem of the parent plant.

**Turgid**   Applied to cells and the plants that they comprise: fully charged with water. A damaging decrease in turgidity causes wilting.

**Variety**   A strain of plant having distinctive features that persist over successive generations in the absence of human intervention. Generally, variety applies to these naturally occurring strains, while cultivar applies to horticulturally developed strains. *See also* Cultivar, Latin name

**Vector**   A transmitter or carrier of disease or infection.

**Vegetative propagation**   The use of plant parts such as cuttings (as opposed to seeds) to create new plants. New plants resulting from vegetative propagation are clones, genetically identical to the parent plant.

**Vermiculite**   A heart-expanding mineral, usually mica, that is used in potting soils for its porosity; sterile.

**Vernalization**   Subjection of plants or seeds to a temperature regime that mimics the natural passage of the seasons. This is done to cause plants or seeds to bloom out of season or at a younger age than would normally occur.

## SOURCES

**Seeds**

Burpee, W. Atlee
Warminster, PA 18974
Phone: 800 / 888-1447
Fax: 215 / 674-4170
  *One of the old-timers. Wide selection of common items.*

Chiltern Seeds
Bortree Stile
Ulverston
Cumbria LA12 7PB
England
  *Very wide selection of flower seeds.*

Cook's Garden, The
PO Box 535
Londonderry, VT 05148
Phone: 802 / 824-3400
Fax: 802 / 824-3027
  *Our own catalog. We specialize in cut flowers, everlastings, and fragrant flowers.*

Far North Gardens
16785 Harrison
Livonia, MI 48154
Phone/Fax: 313 / 522-9040
  *Specializes in rare flower seed and primroses. Catalog: $2.00*

Flowery Branch, The
PO Box 1330
Flowery Branch, GA 30542
Phone: 404 / 536-8380
Fax: 404 / 532-7825
  *Very wide range of flower seeds with good descriptions. Catalog: $2.00*

Fragrant Path, The
PO Box 328
Ft. Calhoun, NE 68023
  *Small company, specializes in fragrant plants of all species. Catalog: $1.00*

Gloeckner, Fred C. & Co.
600 Mamaroneck Avenue
Harrison, NY 10528
Phone: 914 / 698-2300
Fax: 914 / 698-0848
  *Cut-flower seed and supplies for growers.*

Park Seed Company
PO Box 31
Greenwood, SC 29648
  *Old-timer. Very extensive flower listing.*

Pinetree Garden Seeds
Box 300
New Gloucester, ME 04260
Phone: 207 / 926-3400
  *Wide selection; small packets.*

Prairie Nursery
PO Box 306
Westfield, WI 53964
Phone: 608 / 296-3679
  *Specializes in native wildflowers.*

Select Seeds
180 Stickney Road
Union, CT 06076
Phone/Fax: 203 / 684-9310
  *Specializes in heirloom flowers.*

Shepherd's Garden Seeds
30 Irene Street
Torrington, CT 06790
Phone: 203 / 482-3838
*Flower and vegetable seed.*

Stokes Seeds
Box 548
Buffalo, NY 14240
Phone: 800 / 263-7233
Fax: 716 / 695-9649
*A big company with a wide
selection of flowers and
vegetables.*

Thompson and Morgan
PO Box 1308
Jackson, NJ 08527
Phone: 908 / 363-2225
Fax: 908 / 363-9356
*Very wide selection; expensive.*

**Plants**

Bleumel, Kurt
2740 Greene Lane
Baldwin, MD 21013
Phone: 301 / 557-7229
*Perennials, especially
ornamental grasses.
Catalog: $1.00*

Bluestone Perennials
7235 Middle Ridge Road
Madison, OH 44057
Phone: 800 / 752-5243
*Perennial seedlings.*

Busse Gardens
Route 2, Box 13
635 East 7th Street
Cokato, MN 55321
Phone: 612 / 286-2654
*Wide selection of hardy
perennials, both retail and
wholesale. Catalog: $2.00*

Carrol Gardens
444 East Main Street, PO Box 310
Westminster, MD 21157
Phone: 301 / 848-5422
*Comprehensive listing of
perennials, both retail and
wholesale. Catalog: $2.00*

Davidson-Wilson Greenhouses
Route 2, Box 168
Crawfordsville, IN 47933
Phone: 317 / 364-0556
Fax: 317 / 364-0563
*Wide selection of pelargoniums,
especially scented. Catalog: $3.00*

Daylily Discounters
Alachua, FL 32615
Phone: 904 / 462-1539
Fax: 904 / 462-5111
*Specializes in daylilies.*

Klehm Nursery
Route 5, 197 Penny Road
South Barrington, IL 60010
Phone: 312 / 551-3715
*Specializes in peony and hosta,
plus many other perennials.
Catalog: $2.00*

Prairie Moon Nursery
Route 3, Box 163
Winona, MN 55987
Phone: 507 / 452-5231
*Native plants and seeds.
Catalog: $2.00*

Shady Hill Gardens
821 Walnut S.
Batavia, IL 60510
  *Vast selection of pelargoniums.*

Shady Oaks Nursery
112 10th Avenue SE
Waseca, MN 56093
Phone: 507 / 835-5033
Fax: 507 / 835-8772
  *Specializes in hosta. Catalog:*
*$1.00 (bulk); $2.50 (1st class)*

Swan Island Dahlias
PO Box 700
Canby, OR 97013
Phone: 503 / 266-7711
Fax: 503 / 266-8678
  *Very wide selection of dahlias.*
*Catalog: $3.00 (refundable)*

Viette, Andre
Route 1, Box 16
Fisherville, VA 22939
  *Wide selection of perennials,*
*especially good cultivars.*
*Catalog: $2.00*

Wayside Gardens
Hodges, SC 29695
Phone: 800 / 845-1124
  *Full-color catalog of perennial*
*and woody plants.*

White Flower Farm
Litchfield, CT 06759-0050
Phone: 203 / 496-9600
  *Beautiful and informative*
*catalog of perennials and bulbs.*

Wild, Gilbert H. & Son
1112 Joplin Street
Sarcoxie, MO 64862
Phone: 417 / 548-3514
  *Wide selection of daylily, iris,*
*and peony. Catalog: $2.00*

**Bulbs**   Daffodil Mart, The
Route 3, Box 794
Gloucester, VA 23061
Phone: 804 / 693-3966
Fax: 804 / 693-9436
  *Specializes in daffodils, both*
*retail and wholesale.*

DeJaeger Bulbs
188 Ashbury Street
South Hamilton, MA 01982
Phone: 617 / 468-4707

Mary Mattison Van Schaik
PO Box 32
Cavendish, VT 05142
Phone: 802 / 226-7653
  *Small company; quality listing.*

McClure & Zimmerman
1422 West Thorndale
Chicago, IL 60660
Phone: 312 / 989-0557
  *Wide selection of unusual*
*bulbs.*

Skittone Bulb Company
1415 Eucalyptus Drive
San Francisco, CA 94132
Phone: 415 / 753-3332
Fax: 415 / 665-3308
  *Wide range of unusual and*
*hard-to-find, nursery-propagated*
*bulbs.*

Van Engelen
313 Maple Street
Litchfield, CT 06759
Phone: 203 / 567-8734
Fax: 203 / 567-5323
  *Wide selection; quantity
pricing.*

Gardener's Supply
128 Intervale Road
Burlington, VT 05401
Phone: 802 / 863-1700
  *Wide selection of tools and
supplies.*

Leonard, A. M.
6665 Spiker Road
Piqua, OH 45356
Phone: 800 / 543-8955
  *Tools and supplies for
professional nurserymen
and home gardeners.
Catalog: $1.00*

Mellingers
2310 West South Range Road
North Lima, OH 44452
Phone: 216 / 549-9861
  *Very wide selection of tools,
books, seeds, plants, and nursery
stock.*

Necessary Trading Company
PO Box 305
New Castle, VA 24127
Phone: 703 / 864-5103
  *Wide selection of organic
gardening products. Also
available at garden centers.*

**Equipment and
Supplies**

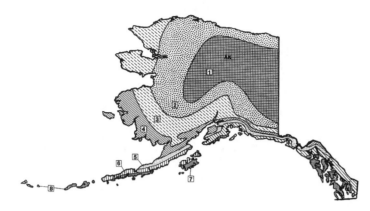

## USDA HARDINESS ZONE MAP

*Range of Average Annual
Minimum Temperatures
for Each Zone*

| ZONE | 1 | below | | $-50°$F |
|---|---|---|---|---|
| ZONE | 2 | $-50°$ | to | $-40°$ |
| ZONE | 3 | $-40°$ | to | $-30°$ |
| ZONE | 4 | $-30°$ | to | $-20°$ |
| ZONE | 5 | $-20°$ | to | $-10°$ |
| ZONE | 6 | $-10°$ | to | $0°$ |
| ZONE | 7 | $0°$ | to | $10°$ |
| ZONE | 8 | $10°$ | to | $20°$ |
| ZONE | 9 | $20°$ | to | $30°$ |
| ZONE | 10 | $30°$ | to | $40°$ |
| ZONE | 11 | above | $40°$ | |

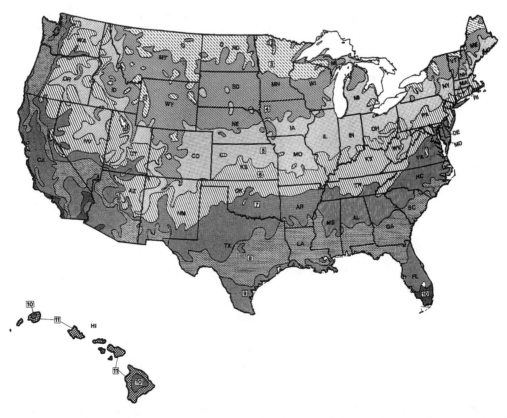

# BIBLIOGRAPHY

*Note:* This listing is of books I own, and represents only the slightest portion of the valuable books available on the subject of flower gardening (and only a portion of those in my library). They are listed alphabetically, by author, with no attempt to rank their importance.

Allaby, Michael, ed. *The Concise Oxford Dictionary of Botany.* Oxford, England: Oxford University Press, 1992.

Armitage, Allan M. *Herbaceous Perennial Plants.* Athens, Ga.: Varsity Press, 1989.

————. *Specialty Cut Flowers.* Portland, Oreg.: Timber Press, 1993.

Bagust, Harold. *The Gardener's Dictionary of Horticultural Terms.* London: Cassell Publishers, Ltd., 1992.

Ball, Jeff, and Liz Ball. *Rodale's Flower Garden Problem Solver.* Emmaus, Penn.: Rodale Press, 1990.

Barnette, Martha. *A Garden of Words.* New York: Times Books, 1992.   (Etymology of flower names.)

Bender, Steve, and Felder Rushing. *Passalong Plants.* Chapel Hill, N.C.: University of North Carolina Press, 1993.   (Regional: southeast United States.)

Bird, Richard. *The Propagation of Hardy Perennials.* London: B. T. Batsford, Ltd., 1993.

Bodanis, David. *The Secret Garden.* New York: Simon & Schuster, 1992.   (Microphotography.)

Brown, Emily. *Landscaping With Perennials.* Portland, Oreg.: Timber Press, 1986.   (Regional: California.)

Capon, Brian. *Botany for Gardeners.* Portland, Oreg.: Timber Press, 1990.

Coombes, Allen J. *Timber Press Dictionary of Plant Names.* Portland, Oreg.: Timber Press, 1985.

Foster, Catherine Osgood. *Organic Flower Gardening*. Emmaus, Penn.: Rodale Press, 1975.   (Regional: northern New England.)

——. *Plants-a-Plenty*. Emmaus, Penn.: Rodale Press, 1977.

Goody, Jack. *The Culture of Flowers*. Cambridge, England: Cambridge University Press, 1993.   (Cultural anthropology.)

Hansen, Richard, and Friedrich Stahl. *Perennials and Their Garden Habitats*. Portland, Oreg.: Timber Press, 1993.

Hill, Lewis. *Secrets of Plant Propagation*. Pownal, VT.: Garden Way Publishing, 1985.

Hudak, Joseph. *Gardening With Perennials Month by Month*. Portland, Oreg.: Timber Press, 1993.   (Regional: New England.)

Johnson, Hugh. *The Principles of Gardening*. London: Mitchell Beazley Publishers, Ltd., 1979.

Kull, A. Stoddard. *Secrets of Flowers*. Brattleboro, Vt.: The Stephen Greene Press, 1976.   (Folklore.)

Lawrence, Elizabeth. *A Southern Garden*. Chapel Hill, N.C.: The University of North Carolina Press, 1991.   (Regional: southeast United States.)

Lovejoy, Ann. *The Year in Bloom*. Seattle, Wash.: Sasquatch Books, 1987.   (Regional: northwest United States.)

Martin, Laura C. *Garden Flower Folklore*. Chester, Conn. The Globe Pequot Press, 1987.

McGourty, Frederick. *The Perennial Gardener*. Boston: Houghton Mifflin Company, 1989.

Powell, Claire. *The Meaning of Flowers*. Boulder, Colo. Shambala Publications, Inc., 1979.   (Folklore.)

Robinson, William. *The English Flower Garden*. New York: Amaryllis Press, 1984.

Stearn, William T. *Stearn's Dictionary of Plant Names for Gardeners*. London: Cassell Publishers, Ltd., 1992.

Thompson, Peter. *Creative Propagation*. Portland, Oreg.: Timber Press, 1992.

Wilder, Louise Beebe. *The Fragrant Garden*. New York: Dover Publications, Inc., 1974.

# INDEX

*Page numbers in italics refer to illustrations.*